AT HOME AFLOAT

at home
Afloat

women on the / waters of the Pacific Northwest

Nancy Pagh

To David and Judith,
At the YWCA, may 19 2005

Thank you so much for
coming to support readings all over
Bellingham. See you at another
one soon!

Nancy
Pagh.

UNIVERSITY OF
CALGARY
PRESS

UNIVERSITY OF IDAHO PRESS
Moscow

University of Calgary Press
2500 University Drive NW
Calgary, Alberta
Canada T2N 1N4

University of Idaho Press
University of Idaho
Moscow, Idaho
U.S.A. 83844-2332

Cataloguing in Publication Data
Pagh, Nancy, 1963-
   At home afloat

Includes bibliographical references and index.
   University of Calgary Press: ISBN 1-55238-028-9
   University of Idaho Press: ISBN 0-89301-253-X

   1. Women and the sea—Northwest, Pacific. 2. Seafaring life—Northwest,
Pacific. 3. Boats and boating—Northwest, Pacific. 4. Sex role—Northwest,
Pacific. I. Title.

G540.P34 2000   305.43   C00-911270-7

 We acknowledge the financial support of the Government of Canada through the Book Publishing Industry Development Program (BPIDP) for our publishing activities.

 The Canada Council for the Arts
Le Conseil des Arts du Canada

The publishers would like to acknowledge the support of International Council for Canadian Studies' through its Publishing Fund in publishing this book.

Portions of this text have appeared previously, in altered form, in the journal *Frontiers* (volume 20, number 3) and *Telling Tales: Essays in Western Women's History* (UBC Press).

Printed and bound in Canada by Friesens Printing.
∞ This book is printed on acid-free paper.

Front cover photograph of Muriel Wylie Blanchet compliments of Janet Blanchet.

Cover and page design by Kristina Schuring.

To Laurie Ricou
trailblazer, mentor, friend

TABLE OF CONTENTS

ILLUSTRATIONS

ACKNOWLEDGEMENTS

I am grateful to the many contributors who read all or parts of this project and who offered useful comments on it at various stages, including: Laurie Ricou, Cole Harris, Jean Barman, Rebecca Raglon, Susan Armitage, Douglas Cole, Randi Warne, Janice Fiamengo, Marian Gracias, Jennifer Lawn, Joel Martineau, Julie Walchli, and Peggy Pace. Susanna Egan offered financial and moral support at a time when I really needed it. This work, born of family experiences on the water, would not have been possible without the journeys that my parents, Sally and Richard Pagh, created together, and that I shared—joyfully—with my sister, Jeri.

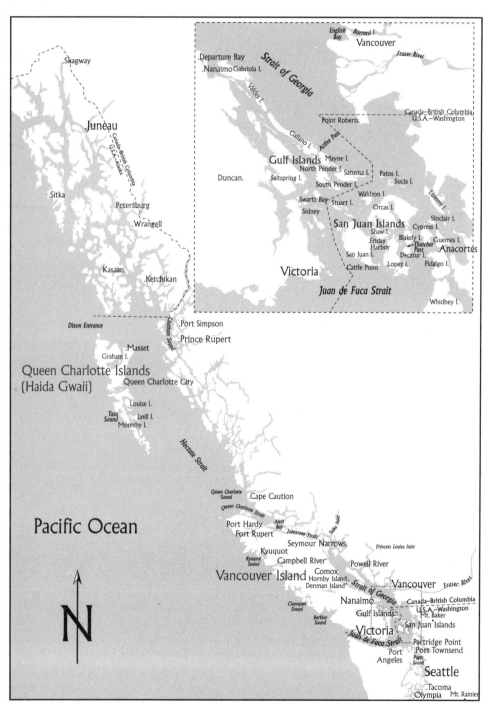

The Northwest Coast

INTRODUCTION

... all really inhabited space bears the essence of the notion of home.
—Gaston Bachelard (1958)

This project may have begun in the late 1960s on an afternoon when I accompanied my father to the marina. It was called Bryant's Marina then and was home port to a modest number of commercial fishing boats and pleasure craft owned by local Anacortes residents.[1] I remember a rainy day, the wooden boards of the docks wet, dark, and slick. It was in no way an exceptional day; my father was simply making a routine visit to check on the boat and chat with the men who frequented the marina. Not yet old enough for school, I trailed along.

What I recall most vividly is the climb to the harbormaster's office. Built of concrete squares, the two-story office perched on the lip of the marina and offered the harbormaster a commanding view over the boat basin. My father and I entered a door at ground level, stepped into a dark corridor, and moved toward a staircase. I remember the sensation of slowly and deliberately crawling up the stairs alone, one by one, in the dark, aware of the voices of my father and the harbormaster hovering above me. The stairs, the walls, and it seemed the air itself were a dark yellow, and as I climbed I could smell the tobacco that Tony, the harbormaster, smoked. Nearing the top stair, my head emerged into the atmosphere of the office at floor level, and I could see the black silhouettes of the two men against the large windows. My father, having by this time finished his conversation with Tony, stood, took my hand, and led me back down.

If I walked to the windows of that office and peered out from the "all-seeing" perspective of the harbormaster, that view made no lasting impression; the perspective of standing on a stair, my face level with the floor, gazing up into an

---

1 Anacortes is located on Fidalgo Island in Washington State (see map).

open room, proved more memorable. In retrospect, the context of that view seems to have contributed to its personal significance: the fact that I was low and small in an elevated space, a place built for men to observe and direct other men on the water, made me suddenly aware of my difference. Perhaps this awareness contributed to a curiosity about difference in marine environments throughout my life.

This project began on a more scholarly level in the spring of 1992, when I took a seminar on travel literature and examined the boating logbooks my mother had written over the course of many summers. I had not read these logs for several years and never in an academic context. Writing about my response to sea literature, I organized my ideas narratively like logbook entries, dividing them into brief sections, each beginning with a geographical place and stated point in time. I opened the project in Monterey with a moment on 11 March 1940, from John Steinbeck's *The Log from the Sea of Cortez* (1941). This is a moment when the men who seek adventure cast off the lines and leave their wives "melting and open" on the dock. In this first "logbook entry" of my voyage to find writings by women who go to sea, I asked, "Why is it that as a reader of sea-travel writing I seem to have to split myself? Part of my imagination is called to sea with the men, and part values the company of women and therefore feels obligated to stay on dry land with them" (Pagh 1995, 127).

With that genesis of this project, I was searching to find and understand written accounts of relatively unheard travelers (including my own mother), and I was exploring what was, for me, a new form of (or challenge to) academic writing. I also began to focus on accounts about Northwest Coast boat travel as a way to re-experience an idyllic time in my life and as a way to connect imaginatively with people who had visited places significant to me. Aware that femaleness has historically been suspect at sea, I was keenly interested in reading the accounts of women on the water. In the thousands of hours I have spent boating, I have rarely seen a woman operating a boat; with my research I was hoping to find a series of offshore heroines I had never met. I began this work, then, with a fairly simplistic desire to discover and celebrate the women participating in Northwest Coast boat travel.

As my work grew in scope, I found that women did indeed participate in the history of Northwest Coast marine tourism, that they wrote and published accounts of their experiences, but that they were not heroines at all; they were real and complex women, inscribing the ideologies of their sex and their time into their travelogues. Because of their gender, women remain significantly marginalized from work on the water.[2] However, women—still somewhat taboo aboard fishing boats and towboats—have made themselves at home aboard Northwest Coast pleasure craft since the first decade of the twentieth century and have defined local cruising as a "family sport." These recreational boaters

---

2 Deckhand Jelena Putnik says of marine-based labor: "Sometimes you have to take on a man's characteristics to succeed in a man's world at a man's job. It would be much nicer if it could just be a person's job" (Jensen 1995, 14).

were predated by upper- and middle-class women who participated in steamship travel along the coast from the late nineteenth century. Their presence on board influenced popular rhetorical constructions of the "Inside Passage" (from Olympia to Skagway; see map on page x) and of the aboriginal people who inhabited that corridor and generated a marine tourist industry along the coast.

I did not set out to focus on powerlessness; indeed, many of the primary texts I consider were written by relatively privileged (White, upper- and middle-class) women touring and cruising in this region. However, as most women with experience at sea know, when a female steps aboard a boat or enters a quayside conversation, power becomes an issue. Western women traveling at sea have traditionally carried the stigma of bad luck and taboo; they enter the marine environment with relatively less opportunity for experience and less authority than men. I found that the ideology of home—essentially, the notion that "a woman's place is in the home"—shapes the expectations and assumptions of both men and women regarding the interests and abilities of women on the water. Those assumptions in turn influence the roles women play at sea, the spaces they occupy on board, and the language they use to describe their experiences and surroundings. There is no single, uniform female perspective at sea, but on the pages of logbooks, diaries, reminiscences, and published accounts, patterns of commonly held beliefs, shared tasks, and connected identities begin to emerge.

To understand and explain these patterns, I have cast off some disciplinary restrictions in favor of an interdisciplinary approach, organizing my analysis around the theme of "home." Reading accounts by female boat tourists between 1861 and 1990, I question the ways that gender influences the roles women play at sea, the spaces they occupy on boats, and the language they use to construct their experiences, their surroundings, and their contact with Native peoples. The chapters are organized to show how women, traditionally forbidden in marine environments, participated in Northwest Coast steam tourism from its initiation and influenced steamship company promotional language. I trace a history of women entering the local recreational boating community and altering it with their homemaking skills and their demand for "houseboats," and I map how domestic ideology can divide the built space of the boat into gender-specific territories. Women who labor in marine occupations (fishers, towboaters) cope with the limitations of a masculine environment. My work shows how female tourists, who typically cruise as "mates" with their captains/husbands, cope with these same limitations while bearing the added responsibility of answering to the patriarchal head of the household; as a result, women who gain access to boats through their domestic abilities can be "ghettoized" in the galley. This reading emphasizes that the "separate spheres" effect of domestic ideology in the patriarchal household is replicated in the home afloat; heterosexual couples occupy gendered territories on the water. These conclusions extend research on the geographies of patriarchal families, which has focused on "how familial ideologies shape men's and women's visions of possible and appropriate ways of living and how many women's responsibilities for domestic work wed them to the home" (Hanson and Pratt 1995, 121). Unlike other studies, my research moves beyond urban and suburban spaces to consider the responsibilities and "work" of recreation.

Rhetorically, I focus on the ways that feminine discourse—influenced by the meeting of homemaking and colonial ideologies—shapes female boat travelers' constructions of Native people, especially Native women. In contrast to studies of British- and European-authored texts (which describe Asian and African travel experiences), my work suggests that along the Northwest Coast in the late nineteenth century, female boat tourists depicted Native women as "counterfeit ladies," emphasizing the tourists' own femininity. I argue that, over time, feminine discourse moved away from a preoccupation with manners and Christian morals. Female marine tourists later used this discourse to portray imagined connections between themselves and Native women and to question their own position as outsiders in a Native world.

The accounts I read show how women's experiences traveling in marine environments differ from literary imaginings about women at sea. Literary critics, novelists, and poets use marine metaphors to symbolize woman's escape from the "social moorings" of gender expectations. The travelers I analyze, in contrast, emphasize their connectedness to the *land*scape and favor relatively home-based imagery (for instance, offering great detail about flora on shore but depicting the seascape as "indescribable"). The exceptions come with a woman—traveling without a husband—defining herself as "captain" (thus giving herself the power and responsibility to read the seascape) and with oral histories recalling girlhood on the water. I hypothesize that frontier girls, particularly, appear to have escaped the gender-specific expectations for domestic role-playing. Free to participate in the marine environment, these adolescents revel in "getting their dresses wet." My analysis questions the notion that woman are naturally more connected to the earth/shore than are men. These female voyagers' links to dry land appear rooted in a patriarchal world-view that limits women, not in any atavistic female desire or instinct.

My ideas branch from and extend ongoing gender-studies research in the fields of English, history, geography, and environmental studies. In the disciplines of English and geography, an interest in British women who visit Asian and African colonies has dominated inquiry into women and travel. I know of no analysis of gender and travel along the Northwest Coast. Literary and historical study of women and landscape has been led by those interested in the North American frontier. Historians working in this field have, until recently, been primarily concerned with the limitations and freedoms White women experienced as they migrated west overland with their families and with women's role as carriers of culture and community in the nineteenth century.

Since the 1970s, issues of gender and space have grown increasingly significant in the discipline of geography. Feminist research in this area has concentrated on the urban experiences of women, focusing on labor and urban landscapes. I found that the extension of theories regarding space, work, and gender into the built space of the boat was appropriate for this project. I also believe that the results of this project may make an important contribution to the developing interdisciplinary field of environmental studies; at the core of this work is my concern for how women construct, and are shaped by, one specific regional environment. In her essay "Approaches to the Study of Women and the Landscape," Janice Monk (1984) tells us that we need "regionally specific" studies to make the field of women and environment more relevant to women's lives; universal theories of gender and environment, she argues, are too essentialist and impractical to be significant on a local level. To date, the study of women and environment has been dominated by Americans working in the Southwest. The most significant text on gender and regionalism, *Regionalism and the Female Imagination* (Toth 1985), includes essays on virtually every region of the United States except the Northwest. As scholars such as Carolyn Merchant (1980) question assumptions about human relationships to the environment, and as thinkers such as Vera Norwood (1988) call for "studies beginning from the premise of the importance of a particular region" (169), my critique of the "home versus nature" polarity in a regional context extends work already done on women, the West, and domestic ideology.

The title *At Home Afloat* is borrowed from Kathrene Pinkerton's (1940) account; she uses the phrase repeatedly when describing her attempts to create a comfortable home in the cramped space of her husband's boat. Perhaps she was alluding to the "at home" custom of upper-class women—an "at home" afternoon was a time set aside by a lady to receive callers in her own element. Yet the ambiguity of the English word "home" prompts a number of questions about my use of it throughout this book. In the introduction to their anthology *Homeground* (1996), Kathryn Trueblood and Linda Stovall describe home as "a word of paradox and antipode" (11). John Hollander (1993) writes that "there is no word so loaded as 'home' in the Romance languages, and English (or German, etc.) sentences containing the word are always variously translated" (38). Etymologies of the term vary.[3] Tim Putnam (1993) suggests the slippery nature of the term by asking, "Does the usage indicate an environment encountered, relationships enacted, and ideal envisaged, or an articulation of all three?" (155). Home may simultaneously invoke all the possibilities that Putnam suggests: as an environment, home can denote a dwelling, landscape, or nation. Each of those environments in turn suggests certain relationships; for example, the idea of a built house as home suggests a dichotomy between indoor and outdoor and a belief that humans are more comfortable and at ease when separated from nature. The dwelling, landscape, and nation each have their ideals, relative to culture and history, but notions of home *all* carry with them a sense of nostalgia and inevitability. Home is our origin; it is the place to which we must return. "Home" is a command option on my keyboard: pressing it, I return the cursor to the left margin, where—in my culture—text begins.

---

3 Hollander claims the word is derived from the Indo-European *kei*, "implying lying down, a bed or couch, and something dear or beloved" (40); with *Home: A Short History of an Idea* (1986), Witold Rybczynski traces the term back to the Old Norse *heima*.

When I use the phrase "at home afloat," I am referring most specifically to a sense of comfort, ease, satisfaction, or contentment (rarely) felt and described by women at sea. That phrase connotes a good deal of irony and tension. As I discuss in more detail in chapter two, women's access to the masculine territory of boats has resulted, in large part, from their homemaking skills. However, the strict limitations placed on women's roles at sea ironically derive from the same domestic ideology that initially allowed them access. The idea of home is not wholly positive. As J. Douglas Porteous (1990) points out, "It can, in its security, its routine, its well-knownness, become a prison" (107). Jan C. Dawson (1996) acknowledges that "some of the most devastating events in peoples' lives, and especially in women' [sic] lives, have historically occurred in the home" (2). Those tensions—between home as a safe place and home as a prison—are particularly distinct in feminist considerations of the notion of home. Alan Trachtenberg (1993) describes the "universal" appeal of the hearth and home with its "fathers and mothers in their place, children secure in the home-based knowledge of what a man is and how a woman differs" (211). He writes that in contemporary society domestic images "shaped by absolute gender roles and sanctioned by sentiment seem outlandishly retrograde, unacceptably patriarchal, and embarrassingly naive" and goes on to describe the common influence of the ideology of the home on our desires:

> *And yet, does not a residue of such sentiment persist in our cultural memory of imagined havens of warmth, shelters against the storm? Is it possible to think about what "home" means without succumbing in some degree to nostalgia for the once-sanctified bourgeois family of European and American cities? Isn't this at least one of the images we unthinkingly set out to re-create when we imagine homes for ourselves, when we go about converting real space into a representation of the homeplace? (211)*

Because the home is seen as "the supreme cultural achievement of women" (Oakes 1984, 28), the territory for "specialized domestic work—women's work" (Rybczynski 70), a space "built by women, since men only know how to build a house from the outside" (Bachelard 1958, 68), the nostalgic hunger for home serves as both praise and a trap for women. In "The Home: A Critical Problem for Changing Sex Roles" (1980), Susan Saegert and Gary Winkel show that "it is almost impossible to imagine a 'home' ... without imagining a caretaking woman in the setting" (41). This close association between woman and the home, they conclude, leads to considerable ambivalence about the significance of home in the identities of contemporary women. In their essay "Feminist Politics: What's Home Got to Do with It?" (1986), Biddy Martin and Chandra Talpade Mohanty review the appeal and power of "home" as metaphor in feminist writings. Finding that a great deal of feminist thinking relies on unexamined notions of home, family, and nation, and is overly preoccupied with finding "safe places," the authors conclude that the women's movement replicates the conditions of the home:

"Being home" refers to the place where one lives within familiar, safe, protected boundaries; "not being home" is a matter of realizing that home was an illusion of coherence and safety based on the exclusion of specific histories of oppression and resistance, the repression of differences even within oneself. (196)

Arguing against the homogeneity of the White, middle-class liberalism of mainstream feminism, the authors suggest that the best work of the women's movement will come not from the desire and expectation for "being home," but rather from the struggle and re-evaluation necessitated by "not being home," not being safe, not being complacent, not repeating the comfortable pattern.

This tension—between valuing the work that women have done traditionally and exceptionally well, and criticizing the patriarchal idea of home that assumes women must occupy this separate sphere—is expressed in my title *At Home Afloat*. As I considered women's participation in Northwest Coast marine tourism, the spaces they share with men afloat, and their constructions of people and landscapes beyond the familiar "homescape," I struggled with that tension, because this region is my home and these experiences are, in many ways, my own. In addition to spending literally thousands of hours on the water, boating with my family, I have worked at a yacht charter company (cleaning and preparing the powerboats and sailboats), worked as the only girl at a marina (attending the gas dock, waxing and painting boats, hoisting them in and out of the water on a sling), worked as a fish packer (I grabbed frozen salmon by their tails as they came out of a glazing machine, then stacked them in crates), and worked as a copyeditor reading scientific manuscripts for the National Oceanic and Atmospheric Administration in Seattle. I came to this project knowing that I felt more "at home" in some of these jobs and activities than in others, and I have attempted to learn about and express some of the reasons why this is so.

One of the most significant contributions of feminism to scholarship has been its questioning of epistemological objectivity. My strategy to use personal memories to introduce chapters is not simply an attempt to interject colorful but meaningless "slices of life" into a theoretical text. These moments are meant to familiarize the reader with some of my "filters"—obviously my gender, but also my nationality, class, and age, and others, such as the size of the boat I traveled on (relatively small compared to those depicted in most of the accounts I analyze) and the geographical area I traveled most frequently (limited to the San Juans group, the Gulf Islands, and the Sunshine Coast).

These filters have inevitably affected my selection and discussion of texts to some degree. I am aware, for instance, that traveling mainly as a power boater has made me more knowledgeable about, and interested in, that form of transportation. Perhaps, then, it is no coincidence that sailing does not figure prominently in my history of regional marine tourism. Traveling by small boat has prejudiced me to believe it is a more "authentic" way to experience the natural environment, compared with passage on the larger steamers or liners. All travelers have their prejudices regarding authenticity; mine may have led to my emphasis on the clichéd perspective of steamer tourists toward landscape.

Valuing the familial closeness that grew from "making do" with a small and less luxurious boat, I am sometimes judgmental of yachters from the higher classes, and I tend to favor texts by middle-class travelers such as Kathrene Pinkerton and "Capi" Blanchet. Readers will undoubtedly discover other cultural, historical, and theoretical biases of which I am unaware.

The effects of using "home" as a synthesizing theme might also be questioned, particularly regarding the issue of class. Much of my original thinking in preparation for this project was based on studies of women in the West—studies that sometimes make use of the "cult of true womanhood." I now understand that Elizabeth Jameson (1987) rightly questions whether the cult of true womanhood is a useful starting point for examining the lives of women in the West. She argues that most frontier women were not Euro-American or upper- or middle-class actors shaped by prescriptions for Victorian respectability. I found the "cult of the home" concept of domestic ideology relevant to the shaping of my own arguments because most nineteenth-century tourists on the coast were British and Euro-American actors of the upper and middle classes. However, that class connection may break down as boat tourism became more accessible to lower classes in the twentieth century. Having personally felt the "woman's-place-is-in-the-home" bias keenly in working-class labor situations, I assumed the Victorian ideology had been recycled and continued to thrive. But I suspect that there are many more subtle distinctions to be made in the interface of home and class.

My interdisciplinary use of the theoretical frameworks of feminist geographers, historians, and literary critics has made this project more rich and fulfilling than it would have been had I pursued it within the rubric of any single discipline. However, I have to acknowledge that this interdisciplinary approach does create its own filters, gaps, and limitations. Working to familiarize myself with, and to address, so many weighty theoretical conversations (regarding postcolonialism, ecofeminism, theories of gender and space) in *one* book inevitably leads to generalizations and gaps that might have been more cleverly resolved were a specialist considering each of the areas I examine. I hope this project will provoke specialists into taking up some of the issues I introduce. For instance, I believe a much more thorough look at colonial discourse in tourist accounts is called for in this cross-border region, where so many cultures have overlapped in such a relatively short span of time. Writing a woman-centered text, I have marginalized and ignored a great deal of interesting and available material written by male tourists; those works also have much to tell—especially regarding the changing natural environment along the coast and visitors' perceptions of it and interactions with it. My research, focused on tourist accounts, has examined women in marine work environments only peripherally but suggests the potential for more analytical study of labor and domestic ideology at sea. Because of limited time and resources, I abandoned my original plan to collect oral histories from boat travelers; I am convinced that such an effort could shed more light on the work I have begun. Because my project is grounded in written texts, I had access to a relatively limited number of boat travelers' experiences. I think it would be profitable to seek out women who captain their own vessels or who succeed at sharing power equitably on the water—those who break through the boundaries I have mapped—to discover how they were able to work those "sea changes."

CHAPTER ONE

Northwest Coast Marine Tourism: A Contextual History

On 9 June 1963, a young couple—married one year to the day—began writing in a flimsy, black, staple-bound notebook, which they titled the "Log of the *Sho-Nuff*." The log begins in Richard's handwriting:

Sun. June 9, 1963

Left on weeks vacation from boat house 8:45 A.M. Look cloudy and overcast. Water conditions a little lumpy to Thatcher Pass, good from there to Henry Island. Followed the Evergreen State [ferry] through the "lumps" to Sidney Spit. Contacted Jimmy on the radio but to much traffic to talk. Had cheeseburgers at Sidney. Left there about 1:00. Got gas in canoe Cove, and then ran to "Rat Cove." Quite windy by now, but nothing but sun. Several big boats at the dock. We had it all to our selves by dusk. One boat left their fish net, and came back an hour later to get it. Had our T-Bones and baked spuds.[1]

His wife, Sally, adds in parentheses: *"(Happy Anniversary!)."*

Richard worked as a laborer at the plywood mill in Anacortes, Washington, where the couple lived, and Sally's first baby was due that August. A reader can tell from their logbook entry that the couple—or at least Richard, the primary writer—were practised boaters. He makes note of windy conditions but is apparently not bothered by the weather. He knows how to follow a state ferry through rough water and how to use the VHF radio, and he makes no mention of having to consult charts for directions through miles of water passages from U.S. to Canadian sites. A good cut of meat is worthy of mention in the day's highlights—perhaps "T-bone" is a code meant to signify a special occasion? Code is not enough for Sally; she opens a dialogue in the logbook by writing a message back to Richard: Happy Anniversary!

---

1 Spelling and punctuation appear as they do in the original logbooks.

Perhaps because Richard operated the boat and Sally needed more responsibilities, or perhaps because Richard got tired of Sally correcting his spelling, Sally took over the task of keeping the logbook the next year. That log, and the others that followed from 1963 to the present, are written almost exclusively in her hand. They record vacation dates, departure and arrival times, weather conditions, and good locations for ice, gas, fresh water, groceries, and fudgesicles. The logbooks tell who owned which boat and where they were seen. They document the temperature of the water in frequented bays, locate good places to swim, and describe the captain of the *Thea Foss* shining his spotlight on a waterfall at night. They give anecdotal names to coves and preserve an image of a crane catching fish one evening at dusk. They preserve a family history—what was said, what was done, what was eaten, what went wrong, where and when vacations happened. Reading them now, it seems to me that they also indicate how—in this watery part of the world and for this family—boat tourism was a normal part of everyday life. On a windy afternoon in 1963, when Sally was overdue with her pregnancy, she writes:

Sept. 5th

Went for a little "joy ride" to see if we could hasten the stork. Had a picnic at Saddlebag [Island] and went for a ride around Guemes Island. Stork paid no attention—

Three days later she adds:

Sept. 8th

Had a "steak out" at Burrows Island—to heck with the stork. Met all the fishing boats coming out as we headed for home.

Because Sally and Richard Pagh are my parents—and I am that baby who would not be shaken loose by a joyride in the boat—these logbook entries begin to suggest the subjectivity I bring to a study of boat travel. I have been a pleasure boater since before I was born and have participated in this activity as a daughter; which is to say that, because my parents have always taken care of me on the water, I have associated boat travel with tenderness, safety, and deep satisfaction. We are boaters, not yachters; we never joined a yacht club. Occasionally we met up with other boating families, but for the most part boating seemed a private family occasion. When I was young, we went out in the boat every weekend (unless there was a funeral or a gale) from about March to September, we fished occasionally in winter, and each summer we took a longer trip north from Anacortes, traveling through parts of the most popular Northwest Coast cruising grounds. For as long as I can remember, boating has been an essential part of my identity; the things that I enjoy, the things that I do well (such as rowing and reading) are things I learned in a marine environment.

To understand the significance of this project, readers must understand that not just *my* identity, but also cross-border Northwest Coast regional identity, have been strongly linked to our marine environment and that, in the Western world, marine environments are traditionally male environments.[2] The centrality—both literal and figurative—of water (in the form of an "Inland Sea" and "Inside Passage" most explicitly) in this region is an important context for regional identity and gender studies in a regional context.

Gender and Regional Identity

The Northwest Coast runs along the western edge of Oregon and Washington State, through Puget Sound and British Columbia coastal waters, and into Southeastern Alaska. Historians, economists, and poets alike have emphasized the significance of water as the defining feature of the region. In his *History of the Northwest Coast* (1884), Hubert Howe Bancroft selects maritime history as his starting point. In British Columbia, written history commonly begins with maritime colonial history and emphasizes the impressions of British sea captains and their crews. Captain George Vancouver's description of a gloomy, monotonous, and desolate landscape in 1792 is a common starting point for B.C. histories. Some American Northwest histories stretch back to Vitus Bering's voyage of 1741-42, which initiated the coastal trade in sea otter pelts, or earlier to Juan de Fuca's disputed arrival in the sixteenth century. American histories of the Pacific Northwest may begin by emphasizing the overland trail experience, but they quickly move toward examining the significance of marine environments. Modern history of the Northwest Coast is a history of changing transportation to navigate the coast and the inland sea and to connect the region—on both sides of the border—to the rest of the world. This history moves from Captain James Cook's ships, the *Resolution* and the *Discovery,* through Vancouver's *Chatham;* Meares' *North-West America* (called the first boat built on the North Coast and launched in 1788); the *Beaver* (the first steamship brought from Britain and used to manage the Hudson's Bay Company outposts from 1836); the *Julius Pringle,* which sailed into Puget Sound in 1853 seeking lumber for San Francisco; the "mosquito fleet" in Puget Sound and the Union Steamship Company line, which connected B.C. coastal settlements from 1889 to 1959 and carried hundreds of Chinese, Japanese, and Native workers to fish plants upcoast; the Canadian Pacific Railway's *Empress of India,* which linked Vancouver to Asia in 1891; the first seine boats to use the gasoline engine on Puget Sound in 1903; the *Komagata Maru,* barred from discharging South Asian immigrants in Vancouver in 1914; the twelve hundred Japanese fish boats impounded by the Royal Canadian Navy at Annieville Dyke in 1941; and the towboats and container ships that still link the coast to other continents.

Margaret Ormsby opens her widely read text *British Columbia: A History* (1958) with a chapter called "Approach from the Sea," that underscores the

---

2 I discuss this argument at length and offer support for it in chapters two and four.

significance of marine transportation. Her use of the present tense shows that in the late 1950s, B.C. identity remained strongly linked to marine transportation and the exploitation of the natural environment. "A coast of indescribable beauty," she writes, "it offers almost every kind of natural challenge to explorer and mariner. Its products are the products of northern seas and forests, and none of these may be obtained without fortitude and effort" (4). South of the border, Daniel Jack Chasan (1981) shows a similar mentality at work as he explores the history of water transportation on Puget Sound in a resource-extraction economy. Washington Sea-Grant researchers Robert Bish et al. (1975) conclude that the water is a symbol of identity in the Puget Sound region (89). Memoirs, essays, and poems confirm the importance of water in defining the characteristics of local topography and a regional psyche on both sides of the U.S.-Canada line. British Columbian writer Gilean Douglas (1983) defines the North Coast of her province as "saltchuck country," and American essayist Brenda Peterson (1990) asks: "What is it about the element of water that shapes and characterizes our Northwest life?" She supposes "our psychic roots might look more like the delicate float of jellyfish than grounded tree ganglia" (128-29).

In both Canadian and American histories, the Northwest Coast region has been depicted as a rugged and inhospitable landscape, a frontier, and a region of seemingly endless natural resources (first otter pelts, then gold, coal, fish, and timber—all transported by water). The more recent transplants to the region, such as Peterson, find themselves at odds with the historical emphasis on "cruel" nature and the frontier mentality; hers, for instance, is a much gentler and aesthetic vision of the potential of local landscape. "I've apprenticed myself to Puget Sound," she writes, "because I believe it will teach me more about living than what I've learned so far. Maybe I hope its watery wisdom will seep into me every night as I lie, listening to the whoosh of waves against my seawall" (132). Her words stand in contrast to the pioneer folklore, songs, and reminiscences of the region, which emphasize the near-impenetrable nature of the forest and the unpredictability of the sea. When the sea is praised in these sources, it is as a last-resort means of provision for the supper table; "When the tide's out, the table's set" was a popular axiom.

Captain George Vancouver admired the pastoral topography of Whidbey Island, settlers sometimes felt they had discovered a paradise (or were duped into believing they could buy property in paradise), and some British Columbia writers emphasized an Edenic vision of the province (Pritchard 1982, 1984). But the more entrenched view of the Northwest Coast is as a proving ground, a region where heroic men battle nature and survive. Historian Carlos Schwantes (1989) suggests that the environment itself has led to the construction of actors in Pacific Northwest history as heroes; that focus on what he calls "the heroic nature-heroic man approach to Pacific Northwest history" has left, he argues, unfortunate gaps in regional history. The explanation behind this approach to regional history, he writes, is that "because nature assumed heroic proportions in the far Northwest, heroic men were needed to tame or subdue it" (xix-xx). Karen J. Blair (1988) notes that "even if this romantic notion was impossible to prove, it remained central to the thinking of generations of settlers and helps to explain why so many newcomers defined progress as taming nature through exploitation" (6). Whether or not we agree that nature assumed heroic proportions in the region, actors who make their way into the regional histories and characters featured in popular regional literary texts have often been made to fit the heroic man stereotype. The memoir of old-timer Archie Binns (1942), raised on a "stump farm" near Shelton, Washington, in the late nineteenth century, provides an example. He describes the project of clearing land this way:

> *In the resulting contest, no one sees more tangible proof of his success than the stump farmer. No profession accomplishes more guileless and ultimate good; no one can have a more secure or more lasting sense of achievement. To have remade part of the earth's surface with his own hands; to have let light into what was once part of the dark forest ... those are the chief rewards of the stump farmer. (13)*

Binns' use of "his" is no accident here; this "sense of having shared in creation" (13) is repeatedly constructed—on both sides of the U.S.-Canada border—as a male responsibility and reward, despite the fact that women also participated in clearing the land. Binns recalls the words of his father when a visitor called at the stump farm; these words clearly speak to the issue of gender history in the region:

> *I recall a tactless visitor who alighted from a livery stable rig and looked about our stumpy clearing with a kind of horror and disbelief. "My God!" he said. "What can you raise in a place like this?"*
> *Father answered, "Boys." (13)*

Many historians now understand pioneer culture—which has dominated the popular concept of Northwest Coast regional identity—to have been what Jean Barman (1991) describes as "a truly male culture" (350). Near the end of the nineteenth century, three times as many white males as white females lived in British Columbia; until the end of World War I, the sex ratio in the province remained more than two to one (Barman 349). Although, as Karen J. Blair (1988) and Gillian Creese and Veronica Strong-Boag (1992) show, regional women's lives have been rich, demanding, and varied, regional histories (such as Ormsby's) have overlooked what Susan Armitage (1988) describes as the importance of the "lives, activities, and values of ordinary women" (233). Instead, Creese and Strong-Boag argue, regional history concerns itself with the values of the more numerous and vocal males. They observe this interest is focused in two main areas: "the economic dimensions of life in the province through the history of business and labour and the conflicts among classes; and the social dimensions of ethnic and racial population variation and the antagonisms and inequalities that have developed" (3). As a result of this limited conception of regional history, they write:

... women have remained absent, either as class actors or as members of ethnic and racially defined communities. This debate [over the significance of labor and race], building on long-standing ideas about the polarization of forces on the B.C. resource frontier, has for the most part failed to move beyond a fascinated preoccupation with men and, occasionally, a male perspective on women. (3)

In her essay in *British Columbia Reconsidered* (1992), Daphne Marlatt describes how, "In this most western of provinces, at the edge of the continent, we live in a culture not yet disengaged from its frontier roots." Because females "have never figured as cultural heroes in the macho scheme of things"(296), women's writing is needed; it subverts the heroic by paying attention "to the little things that the heroic through-line of action ignores as background" (303). Its language can "comment on the stereotypes hero and heroine represent" and attempt to escape from them (302). One of the most common stereotypes regarding hero and heroine is the idea that the hero travels while the heroine remains at home. Gillian Brown (1990) comments on the plethora of American literature recording this masculine desire for freedom and the feminine will toward domestication: Huck Finn versus the "sivilizing" Widow Douglas.[3] The woman's sphere, the domestic, is defined by patriarchal culture as that from which the male must escape "in order to establish and preserve his identity" (5).

Marine travel literature by women—a relatively large body of Northwest Coast travel writing that has been overshadowed by interest in male exploration literature—subverts the concept that travelers desire escape from the domestic sphere; domesticity and travel (previously polarized concepts) coexist in these accounts. This literature demonstrates the power and appeal of the idea of home in a natural environment (the "rugged" frontier and the sea) and in a built environment (the boat), which could both be characterized as "masculine." These accounts are valuable because they are written from a perspective not often considered in Northwest Coast regional studies; they are generated neither by explorers, nor traders, nor missionaries, nor settlers, but by women who were mobile and who had the leisure to observe and record the world and the people around them. Traveling by water, on the regional "symbol of identity" (Bish et al. 1975), these women articulate many journeys that share—to a degree—a common method of transportation and a common route over a period of about one hundred and thirty years.

---

3 The terms "masculine" and "feminine" are not synonymous with "male" or "female." "Female," for example, refers to the conventionally accepted definition of being biologically "not male." "Feminine" refers to the malleable social expectations for how females should act and think.

Cruising and Steam Beginnings

"Cruising" is a word and an activity that has much changed over time. The term was in use as early as 1712, when Woodes Rogers published *A Cruising Voyage Round the World*. At the time of early Russian, Spanish, and English exploration of the Northwest Coast, the term "cruising" was used to describe traveling "to and fro" by ship.[4] Because the region was penetrable almost exclusively by water corridors, and because the earliest written records of the Northwest Coast (I am thinking particularly of Steller, Mourelle, Cook, and Vancouver) are accounts written from the perspective of men exploring the coast by boat, this body of literature could arguably be classified as "cruising literature."[5] Clearly the mapping, claiming, and dividing of this New World territory depended upon boat travel, and the earliest recorded impressions of its landscape and inhabitants are conditioned by the voyage experience and by the discourse seafaring men used in their journals and logbooks. Even two hundred years later, the discovery, cataloging, and ownership of Native culture along the coast was largely conditioned by boat travel. In the 1930s, for example, Frederica De Laguna collected information for *The Archaeology of Cook Inlet, Alaska* (1934) using a series of vessels. De Laguna uses the term "cruise" to describe the research process: "The *Chugach* took us for a ten-day cruise around the Sound, stopping at ... villages where we had an opportunity to talk to the natives, and also touching at a few of the ancient village sites" (8). "In all," De Laguna writes, "we traveled about 440 miles in our skiff" during one summer of their work, and although the marine environment made travel possible, "owing to the extreme range of the tides ... travel is very difficult. It is possible to go only with the tide" (8).

In *The Hidden Northwest* (1972), Robert Cantwell claims that Northwest regional literature opens with Don Francisco Antonio Mourelle's *Voyage of the Sonora* (1780). He writes of Mourelle: "He saw the land from the deck of the *Sonora*" (247). The implication of this perspective in Northwest Coast exploration literature probably warrants a study in itself. In this project, however, I define "cruising" in more modern terms; I use it to connote travel by oar, sail, steam, gasoline engine, or diesel, undertaken in significant part for pleasure, and either individually or with a small group of people. I do not use "cruising" in reference to taking passage on an ocean-going vessel or commercial steamer. Cruising literature is the product of a private tour or vacation; it tends to include anecdotes and descriptions, and its author frequently adopts a tone of

---

4 The Oxford English Dictionary traces "cruising" to seventeenth-century Dutch origins: "*kruyssen op de Zee*." It defines the verb:

> To sail to and fro over some part of the sea without making for a particular port or landing-place, on the look out for ships, for the protection of commerce in time of war, for plunder, or (in modern times) for pleasure.

5 Because the overland explorations of Lewis and Clark, Alexander Mackenzie, Simon Fraser, and David Thompson depended substantially upon boat transportation, one might also argue that significant portions of their accounts are also cruising literature.

spectatorship or high adventure. Even given this more modern definition, cruising literature of the region remains strongly linked to the social history and topography of the Northwest Coast, to the settler's urge to create a home in an environment perceived as sometimes pastoral and welcoming, but often cruel and inhospitable.

Cruising began in the southerly portion of the Inside Passage, at roughly the same time in the areas now known as Washington State and southern British Columbia. Ezra Meeker's 1905 account, "A Cruise on Puget Sound," describes traveling by boat with his brother Oliver in 1853—at a time when "the Sound was a solitude so far as transportation facilities, with here and there a [sailing] vessel loading piles and square timber for the San Francisco market. Not a steamer was then plying on the Sound; not even a sailing craft that essayed to carry passengers" (2). Meeker begins his account by emphasizing the brothers' anticipation of action:

> So, when we cast off the line at Olympia, on or about the 28th day of May, 1853, we were assured of one thing and that was a concert of action, be there danger or only labor ahead. Neither of us had much experience in boating, and none as to boat building, but when we decided to make the trip and discarded the idea of taking a canoe we set to work with a hearty good will to build us a skiff out of light lumber. (2)

Sounding much like a tourist embarking upon a well-deserved vacation, Meeker describes the start of the voyage as idyllic:

> Nothing can be more enjoyable than favorable conditions in a boating trip, the more especially to those who have long been in the harness of severe labor, and for a season must enjoy forced repose. And so we lazily floated with the tide, sometimes taking a few strokes with the oars, and at other times whistling for the wind, as the little town of Olympia to the south became dimmed by distance. (3)

But the pioneer Meeker[6] also describes how little the brothers knew about the geography of Puget Sound and the effects of the tides upon their progress. "Poor innocent souls," he writes, "we thought we could follow the shore line and thus avoid danger, and perhaps float with the tide, and thus minimize the labor, and yet keep our bearings" (3). His words illustrate how little the pioneers in the mid-nineteenth century knew of the region and how unfamiliar boat travel was to the overland settlers. At the end of their first day, the brothers "talked and pulled and puzzled until finally it dawned upon us that the tide had turned and we were being carried back to almost the spot from whence we came" (3). The author relishes their inexperience and ineptitude at making progress or finding adventure on their first day out. There are no gruesome or serious consequences

---

6 Meeker lived his later life in relative fame, as the "only adult survivor" of the 1850s overland trail experience (Meeker 1908).

for the young men's innocence; as a result, the text reads more like Jerome K. Jerome's humorous *Three Men in a Boat* (1889) than a nineteenth-century tale of "noble" adventure.

The Meekers appear to have no fixed schedule for their cruise, and clearly the overall experience is extremely pleasant:

> *Did you ever, reader, take a drive, we will say in a hired outfit, with a paid coachman, and then take the lines in your own hands by way of contrast? If so, then you will realize the thrill of enjoyment where you pull your own oars, sail your own craft, cook your own dinner, and lie in your own bed of boughs, and go when and where you will with that keen relish incident to the independence and uncertainties of such a trip. (18)*

Meeker's travel-writing aesthetic emphasizes independence, ingenuity, and self-reliance. No yachtsman, Meeker completely lacks interest in, or awareness of, the conventions of yachting; he tells of his sense of accomplishment through descriptions of labor and he uses no nautical jargon. The two brothers row and camp their way north along Whidbey Island and west to Port Townsend before heading home. Not until several pages into the account does Meeker acknowledge that he is floating through Puget Sound looking for suitable land to stake a claim (10).

Like so many cruising narratives to follow Meeker's, this account attempts to offer ethnographic information about the Native people of the coast; he describes villages, songs, language, and food. He records the important role Native women played in transportation: "Then here came two well-manned canoes creeping along shore against the tide. I have said well-manned, but in fact, half the paddles were wielded by women, and the post of honor, or that where most dexterity was required, was occupied by a woman" (9). Meeker's travel narrative documents the maritime skills of women in a non-Western society. It also shows that it was impossible to cruise Puget Sound in a small vessel in 1853 without meeting and interacting with living Native culture at every turn in the landscape. Fenton Aylmer's *A Cruise in the Pacific* (1860) confirms that virtually the same could be said regarding the earliest pleasure boating north of the Juan de Fuca Strait. When Aylmer was on leave from his British naval vessel in Victoria, he hired a craft and crew for a cruise:

> *I proposed to four friends to get leave for twelve days, and by clubbing our resources together, engage a good boat and competent crew, and start on our expedition.*
>
> *Having ascertained all we could relative to our route, and the best manner of behaving to the tribes we were likely to meet, we set sail up the Gulf of Georgia, intending, if possible, to get round the island.* [7] *(123-24)*

---

7 Aylmer, his friends, the crew, and a hired "Yankee hunter" took their first rest at Newcastle Island, then visited a Native village a four hours' sail north of Nanaimo. Shortly after, word reached the party that because of a Native insurrection on the west coast of Vancouver Island, their naval ship had departed Esquimault. Aylmer and the others immediately sailed south, curtailing their cruise to rejoin their naval ship.

Clearly Aylmer regarded interaction with Native peoples as inevitable; it was essential that his party attempt to understand "the best manner of behaving to the tribes" to make a cruise.

Although Meeker is told there are no "transportation facilities" on Puget Sound, a Native community gives Meeker and his brother venison, and a "native matron" teaches them how to find and cook clams. Native people provide the brothers with lessons in Chinook jargon, the language necessary for coastal travel. And, perhaps most important, Natives knew the landscape. Meeker admits: "We did not really know whether we would go twenty miles or a hundred; whether we would find small waters or large; straight channels or intricate by-ways; in a word we knew but very little of what lay before us" (2-3). Although Meeker does not recognize them as "transportation facilities," Native camps are a great aid to the brothers on their cruise.

The conflicts that arrived as settler and Native cultures overlapped never enter Meeker's narrative directly; like Theodore Winthrop, who traveled Puget Sound by canoe later that same summer, Meeker seeks the future in the landscape through which he rows. Winthrop (1862) is still known for his firm belief that the grand landscape of the Oregon Territory would inspire "new systems of thought and life" (129) and free Americans from tyranny (a great irony, given that the settlement of the territory created domination over its aboriginal inhabitants). Meeker wanted to find suitable farmland to settle with his wife and family and to profit from the land; his use of boat touring to participate in the imperialist project to commodify the landscape, and to marginalize the people living upon it, is a subtext we can recognize and name in retrospect. His conviction that the Pacific Northwest was the ideal setting for his own idyllic future is reflected in the pastoral rhetoric of his cruising narrative.

While traveling north of the border, Charles Barrett-Lennard appeals to the potential colonial emigrant of the period in his *Travels in British Columbia, with the Narrative of a Yacht Voyage Round Vancouver's Island* (1862; see map 2). In contrast to Meeker's idyllic prose, Barrett-Lennard makes use of high-adventure discourse and nautical language. He writes in his preface, composed at the Royal Thames Yacht Club, London:

> *The interest which at the present moment attaches to everything connected with British Columbia and Vancouver's Island, has induced me to believe that a narrative of personal adventure and experience in these still comparatively unknown but highly important colonies might prove not only acceptable to the general reader, but of practical utility to the intending emigrant. (v)*

Barrett-Lennard departed England in September 1859, carrying his cutter-rigged, twenty-ton yacht,

> *... which I took out with me on the deck of the ship in which we made our passage to Victoria. On my arrival in the colony I had her thoroughly fitted for sea. After various prepatory trial trips on the channel in the neighborhood of Victoria, to test*

her sea-going qualities, we started in the month of September, 1860, on our cruise round the island, which we expected would take us about six weeks to accomplish, but we soon found that we had not made sufficient allowance for the difficulties we should encounter in our expedition. (27-28)

His account marks the first instance of yachting off the Northwest Coast—a long-established activity in Britain and Europe. Yachts originated as small Dutch war vessels, or *jaghts*, before 1599, and "by the middle of the [seventeenth] century a person of power and wealth possessed a yacht" for pleasure (Heaton 1966, 29; see also Clark 1904). By 1702—the yacht having been introduced to England by Charles II—there were "literally hundreds of private yachts, varying in size" (Heaton 28) in use by the Dutch and English:

... when King Charles II of England spent part of his exile in Holland he was introduced to yachting and formed an enthusiasm for the sport which lasted his lifetime. And it is to King Charles the English owe the introduction of yachting to England. For no sooner had the news of his Proclamation as King on the 8th May 1660 in Westminster Hall, London, reached the Prince of Orange than the latter immediately placed a yacht at the service of the English King. (Heaton 29; see also Phillips-Birt 1974)

Yachts—created initially as vessels of war and later used by persons of privilege—are thus associated historically with empire, with power, with defending and extending the homeland, and with creating what Mary Louise Pratt (1992) calls "the 'domestic subject' of Euroimperialism" (4). Because of this link, and because of the harsher weather, tidal, and topographical conditions found north of Puget Sound, Barrett-Lennard aboard his yacht adopts a tone very different from Meeker's. Natives are not friendly, interesting, or helpful; rather "They appear insensible to anything like chivalry or generous feeling, killing and slaying with remorseless cruelty, undeterred by any sentiment of compuncture" (41). Barrett-Lennard makes these claims despite the fact that a Native man "accidentally become [*sic*] one of our crew," and for a period of time during the two and one-half month cruise made himself useful (101). His emphasis on the crude and cruel nature of Natives implies legitimization of colonial rule.

Barrett-Lennard draws attention to the adventurous side of cruising throughout his narrative, playing up the danger of the Natives and of the natural environment. "We were much impressed during this cruise by the natural beauties of Nootka Sound" (100) he writes, but he emphasizes the drama of "our struggle with the elements," "the pitiless pelting rain," and "our narrow escape" from the tides and sunken rocks. Even kelp poses a threat to yachts and brave colonialists:

I have seen a vessel of forty or fifty tons, with a fair breeze, brought up dead, as if at anchor, by coming suddenly on a bed of kelp, and woe betide the hapless wight whose fate it may be to get entangled, while bathing, among the treacherous rope-like stems, and long, leathery leaves of this Brobdignag, submarine growth:

he is caught, like a fly, in the meshes of a spider, and with as little chance of escape.
To this fact I can testify, from several painful cases of brave fellows and capital
swimmers who thus lost their lives during my stay in the colony. (17)

In this way, Barrett-Lennard engages in the common strategies of what Rebecca
Stott (1989) calls the "man-made discourse" of imperialist travel writing, a gendered discourse that emphasizes the importance of the (White) male experience
and (White) male camaraderie. This "adventure narrative" genre, as Martin
Green (1979) describes it, is "the energising myth of empire" (xi) and depends
upon "settings remote from the domestic" within which a central character can
engage in a series of exploits to prove his courage, leadership, strength, cunning,
fortitude, and persistence (23). While it has become more common to deconstruct the narratives of eighteenth-century Northwest Coast travelers in light of
imperialist discourses and agendas,[8] readers should understand that some nineteenth-century (and even some twentieth-century[9]) tourists mimic and applaud
this discourse while traveling in its wake. The extent to which female boating
tourists adopted and resisted that discourse when they began to travel the region
in "floating homes" is the topic of my third chapter.

For male and female settlers living on the Northwest Coast and coastal islands
during the latter half of the nineteenth century, boat travel was not a swashbuckling male adventure; it was an integral part of everyday living. Because the
water of Puget Sound, the Strait of Juan de Fuca, and the Inside Passage between
Vancouver Island and the mainland connected—and stood between—nearly
everyone and everything, boat travel was essential. In his history of Puget
Sound, Daniel Jack Chasan (1981) shows how during settlement "The Sound
itself was and would remain central in the most literal sense: the towns were
on the outside and the water was in the middle" (3). Even after the Northern
Pacific railroad arrived in Tacoma in 1883, the "rowboat still was and would
for decades remain a standard means of transportation; one might row to the
store, row to school, row to catch the steamboat, even row across the lower
Sound" (Chasan 15). Farther up the coast, this situation extended into the twentieth century. Eustace Smith recalls his 1900 upcoast honeymoon in an aural
history (prepared from 1964 recordings by David Day [1983]):

---

8 See, for example, Robin Fisher and Hugh Johnston (1993); Barry M. Gough (1992); Beth Hill
(1983); Lionel Kearns (1984); Noel Currie (1994). Some literature produced by nineteenth-century
traveling coastal missionaries has been reconsidered in light of postcolonial studies; see Robin Fisher
(1977).

9 I would argue, for example, that Joe Upton's *Journeys Through the Inside Passage: Seafaring
Adventures Along the Coast of British Columbia and Alaska* (1992) and Nan Nicolls' *North
of Anian: The Collected Journals of Gabrielle III Cruises in British Columbia Coastal Waters
1978-1989* (1990) could both be read as deliberate extensions of eighteenth-century Northwest
Coast exploration discourse.

So we set out in that rowboat full of goods and a small sail, left Comox for Beaver Cove. Sounds almost crazy now, setting out in that little boat with my child-bride and following that fierce ragged coastline all the way up, through the riptide at Seymour Narrows. (How many ships went down there? I can't remember. A lot of big ones.) Yes, through the Narrows, past—or rather wide around—the great whirlpool at Ripple Rock. Up the coast—and this was winter, so we'd have to lay in quite often because of the bad storms. Then when it would clear, we'd shovel the snow out of the boat and start up again. It took us more than a month to end that odyssey. I guess that was our honeymoon. Come to think of it, it wasn't such a bad honeymoon at that. (273)

Describing 1950s transportation connecting the isolated British Columbia coastal communities between Vancouver and Prince Rupert, Gilean Douglas (1983) writes:

... if you couldn't get at these pioneers by land, and the air was too expensive for anything except emergencies, what did you do? You got yourself a boat and took to the highways and byways of the sea. Everyone did it: ministers, doctors, lawyers, merchants and some beggar-men and thieves too. There were dental dories, hospital ships, barber boats and craft which carried salesmen selling everything from pots to photographs, groceries to garments. (230)

Small-boat travel was a necessity for settlers along the Northwest Coast; it was augmented with steamship service made widely available largely as a result of the Fraser River gold rush of 1858. The Hudson's Bay Company introduced steam to the North Coast when it brought the steamer *Beaver* from Britain to Fort Vancouver in 1836. But with the discovery of gold, side-paddle steamers were immediately brought to the region from the Sacramento River, where they had been used in the rush of 1849. The steamers were modified into stern-wheelers to suit the shallow banks of the Fraser River and later the coast (Marine Retirees Association 1977), and they were soon widely used in freight and passenger service. Archie Binns (1942) recalls the steamboat design "best suited to Puget Sound" and the development of the ship-building industry in Washington Territory:

... it was a shoal-draft stern-wheeler with two or three feet of freeboard amidships and a high superstructure that put the pilot house at least three decks up. A high, thin smokestack, painted black, made her appear even taller than she was. The steamers were invariably painted white and the enclosure of the lower deck, pierced by innocent house windows, accommodated freight and the crew's quarters. On each side was a sliding barn door through which passengers or freight could be received from a small boat alongside, or discharged. The stern-wheeler never had the side-wheeler's look of compact power or its seagoing abilities, but it took kindly to the sheltered inland waters, and was cheap to build and economical to run. (30)

The shape of steam travel changed again with the coming of railways to Washington and British Columbia, and with the advent of the Klondike gold rush in 1897. In 1891 the *Empress of India,* first of the original three Canadian Pacific Railway ships, was launched into service to Asia. When Seattle's *Queen* initiated transportation to the Klondike via Skagway, it opened the door for eventual tourism through the length of the Inside Passage to Alaska. During the same period, British Columbia's Union Steamship Company (established in 1889) was transporting freight, loggers, miners, cannery workers, and settlers upcoast. Gerald Rushton (1974) describes a typical dock scene late in the nineteenth century:

> *From seven in the morning, at the bustling little dock, freight of every variety was steadily unloaded in the small Union shed from a succession of horse-drawn wagons and drays, and handled on boards or with hand trucks through the forward side-doors of the* Comox. *Freight included flats of groceries, sacks of feed and bales of hay, barrels of beer, pipe and household effects, oil drums, and crates of live poultry and pigs. The larger livestock had to be held back for a freighter. The sides of beef and perishables went on last. It was an animated scene when, just before sailing time with most of the passengers already embarked, the mail van arrived and the coast's most welcome item, some forty or fifty mail sacks, would be passed aboard by hand. (25)*

By the year the Union Steamship Company was established in British Columbia, 892,000 local passengers were being carried by steamers on Puget Sound alone (Wright 1895, 363). Steam tourism—by this time long popular in England—grew out of the necessity for boat travel along the Northwest Coast.

Steam Tourism

During the Victorian period (1837-1901) the railway and the steamship greatly enhanced the comfort and speed of travel while reducing its cost; as a consequence, foreign travel became commonplace for middle-class Britons. Travel writing satisfied the Victorian appetite for both romance and fact, and as a result, nineteenth-century accounts of voyages and travels flooded the English market and fueled a desire for would-be travelers to discover and describe the more distant colonies (Corwin 1988; Distad 1988; Thurin 1988). As I discuss at length in chapter three, there is a great deal of interest in the experiences and accounts of Victorian women travelers (particularly those who visited Africa and Asia) and some degree of controversy about how to read these colonialist texts. There is no doubt, however, that whatever their motives, Victorian women traveled as no previous generation had.

But the Northwest Coast was a long way for English women to come—farther than Africa, farther than Asia. Frances Barkley was the first known European woman to make the voyage; she sailed to Vancouver Island with her husband, fur-trader Captain Charles Barkley, in 1787 and returned again in 1792. During the nineteenth century most women who arrived by ship from England came around Cape Horn to settle, not to travel. Consequently, as a tourist market for steam travel developed along the coast after the mid-nineteenth century, the participants tended to be mostly Americans (who often traveled by train across the continent to San Francisco or, later, to Portland and Tacoma) and wealthy Britons who could afford the extended journey.

One of the earliest records of women touring the region is an 1861 account written by Sophia Cracroft, who describes accompanying her aunt, Lady Jane Franklin. Franklin and Cracroft traveled the Northwest Coast by boat twice (in 1861 and again in 1870), following the disappearance of Franklin's husband, Sir John Franklin, in 1846 during an Arctic expedition.[10] Lady Franklin may have been searching for some word of her missing husband, but Cracroft's accounts of their travels between Victoria, Sitka, the Fraser River, and the Columbia River are more concerned with Native villages and the purchase of Native "curios," the lifestyle of settlers, the comforts of their ship, the natural setting, the honors accorded to Lady Franklin,[11] and the unacceptable presence of Americans on board the vessels. When traveling up the American Columbia River—which they find inferior to the Fraser River in British colonial territory—Cracroft writes:

Of course everyone had to be introduced & then each one had the usual string of questions "Well Madam—how do you like our country? I guess you find it very wild" — "Well Madam—you've travelled a great deal but I guess you don't often see such fine scenery as this?" Then, we were asked by everyone if the Columbia was as fine as the Fraser, & they seemed much disappointed when I said that the scenery of the Fraser was the finest. Every American puts personal *feeling into these questions, & this often provokes me to answer with the strictest truth. (Smith 1974, 85; her emphasis)*

This reaction typifies the anti-American response of female tourists from Europe and Britain to travel in the New World at the time. Marion Tinling (1993) writes in *With Women's Eyes: Visitors to the New World, 1775-1918* that "Many travelers did not like the manners of Americans, and they resented being asked, over and over, 'How do you like our country?'" (xiv).[12] As I explore in greater detail in chapters three and four, Cracroft wrote much more enthusiastically

---

10 These travels are recorded in *Lady Franklin Visits the Pacific Northwest* (Smith 1974) and *Lady Franklin Visits Sitka, Alaska, 1870* (Cracroft 1981).

11 For instance, Cracroft describes how the two women were paddled through a section of the Fraser River by Natives of Yale in a ceremony bestowing the name "Lady Franklin Pass" on a site in the river canyon. The name was announced on a white banner suspended from a long pole stretched over the river from the rafters of a salmon-drying shed.

12 Tinling's work considers the accounts of twenty-six women visiting the New World; however, none of them visited the Northwest Coast. The absence of contributions from the region in her text—despite their availability and their relevancy to her ideas—underscores the need for a regional study of women's travel writing.

about people and landscapes that reminded her of the culture and landscape of her homeland.

Because of the distances involved in traveling from England to the Northwest Coast, and perhaps because British Columbia and Canada have never captured the British imagination as have the colonial tropics, it was the American passengers who dominated coastal steam tourism and demanded an industry to take them upcoast. British Columbians of the late nineteenth century appear content with steamship excursions limited to the south coast or around Vancouver Island, and they did not publish travel accounts widely. In an unpublished manuscript, "Diary of a Voyage Around Vancouver Island 1879," Mary Wilson[13] recounts departing Victoria on 13 August of that year for a pleasure voyage. Vancouver Island politician Amor De Cosmos, and the father and sister of the now-famous painter Emily Carr, enjoyed the trip as well. But apparently there was little Canadian interest in reading such accounts.[14]

In 1867 the United States purchased the Alaska Territory from Russia; shortly thereafter Americans were riding government and commercial vessels to observe and describe for eager American readers the new American colony and its native inhabitants. Tourists rode freight steamers or—as George Wardman did in the summer of 1879—received special permission to travel aboard government revenue steamers (Wardman 1884). One of the first detailed accounts of Alaska steam travel was penned by Eliza Ruhamah Scidmore (1885), an early editor and contributor to *National Geographic*. Women were consistently present as tourists in the steamship era. In 1888 Massachussetts-native Abby Johnson Woodman climbed aboard the *George W. Elder* (figure 1)—the first iron steamer to ply to Alaska—and traveled from Victoria to Sitka (her sea voyage began in April from San Francisco). Her account, *Picturesque Alaska: A Journal of a Tour Among the Mountains, Seas, and Islands of the Northwest, from San Francisco to Sitka* (1889) was immediately published by the large Boston publishing house Houghton, Mifflin and Company. Although she is scathing in dismissing "lazy" and "poor" Alaskans in Juneau, Woodman is ignorantly charitable in her assessment of the Canadians she meets in British Columbia; she asserts that they "are very like our people though as yet not of us, a mistake which time will rectify" (69). Given the booming interest in Alaska travel, and the fact that the province of British Columbia stood in the way of connecting Alaska with the American continent, Woodman assumed the Inside Passage would inevitably be controlled and populated by Americans.

In August that same summer, E. Katharine Bates, a world traveler and native of England, also toured aboard the *George W. Elder* to Sitka; she describes the voyage in *Kaleidoscope: Shifting Scenes from East to West* (1889). Unlike

13 Mary Wilson, "Diary of a Voyage Around Vancouver Island 1879." Olive Wilson Heritage Collection, Box 1. British Columbia Archives and Records Service, Victoria. Add.MSS. 1245.

14 In researching this project I found a plethora of published accounts written by American tourists traveling to Alaska. In contrast, I found relatively few cruising accounts authored by Canadians; those I did find were often unpublished or self-published.

Figure 1. The George W. Elder at Sitka, Alaska (Unattributed photo from Wright 1895).

Woodman, who focuses her attention beyond the ship and toward the "sublime" storms and "squalid poverty" of the coast, Bates is much concerned with comparing the steamship service on the Northwest Coast to service elsewhere in the world. It does not compare well:

> ... *I am sure that if our hundred and twenty passengers had been asked, and* had spoken the truth *without fear or favour, seven-eights of them would have admitted the truth of what I am about to say.*
>
> *The G.W. Elder is a 1,200 ton freight steamer, and in no way fitted to carry passengers unless the numbers were reduced very much below the figure on the occasion of our excursion. (226, her emphasis)*

Passengers are squeezed three into each cabin, meals are badly planned and poorly cooked, and in general "the accommodation on board the Alaska Steamers leaves a great deal to be desired" (225). Bates—who probably had more experience with steam tourism than had the people responsible for the newly created tour to Alaska—concluded:

> *The Alaska expedition has much novelty to recommend it, and the beauty and wonders of Glacier Bay can scarcely be exaggerated. But so long as the world lasts, mental impressions must and will depend to a great extent upon physical conditions, and I think the Pacific Coast Steam Shipping Company might materially improve these. (262)*

Bates was correct to conclude that steamship companies would have to do better than corral passengers in old freight steamers; tourists—especially female tourists—wanted a taste of adventure in their trip north, but they also wanted to be surrounded during the cruise with the comforts of home. Matilda Barns Lukens (1889) carefully describes the significance of a home-like environment when she traveled with her husband aboard the new Pacific Coast Steamship Company vessel *Corona*:

> *Our morning after leaving Seattle was given to arranging our state-room and getting our small luggage conveniently placed. We made thin curtains for our windows out of material which we had bought in Portland, and hung them to our great satisfaction.... Before the afternoon was spent we had become* quite at home *in our new quarters and prepared to enjoy all the delights promised in this northern journey. (9, my emphasis)*

Mary Holbrook—also from Portland—is pleased to enjoy the comforts aboard "the fine English steamer" *Islander* during her northern tour. In her unpublished account "Jottings by the Way,"[15] she writes that she is as comfortable as she would be at home (2), the result of a piano on board, the excellent French cuisine, the sermons offered, and the presence of other women and even children.

After the turn of the century, steamship companies began to compete vigorously for Alaska-bound American tourists. Travelers interested in seeing the mountains and inlets of British Columbia would board slow freighters carrying cattle, sheep, horses, grain, lumber, and mining supplies through the Inside Passage rather than join passenger ships that sped past the scenery up the west coast of Vancouver Island. In "The Voyage of All Voyages" (1906), Ella Higginson explains to readers of *Washington Magazine* that the Northwestern Steamship Company is the company of choice as it is the only one running up "the inside route" to Alaska. Shortly after, the Pacific Coast Steamship Company[16] created a route through the Inland Sea; by 1910 the company was distributing a promotional brochure entitled *Alaska Via Totem Pole Route: Season 1911*, in which it claims: "The Pacific Coast Steamship Company operated the first vessels to Alaskan waters via the famous 'Inside Passage' which enables the tourist to visit this wonderful country by a calm water-way" (13). In an attempt to appeal not only to totem stalkers but also to women supposedly faint-hearted at the thought of crossing rough water, the brochure emphasizes the "calm" waters of the Inside Passage and assures the reader: "These are not 'excursions' but cruises de luxe" (5). As coastal tourism developed into bigger business, steamship company promoters aimed their advertising

---

15 Mary H. Holbrook, "Jottings by the Way." Self-published, 1892. British Columbia Archives and Records Service, Victoria. NWp/971M/H724j.

16 Pacific Coast Steamship Company, *Alaska Via Totem Pole Route: Season 1911*, San Francisco, 1910 [promotional brochure]. Univ. of British Columbia Special Collections, Vancouver. SPAM 13881.

even more directly toward women, who were perceived to desire comfort and romance. In *Sailing Sheltered Seas*[17] the Alaska Steamship Company emphasizes "gay deck sports," "dancing on sheltered seas," and "the famous Inside Passage—a thousand-mile ocean lane so subtle in its witchery that it has become 'The Lovers' Lane of the Seven Seas.'" The same company assures potential voyagers in *A Trip to Wonderful Alaska*[18] that "There is always an air of romance about a ship. Often many new acquaintances are formed, and in some cases end in close friendship in which confidences and knowledge are exchanged." In an appeal aimed directly at female tourists, the same brochure claims Alaska is "a country which is a fairyland of agreeable surprises." By 1926 even the Union Steamship Company was advertising British Columbia as "the Coast of Romance."[19]

The notion that the Inside Passage was "the Lover's Lane of the Seven Seas" was in large part created and recycled by women's travel accounts, accounts reflecting the gender-specific discursive pressures on Victorian women travel writers. While these pressures certainly had negative effects upon the women travel writers (for instance, women were expected to apologize for their work and were frequently regarded as liars because of their gender; see Mills 1991), the romanticizing of the Inside Passage did help generate a steady stream of female tourists to the region and profits for the steamship companies. With or without the romantic hype, women from Septima Collis (*A Woman's Trip to Alaska,* 1890) to May Kellog Sullivan (*A Woman Who Went to Alaska,* 1902) to Alberta L. Weed (*Grandma Goes to the Arctic,* 1957) have published titles that recognize a lively female presence in Northwest Coast marine tourism from its initiation.

---

17 Alaska Steamship Company (Seattle), *Sailing Sheltered Seas,* 1936 [promotional brochure]. Univ. of British Columbia Special Collections, Vancouver. SPAM 13282.

18 Alaska Steamship Company (Seattle), *A Trip to Wonderful Alaska* [Facsimile of promotional brochure dated MDCCCCVI [*sic*], The Shorey Book Store, Seattle, 1965, SJS#63]. Univ. of British Columbia Special Collections, Vancouver. SPAM 13281.

19 Tourists—particularly Californians—had to be limited on board Union Steamship Company ships in 1925 to allow space for local coastal travelers (Rushton 108). However, company general manager, Harold Brown, acknowledged that same year that "The British Columbia coast is as beautiful and interesting a section as there is in the world and it deserves the best provision for tourists" (Rushton 100). In 1947 the company began operating tourist cruises to Alaska via the *Chilcotin;* it was the most successful cruise ever run by the company.

The Gas Engine and Recreational Boating

The founding of both the Royal Victoria Yacht Club and the Seattle Yacht Club in 1892 indicates significant interest in recreational sailing and racing at the same time on both sides of the U.S.-Canada border. Nearly forty years after Ezra Meeker and his brother pushed off from a quiet shore near Olympia and relied upon the guidance of Native people, official yachting "transportation facilities" began to spring up to service boat travelers—initially the owners of sailing vessels, then powerboaters.

The arrival of the gasoline engine on Puget Sound in the summer of 1903 (Chasan 1981) and on the Fraser River in 1907 (Meggs and Stacey 1992) revolutionalized regional seine and gillnet salmon fisheries. By 1911 British Columbia's south coast fishery had almost entirely converted to gas—translating into the loss of jobs for boat-pullers (figure 2) and the increased size of vessels that could go farther and faster and carry more fish. The technology had an impact on pleasure boating as well; in general, powerboaters could travel faster and with less regard for wind and tidal conditions. As gasoline engines became more reliable, it took less human power to cruise and to maneuver vessels; as a consequence, people could travel alone or in small groups, such as families. The wider and more stable design of the powerboat brought more spacious and brightly lit interiors and more comfort. And with their relatively flatter bottoms, powerboats could enter shallow bays and come closer to shore.

A July 1907 contribution to *Pacific Monthly* (Pratt 1907) marks the beginning of what would grow to become a large and profitable segment of local marine industry. The author describes:

> ... *scores of other fine launches ... already chugging off across the brine, and scores more are casting loose the hawsers. In fact, it is quite a sight of a Sunday morning to see the pleasure-seekers speed away in their handsome motor boats for "realms unknown." The bay is fairly dotted with the launches outward bound and the air is so pregnant with gasoline explosions that it sounds like an Oriental New Year's. (114)*

Already "the doughty motor-boat sportsmen of Puget Sound," he writes, "have spent thousands of dollars in outfitting handsome pleasure cruisers" (117). Henry Bell-Irving, a Scottish immigrant to the Vancouver area who formed the Anglo-British Columbia Packing Company and established the Bell-Irving Insurance Agencies, was an early powerboater north of the border. As the 1907-09 log of his boat the *Beatrice* confirms, yachts were becoming a more common sight on the inland sea yet were rare enough to elicit enthusiastic waving between boaters.[20] On a cruise from Vancouver to Seattle, the occupants aboard the *Beatrice* picked up a load of strawberries and cream at the Fidalgo Cannery in Anacortes on 30 June 1907, then continued south. The log records:

---

20 Bell-Irving Family Fonds, *Log of the Launch "Beatrice," 1907-09*. City of Vancouver Archives. Add.MSS 592, Vol. 2, File 2.

Figure 2. A Native woman works as a "boatpuller," fishing near the mouth of the Fraser River, 1913 (photo courtesy of the B.C. Archives and Records Service, F. Dundas Todd Collection #HP84113).

> *Passed Partridge Point @ 5 P.M. and began to feel the floodtide into the Sound.*
> *7 P.M. passed the Linda quite close & the following yachts. Hiawatha. Fourwinds.*
> *Madeline. Brittannia Swife Ceauuck (?) Intrepid. Wideawake. Silver Spray....as*
> *we passed each yacht cheered as just as [sic] if they had not seen Human beings*
> *for years. (12)*

The enthusiasm of the *Beatrice* passengers seems only to be dampened by the failure of the engine, which was occasionally clogged by "dirt" (20).

An anonymous writer first published in 1908 expresses his mistrust of the new gas-powered boats with "The Cruise of the *Mineola*." As a guest who boards a thirty-five-foot pleasure boat in 1907, he notes:

> *A gasoline engine boat had never impressed me favorably, in fact I had always*
> *been possessed of a more or less wholesome dread of the things. This one seemed*
> *to be all right, however, and besides we were taking out on this trip a young*
> *fellow who knew all about gasoline engines. Anyone could tell he knew all about*
> *them—he handled this one so gingerly. (28)*

The author soon recovers from his apprehensions and from his first turn at the wheel enjoys the pleasure of motor boating from Vancouver to Victoria and the San Juan Islands on a ten-day cruise:

So for the next two hours I, the man who but yesterday was mixed up in puny affairs of business, guided the packet down that wonderful channel all by myself. To feel her answer my slightest touch thrilled me and the spirit of the whole scene, the mountains, the deep silent waters of the channel, the clear brilliant sunlight and the cool green slopes of the hills all entered into my very being, until I forgot that there ever was any other existence than this or cared whether there would be any other. (30)

Even without the engine throbbing, the author revels in the motion of the small *Mineola* and the natural scene surrounding him. Unlike steamship travelers of the time, who emphasized the distant majesty and grandeur of Inside Passage scenery in their travelogues (see chapter four), this author acknowledges the "mighty" mountains but also notices and describes the environment closer at hand. Anchored at Sucia Island in Washington State one night, he goes on deck at ten o'clock to inspect the riding light; at two o'clock he is still gazing out over the water:

Around about us lay the islands, the clear spots and beaches thrown into relief by the dark shadows of the woods. The little ground swell coming in from the Gulf gently rocked Mineola, *and passing on broke with a ripple on the beach, intensifying the silence of the night. (35)*

"The Cruise of the *Mineola*" shows the differences between steamship tourism and small-boat cruising, and illustrates how much closer the traveler is to the natural world on a smaller craft. "I awoke this morning with the smell of fresh bacon and coffee in my nostrils and heard a big splash overboard," the author writes on 26 July; "I turned out at once and joined the bunch in a swim three times around the packet" (35). Unlike steamship tours—which by this time had developed into prescheduled stopovers at the largest coastal towns—the cruiser often has no fixed schedule:

I was awakened this morning by the pitter of rain on the cabin top. The high wind from the S.E. of yesterday afternoon and evening, [sic] had brought it up, and it is now coming down steadily and persistently. We decided that as we were very snug at this anchorage, and were in no rush, that we would stay where we were to-day. (31)

While Canadians were cruising south into Washington in the first decade of the twentieth century, Americans of the period were particularly interested in entering Canadian waters by boat, occasionally continuing on to Alaska. But whereas the gasoline engine led to uniformity in the fishing fleets on both sides of the border, its adoption in a variety of ways by recreational boaters led to a transformation in the social dynamics of cruising. The two narratives that follow, which describe cruises undertaken within months of each other, demonstrate how varied cruising experiences were becoming at the time.

Figure 3. *Calcite* makes "a triumphant return" with "hunting prizes displayed on the bow" (photo by McCormick in McCormick 1969).

Wealthy businessmen such as Vancouver's Henry Bell-Irving were among the first to enjoy motor yachting. In September 1908 American and Canadian passengers aboard the fifty-foot gasoline-powered yacht *Calcite* embarked on a hunting and fishing trip up the British Columbia coast (figure 3). The party consisted of J. A. McCormick, a Seattle photographer and author of "Cruise of the *Calcite*" (collected 1969); John S. McMillin, owner of the *Calcite*,[21] president and general manager of the Tacoma and Roche Harbor Lime Company, and commodore of the Roche Harbor Yacht Club; Fred H. McMillin, captain; and R. P. Butchart, a Vancouver Island businessman whose wife was to transform his abandoned lime quarries into the now famous Butchart Gardens. To conserve their energies for salmon fishing at Campbell River and bear hunting in Jervis Inlet, the party relied on a working crew: first officer Harry Horst, chief engineer Guy Wheeler, and "last, but most important, our chief steward, Jim Nagioka, a man with a yellow skin but a white understanding when it came to tickling the palate of the hungry horde aboard our good ship" (185).

At the same time, the gas engine enticed Sidney R. Sheldon to travel to Alaska in an eighteen-foot steel boat. In the spring of 1909, Sheldon (on faculty at the University of Idaho) and two friends (an assistant professor and a student) departed Seattle for Skagway. The assistant professor, "not built for a seafaring life" (Sheldon, 1959, 39), left the party at Nanaimo, but the other two cruised to Skagway in two months. The men made use of the sail they had added to their

21 The word "calcite" refers to a mineral form including common limestone; the owner of the yacht *Calcite* made a fortune selling limestone from Roche Harbor on San Juan Island.

Figure 4. "The houseboat has arrived" (unattributed photo from Pyle and Pyle 1910).

craft, as their engine frequently broke down. However, even the more monied yachtsmen of the period were figuratively in the same boat; Sheldon writes:

> *Captain Shrove had brought his yacht into Port Simpson under sail as he was having trouble with his engine and the repair men in Alaska had not been able to diagnose it. We offered to look it over. Luckily we discovered the trouble, dismantled the engine, had repairs made at the shop and reassembled it. It worked perfectly. (43-44)*

By this time, women on the Northwest Coast had a significant history of traveling by boat: Canadian women immigrated to British Columbia by ship, and Canadians and Americans of both sexes relied upon steamers and small craft to move themselves and their supplies within the region. But mass marine travel for pleasure was just beginning to open up for women in the first decade of the twentieth century. For three decades wealthy women had enjoyed steam tourism through the Inside Passage; with the coming of the gasoline engine, cruising became an activity that middle-class and eventually working-class women would enjoy and influence.

By 1909 the gas-powered houseboat (figure 4) was available for charter by middle-class couples or small parties. In "Six Hundred Miles in a Houseboat: A Leisurely Cruise Along the Coast of British Columbia in the First Modern Houseboat in Pacific Waters" (1910), Joseph and Annie Pyle write: "If the gasoline engine has made aviation practicable, its transformation of the houseboat is scarcely less startling" (13,295). They continue:

> *For from one-fourth to one-tenth of the cost of an ocean-going yacht, a man may to-day build a houseboat giving equal comfort, from one-half to two-thirds the*

Figure 5. "Deep, restful sleep in roomy beds, to the soft accompaniment of waves that, in our cosy anchorages, lapped the sides of the *Lotus* and lifed her just enough for a lullaby" (unattributed photo from Pyle and Pyle 1910).

speed, and quarters far more homelike and adaptable to living purposes. He can operate it for a small fraction of the cost. (13,295)

With the houseboat came the opportunity for middle-class cruising; one did not have to rely upon an invitation to board the yacht of a Henry Bell-Irving or John McMillin, or have the knowledge to build and repair a small boat. Houseboats—cheaply built, and operated and maintained by an enterprising owner—could be chartered for a summer's cruise. The relatively low cost was a significant factor in the middle-class initiation into Northwest Coast marine tourism, but the homelike atmosphere of this boat was especially appealing to women (see figure 5). "She is equipped with every possible comfort and convenience for cruising," writes Florence Kell of the chartered forty-eight-foot *Restless* (1911, 9). On a two-week cruise up the British Columbia coast, Kell uses the term "apartment" to connote how at home she felt on board the *Restless* in the midst of spectacular scenery: "On returning to our floating apartments we sat on deck for hours charmed with the marvelous splendor of a perfect July night" (11). The Pyles, in addition to advertising the house-boat as an antidote "for a people whom the growing habit of outdoor life and summer vacation is gradually rescuing from the doom of overwork and nervous exhaustion," emphasize that it "can be made as comfortable as your own

Figure 6. After World War II, boats grew smaller, cheaper, and more popular (photo courtesy of Richard Pagh).

home" (13,302). For Annie Pyle, the comfort of "your own home" afloat was achieved with the on-board help of a skipper, an engineer, a sailor, a Japanese cook, and his wife as steward and housemaid—all paid for by the charterer.

Mass marine tourism would remain off limits for the working class until after the Second World War. But in the decades between 1910 and 1950, cruising the southern Northwest Coast became extremely popular for the middle class, and that interest changed the size and shape of cruising vessels and stimulated an industry in transportation facilities, which took shape in the form of resorts. In the 1920s, Kathrene and Robert Pinkerton—acknowledged as the first family cruisers of the region (Lillard 1991)—remodeled their boat into a live-aboard cruising vessel (see chapter two). By the 1940s, wooden power cruisers (outnumbering sailboats by several times) were available in a variety of new stock models (Ogden 1948, 703). Middle-class "amateur yachtsmen" who "crowded" into the safe inlets of southern Puget Sound on summer weekends often purchased these vessels. In "Puget Sound and Vancouver Waters" (1948), Charles Ogden describes the popularity of regional cruising:

> The waters of Puget Sound and the coast of British Columbia offer the yachtsman
> a variety that is hard to find any place else in the world. There is cruising to
> suit the taste of every man, from the one who prefers to move from one resort
> with its city conveniences to another of the same type, to the one who enjoys
> his own exploring of out of the way places, some of which have not yet been
> charted in detail. (679)

Catering to the interests of upper- and middle-class boaters, a resort industry bloomed on both sides of the border; Ogden notes that by 1948 there are "many resorts in both the San Juan and Gulf Islands. As a matter of fact, this is a business that has expanded rapidly in recent years" (691). But despite the resorts, a popular movement of "family cruising" was growing as smaller and cheaper boats (made possible by smaller and cheaper gas engines, and later by the invention of fiberglass; see figure 6) entered the recreational boating industry and as marinas and state and provincial marine parks provided services. By the late 1940s, Ogden observes, "Many yachtsmen do not belong to clubs at all, and many of those who do belong take no part in the programs offered by their clubs, but use them as a place to moor their boats and to meet kindred souls and swap yarns and information about their cruising" (712). With Power Squadron courses and manuals available to replace the yacht club as a source of information, and with the coming of the modern marina (offering fuel, ice, motor repairs, moorage, laundromats, showers, groceries, restaurants, etc.) to replace the club as a necessary facility, working-class boating began to boom. In "Northwest Dividends for Small-Boat Yachtsmen" (collected 1969), Bruce Calhoun explains that "Cruising in the Pacific Northwest, as elsewhere, is a way of life attracting more and more families every year. Formerly enjoyed only by the affluent in palatial yachts, [the experience is] now within reach of almost anyone." He continues:

> The difference is the small cruiser, either outboard or inboard/outdrive. The amazing development of this craft since the early 1950s, with its trailerability, its speed, its easy maneuverability and its modest cost, means that literally hundreds of thousands of boaters scurry back and forth each summer. (8)

In 1954 a Seattle teacher describing a cruise wrote that along the shores of the greater Seattle area "It appears that every hundred feet one sees a dock and boat moored" (H.D. Brown 1954); but with the smaller, trailerable craft, boat owners did not need to own shorefront property or pay to moor their vessels.

The "hundreds of thousands of boaters" in the 1950s, described by Calhoun, stimulated rapid growth in industries related to marine tourism. New boaters challenged traditional land use along the waterways; in a region where logging had been king, scenery grew into a commodity. For instance, numerous Washington State yacht clubs combined efforts in the early 1960s to purchase Sucia Island (previously a logging area in the San Juans) and turned it over to the state Parks Department as a haven for boaters. Chasan (1981) describes the effect of this transformation on Puget Sound:

> Since the immediate post-war period, recreational boating and saltwater sport fishing had become major pastimes and the bases for significant industries on the Sound....
> As the regional economy and the regional population grew more sophisticated, the Sound and the forests were valued increasingly as amenities, as objects of

contemplation and settings for avocational activities. People with money and sophistication and a taste for political combat were acquiring a significant stake in the Sound that had nothing to do with pulp production or merchant shipping or the canning of salmon. (115)

Boating rapidly became not just a pastime of the "people with money and sophistication" but a way of life strongly associated with family and with regional identity. "Boating is a Family Sport" reads a 1958 headline in the *Seattle Times* (Clark); "1 of 6 Seattle Families Owns Pleasure Craft" announces another in 1961 ("One of"). Specific issues—particularly spatial issues—arose with women participating in family cruising, and that is the subject of my second chapter.

By the 1970s boating had become a mass-market hobby in the Olympia-to-Vancouver corridor. Robert Bish et al. declare in the study *Coastal Resource Use: Decisions on Puget Sound* (1975) that in the Puget Sound area, boats per capita were the highest in North America (49).[22] Arguing that water's "physical presence and image have strongly influenced how residents of the region have organized themselves geographically and economically," Bish et al. conclude that "the Sound provides a symbol of identity and invites life styles which interrelate land and marine environments in ways that are probably unique in the United States" (89). As a result, the study forecasts overcrowding at Puget Sound marine parks.

Inside Passage boating can be mapped to some degree on a series of frontiers settled in a south-to-north pattern. As the southerly end of the Inside Passage grew crowded, boaters ventured farther north to escape each other's society. In 1948 Ogden describes sheltered coves near the Tacoma Narrows as "crowded with cruising boats on the weekends throughout the usual cruising season.[23] There are some other [inlets], however, not so popular, that have real charm" (682). As the "remoteness" of cruising grounds moved from Puget Sound up the coast of British Columbia, state and provincial governments invested in property to preserve it in a "natural" condition for pleasure boaters seeking their idea of pristine wilderness. With the "discovery" of each new and more distant paradise came a tribe of boaters. Writing in Canada's *Western Living* in 1977, Olga Ruskin describes the popularity of British Columbia's upcoast Desolation Sound, which became a marine park in 1973:

---

22 In a 1977 look at the Seattle Boat Show, Robert Horsley and Eric Carlson observe that "What used to be the plaything of the elite is increasingly becoming the province of middle America" (9); "What used to be an exclusive hobby is now a mass market. The growing interest in boating sparked a similar interest on the part of big business. Corporate giants like Chrysler ... now compete for a market worth about $30 million a year just locally" (10).

23 Official boating season runs from the first Sunday in May through Labor Day weekend in September. "Opening Day" continues to be celebrated with ship parades, regattas, and other maritime events.

Desolation Sound is one of these [places accessible only by boat], a beautifully rugged area of fiord-like scenery offering delightful anchorages, warm water for swimming and a feeling of being away from civilization—if you're lucky enough to escape the other boats. Ten years ago Desolation Sound was far from the maddening crowd but boaters converge upon the area today in droves because of the recreational opportunities. (18)

Ruskin's warning brings to mind Muriel Wylie Blanchet's (1961) indignation when, in the 1930s, she takes her family by boat to Princess Louisa Inlet only to discover that they must share the place with another human for the first time. "After all, *he* was the intruder," she writes; "this man and his log-cabin made the first thin wedge of civilization that had been driven into our favourite inlet" (29).

Contemporary competition for space on the water is especially antagonistic between upper-class yachters and working-class locals, and the situation is not particular to the Northwest Coast. A Chesapeake Bay crabber in Lila Line's *Waterwomen* (1982) describes a run-in with a yachtsman:

One time we were out there putting on brand new five-inch net when this big yacht coming up from Florida got right on top of us and he throws her in reverse. Well, he just wound the nets in his wheel, so we had to go to him and cut him out, and here he's sitting up there, you know, in this great big yacht, I mean it was big, drinking a mixed drink, and he's saying how sorry he is, you know, and he pulls out a twenty-dollar bill. (8, her emphasis)

Michael Modzelewski complains about the noisy, rude, and drunken power yachters anchoring in Freshwater Bay in *Inside Passage* (1991). And somebody should have complained when a more recent Bell-Irving and party invaded the village of Kyuquot aboard a sailing yacht. Bell-Irving records the following log entry in Nan Nicolls' *North of Anian* (1990):

After dinner we again played the full tape of "Evita." This turned it into a two-candle, two-bottle-of-Port dinner. For the first time the evening sky was clear with stars and a lovely quarter moon. The whole village must have shared our concert because it was played at near full volume, but there were no complaints. Perhaps they enjoyed it as much as the crew of Gabrielle III—*a beautiful anchorage and a memorable evening. (11)*

Bell-Irving's entry records more than common rudeness. His words suggest he believes himself a civilizing force, anchored on an outpost.

Southeastern Alaska has grown to be constructed as the last frontier: "Alaska is not just a place one has reached,— [sic] it is an achievement, an experience, a feeling. Here is all man could wish of primitive untouched wildness," writes Betty Nunn to open her cruising account (collected 1969, 222). But then north of the Inside Passage—beyond Yakutat—becomes the final cruising frontier:

These shores were uninhabited and desolate beyond words.... Under the stygian black canopy the lower spurs of the St. Elias range and innumerable coiling rivers of ice had an evil glitter in the sea beyond the wooded plain.

As my boat rose to the crests of these huge seas, the grim black coast and sky seemed to stretch on forever. This was the real Alaska I had imagined from the story book. The last frontier indeed; and never so named in jest. (Hill 1983, 240)

The vast majority of Northwest Coast pleasure boaters will never travel north of the Sunshine Coast. Limited by the time span of a vacation from the urban centers of Vancouver or Seattle and by the open water of Queen Charlotte Sound, most are content to explore the southern Inside Passage. But from the accounts of those who have ventured north—accounts that recycle the rhetoric of colonial exploration, emphasizing the "primitive," "wild," "desolate," and "dangerous" coast (the antithesis of the contemporaneous, the tame, the decorative, the safe home)—there remains the firmly planted notion that another frontier awaits the adventurous boater.

Homemaking Tourists

As I sought to understand a history of women traveling the Northwest Coast for pleasure and sought to place their accounts in the context of this marine history I have just charted, two broad notions occurred to me. The first is that power is a very complex issue when applied to this history. It is true that in this region, as elsewhere, access to boat travel was quite limited for Western women while that form of travel was strongly associated with power. Marine explorers, traders, and claim-stakers were men. As boat travel became less an instrument of imperialist and nationalist power and more of a pastime, and as the lower classes gained leisure and a form of transportation of their own, women were invited aboard as homemakers and caregivers afloat. A few women even began to travel without spouses. However, the working-class female tourists who did enter the marine environment (particularly in the 1950s, 1960s, and 1970s; since the 1980s boating has grown less and less affordable for the working class) appear to have been exclusively White. Try as I might, I could not knowingly find one tourist account in this genre penned by a non-White woman of any class, with the exception of one Jewish author from the nineteenth century (Septima Collis). How can I explain the fact that minority women work in marine environments along the Northwest Coast (particularly in shore-based fish processing) but are not present in the travel literature I have examined? Have they been denied this travel experience? Have they a history of disinterest in tourism generally or boating specifically? Or are they out there, traveling on the water and not writing accounts of these experiences? I have had to confront the knowledge that I cannot easily categorize female marine tourists as "powerless" or as "privileged" because these notions are so relative given this context.

A second broad idea is clear: a pattern of shared sensibilities and responsibilities began to take shape as I read the literature I have found. Because ship travel had been an experience relatively closed to women before the Victorian era (see chapter two), this pattern emerged as women stepped into a new arena and relied upon "feminine values" for support in a strange environment. These values are based on woman's long association with the home and with the work accomplished in the domestic sphere. Women's experiences afloat—along the Northwest Coast and throughout the world—may vary over time and with nationality, class, region, and craft. Yet, transcending these distinctions, Western women's experiences on the water exhibit remarkable similarities; these similarities are shaped largely by gender expectations and by the connected concept of women's separate, domestic work.

In *Home: A Short History of an Idea* (1986), Witold Rybczynski traces the origin of the idea of "home" to seventeenth-century Dutch society, where the home was first defined as a separate space. "The world of male work," he writes, "and male social life, had moved elsewhere. The house had become the place for another kind of work—specialized domestic work—women's work. This work itself was nothing new, but its isolation was" (70-71). The "feminization" of the home, Rybczynski explains, meant that the home became "a feminine place, or at least a place under feminine control," and it introduced a concept that had not previously existed: domesticity. Describing domesticity as a "feminine achievement" grounded in the Dutch pride in tidiness, he points out that "homely domesticity depended on the development of a rich interior awareness, an awareness that was the result of the woman's role in the home" (75). This appreciation for the "feminization" of the house saturates the western idea of the home. For example, German philosopher Georg Simmel wrote in 1911:

> The home is an aspect of life and at the same time a special way of forming, reflecting, and interrelating the totality of life.
> To have accomplished this is the immense cultural achievement of woman. The home is an objective entity whose distinctiveness can be compared with no other. It has been stamped by the special abilities and interests, and emotionality and intellectuality, of the woman, by the total rhythm of her being. (92)

"On the whole," he concludes, "the home remains the supreme cultural achievement of women" (97). In *The Poetics of Space* (1958), French philosopher Gaston Bachelard relies upon this entrenched connection between femininity and "keeping house" when he writes:

> A house that shines from the care it receives appears to have been rebuilt from the inside; it is as though it were new inside. In the intimate harmony of walls and furniture, it may be said that we become conscious of a house that is built by women, since men only know how to build a house from the outside. (68)

Feminists tend to be much less celebratory of the creation of separate male and female spheres, focusing instead on patriarchy's capitalizing on women's unpaid labor. In reference to the history of changing economic organization in

England, Doreen Massey and Linda McDowell (1984) write that by the nineteenth century "the separation of men's and women's lives was virtually total: men were the breadwinners, women the domestic labourers" (193). As a result, unpaid work in the home was the only option for women (see also Carolyn Merchant 1980; Karen Davies 1989). Having neither the power nor the inclination to dismiss the domestic arena as undeserving of their talents, nineteenth-century women in the northern United States worked "to exalt home tasks and values and to depict a nation in crying want of domestication" (A. Douglas 1975). In "The Home and the Family in Historical Perspective," Tamara Hareven (1993) shows that at this time,

> Homemaking became an occupation in itself, one that demanded physical and material resources, planning, and the persistent following of changing fashions. As one writer in mid-century put it, a house "is not only the home center, the retreat and shelter for all the family, it is also the workshop for the mother. It is not only where she is to live, to love, but where she is to care and labor. Her hours, days, weeks, months and years are spent within its bounds; until she becomes an enthroned fixture, more indispensable than the house itself. (235)

With the ideology of homemaking came a vast body of advice literature written by women. Conditioned to accept that work within the home would be performed by a woman whose most significant job was caring for her husband and family, these writers created a genre of domestic management texts that flourished from the mid-nineteenth to the mid-twentieth century.[24] These texts emphasized efficiency and the "scientific" nature of housewifery and contributed to many of the comforts people working in the home now take for granted (the overhead shelf, the correct height of work counters, the dishwasher; see Rybczynski 1986, 171). From the mid-nineteenth century through the heyday of 1960s suburbia, no aspect of the home was too trivial for women to study. The resulting literature reflected a widespread belief that the private home was the heart of human society and that a woman could be valuable—if secondary—as the God-appointed and "natural" caretaker of that home. Given the thorough wedding of female identity with the symbolic ideal of the home, women carried the baggage of the home with them wherever they traveled—whether or not they were literally homemakers.

A home, as Mary Douglas points out in "The Idea of a Home: A Kind of Space" (1993), is not necessarily a house: "[Home] is always a localizable idea. Home is located in space, but it is not necessarily a fixed space. It does not

---

24 Some of these texts include: Beecher (1849), *A Treatise on Domestic Economy;* Beecher and Beecher Stowe (1869), *The American Woman's Home;* Frederick (1914), *The New Housekeeping: Efficiency Studies in Home Management;* Pattison (1915), *Principles of Domestic Engineering;* Balderston (1921), *Housewifery: A Manual and Text Book of Practical Housekeeping;* and Gilbreth et al. (1954), *Management in the Home: Happier Living Through Saving Time and Energy.* For a history of domestic pioneers, see Dolores Hayden (1983).

need bricks and mortar, it can be a wagon, a caravan, a boat" (263). The imperative to create a home afloat affected the sensibilities of women touring the Northwest Coast by steamer and by pleasure craft. It shows itself in the discourse of upper- and middle-class women who portrayed Native peoples as children, Alaska as a land in need of a mother country, and the Inside Passage as a matrimonial shopping mall. It is even more evident in the narratives of women traveling with their families on small boats. Because the social dynamics on board a family boat imitate those of the family home, the domestic responsibilities for cooking, childcare, and decorating and cleaning the interior fall inevitably to the "first mate." This fact is made clear not only with narratives written by both men and women, but also by the considerable advice literature written by and for women boaters, which bears such titles as *The Woman's Guide to Boating and Cooking* (Morgan 1974), *Galley Slave's Guide* (West Vancouver Yacht Club, Ladies Sailing Group 1969), and *The Yachtsman's Mate's Guide* (Livingston 1980).

Undoubtedly, women have been confined and limited at sea by the widespread assumption of a connection between femininity and the idea of the home. And yet, the slowly growing acceptance of women on the water also appears linked to assumptions about her connectedness to homemaking; as boating has grown in popularity as a family activity, women have become a stronger presence in the marine environment. In turn, their presence has influenced boat design (see chapter two) and has translated into the development of more on-shore facilities catering to women (for example, showers and laundries). Many—I would even argue most—women boaters take some pleasure in acting out their domestic roles on the water and would have absolutely no interest in boating without their husbands.

Femininity—linked traditionally and so emphatically to the idea of the home and to women's work within the domestic sphere—both enables and limits women traveling in this region's marine environment; it defines the normative boundaries for women afloat. Thus the complexities and varieties of women's experiences and perceptions afloat along the Northwest Coast, which I explore throughout this project, must be read within the context of the idea of "home."

CHAPTER TWO

Space for the Mate:
Superstition, Ritual, and a Woman's Place

Aboard our twenty-seven-foot cabin cruiser, my family knows where I spend most of my time: in "Mama's bunk." The bow of our boat is V-shaped, and inside the cabin, below the deck, are two berths: Dad's bunk on the right (starboard) and Mama's bunk on the left (port). The berths are mirror images of one another, each about three feet wide at the head (where you can stand between them), tapering to a narrow place where the ends of my mother's and father's sleeping bags overlap. The bunks are the same size; each has a mesh hammock for stowage drooping down onto the sleeping bag. Each bunk has a shelf along its length, stuffed with books and magazines, beach towels, extra blankets, fishing tackle, gloves, and flashlights. Superficial differences distinguish the bunks; the magazines on the right are *Motor Boating & Sailing, Sea,* and *Rudder,* and those on the left are *Good Housekeeping, Ladies Home Journal,* and *Woman's Day.* But to me—someone who, my family would tell you, "practically lives in Mama's bunk" when we are boating—there is an important difference between these two spaces.

Mama's bunk is comfortable. It is, as far as I am concerned, the only truly comfortable space on board. A thermodynamic miracle, Mama's bunk is warm in spring and fall. In the summer—with the deck hatch open above me and catching a breeze—it is the coolest spot on board. I can stretch out there, my feet just near the anchor chain and my head separated from the oven by a wooden partition. I read and nap and listen to the sound the water makes against the hull. I am out of the way, out of the traffic on board, and no one interrupts my thoughts. It smells nice—like my mother, and salt, and the slightly musty pages of books left on board over winter. Until my mother kicks me out of her space and I head back to the cockpit, where my own cold and slightly damp sleeping bag lies on a foam pad, I feel at home there. Mama's bunk reminds me that there are certain territories and comfort zones on boats, just as there are in homes.

As my description of Mama's bunk and what I do there hints, pleasure boating is vacationing. A good deal of planning and labor are required before, during, and after any cruise—much more than would be necessary for a tour on a steamship or an ocean liner; but essentially, cruising is meant to be recreation. Since the combination, in the first decade of the twentieth century, of the gas engine and the private pleasure craft, Northwest Coast cruising has been a vehicle for upper-class yachtsmen and, later, middle- and working-class boaters, to treat themselves to a scenic "paradise" and quiet retreat. The accounts of these vacationers could be stereotyped as tedious or self-indulgent; logbooks and narratives about cruising are more likely to disclose routine activities on board, family anecdotes, and how "Amy cooked the ham as we came along" (Barrow 1985, 8) than to grip readers with tales of adventure. Adventurous action does occur in descriptions of the occasional stranding on a reef, crossing the Georgia Strait, or an unexpected gale. Descriptions of the natural environment—the discovery of an unexpected waterfall or the power of the Yaculta Rapids—tend to be the most dramatic moments in cruising accounts. I will consider some of those moments in chapter four; in this chapter, I want to set aside those passages about the natural environment to consider the subtle drama of men and women sharing a limited, built space that has traditionally been the domain of men. Read in this light, the self-absorbed or mundane jottings of vacationers have a great deal to say about the literal and figurative place women occupy on the water.

Space and Gender Politics

Space, as geographer Doreen Massey (1992) writes, seems to be on nearly everyone's agenda in contemporary academic circles. The terms "space," "place," "location," and "positionality" are exercised frequently in scholarly debates concerning identity and power—debates about the lived practices within, and metaphorical meanings of, particular spaces. Massey has written that, with the recent popularity of the term "space" and the multiplicity of definitions that have sprung up with its usage, space is an idea that is losing political significance. Instead, she points out, space is becoming equated with stasis in scholarly rhetoric. In Western culture time is generally aligned with history, progress, civilization, science, politics, and reason, while space is left as the absence or opposite of these things: stasis, reproduction, nostalgia, emotion, aesthetics, and the body (257). A result of this dualism, Massey writes, is the denial that the social and the spatial are in fact interrelated (not opposite poles) and inseparable.

Agreeing that "space is a social construct" (an idea that originated with radical geography in the 1970s), Massey explains that "society is necessarily constructed spatially, and that fact—the spatial organization of society—makes a difference to how it works" (254). If space influences how society works and changes, then space is also implicitly political. Drawing on feminist theory, Massey concludes by arguing toward an "alternative view of space" that resists relying upon irreconcilable dichotomies; space and time differ from each other, yet neither should be understood as the absence of the other. Space, she urges us to understand, is "full of power and symbolism, a complex web of relations of domination and subordination, of solidarity and co-operation" (265). As she writes elsewhere,[1] space can no longer be analyzed only through the male heterosexual experience and generalized onto all others; the gendering of spatiality (in concepts such as "modernity," for example)[2] is due for reconsideration.

Two previous studies of this "gendering of spaciality" are particularly relevant to my research on gender and boat travel and served as models for my work. Moving between women of the Andes, Greece, Iran, Yorubaland, South Africa, and the British House of Commons, the essays in *Women and Space: Ground Rules and Social Maps* (Ardener 1981) map the social conventions that have prevented women from entering (male) space. Mobility is linked explicitly to safety and freedom; editor Shirley Ardener writes that "if women are not encouraged to ride bicycles or horses, to paddle canoes or to learn to drive cars, or to own these means of transport, their freedom to enter spaces may be relatively curtailed in comparison to men's" (21-22).

I too am interested in mapping the exclusion of women from space—in this case, the Western taboo against women on boats. Certainly the long history of exclusion of women from water transportation (much like their restriction in most forms of travel) has at times interfered with their ability to move from place to place, with their freedom to disconnect and to arrive. As Mary Morris (1992) has written, women, denied the freedom to roam outside themselves, turned inward toward their emotions, and historically these would-be travelers have had to concern themselves with waiting rather than with moving. I think that if there is a "master" narrative for women and the sea, it has been the story of waiting for the husband, the father, the son to come home.

But exclusion from the spaces that allow the opportunity to move and to travel limits more than a woman's freedom. As Daphne Spain argues in *Gendered Spaces* (1992), spatial segregation also affects the distribution of knowledge and power in society. It is precisely in the spaces traditionally "closed" to women (the boardroom, the locker room, in her examples) that knowledge—and thus power—is transferred.

I am not arguing that sea captains hold the secrets of the universe or that boats are the world's greatest campuses. I am, however, suggesting that because of their unique history as a restricted space, and because of the highly limited nature of their small space, boats offer a significant location for charting the "invasion" of females into a traditionally masculine territory. On a local and practical level, this invasion has important implications in the recreational boating industry; for instance, boat design must cater to a family experience nowadays. On a more global and academic level, this history of exclusion should have implications for theorists such as Paul Carter (1988) and Rockwell Gray (1992) who, without considering the significance of gender, argue that travel or the

---

1 See "Flexible Sexism" and "Space, Place, and Gender: Introduction," collected in Massey (1994).

2 See Griselda Pollock (1988) and Susan Ford (1991) on the notion of the "female gaze."

voyage is the ultimate metaphor for "spatial history" (Carter) or is "the essence of human life" (Gray 49).

In this chapter I map the spaces that women have entered as they traveled by boat along the Northwest Coast, and I analyze several published narratives as case studies to explore the spatial issues surrounding women's growing participation in regional pleasure boating (and, to a limited degree, fishing). I am working from a premise Ardener explains in *Women and Space:*

> *Some people reject the idea that men and women, individually or collectively, live in different worlds. But I would suggest that it is not adequate to say that men and women merely have a different viewpoint, as if they are seeing "the same thing" or observing the same hard "reality". Their social constructions and their experiences of the world must often (but not always) differ fundamentally if only as a result of their accumulated experiences and the way these will inevitably affect their perceptions. (19)*

When we look at women on the water, their accumulated experiences do not begin when a woman first steps aboard a boat. Both patriarchy and a long history of superstition restrain women from the built space of a boat; this history continues to translate into the real exclusion of women from working boats. This history influences (perhaps even dictates) the sphere allowed to women when they boat for pleasure; for that reason, in this chapter I offer a brief overview of the taboos against women at sea and the effects upon women who have worked against these superstitions.

A number of the gender-specific "little tactics of the habitat"[3] expressed in published boating narratives are also explicitly described and encouraged in boating handbooks, guides, and manuals. This material shows that homemaking was and is a strategy used by women to make a place for themselves in this traditionally masculine space. By creating a home afloat in the interiors of pleasure boats, women invent a space within which they feel comfortable. This feminization of the cabin has two important effects: it makes a woman's presence on board seem more legitimate or natural (she suits the setting), and it ghettoizes her below deck as she performs the duties of homemaking. By considering some worldwide cruising and instructional literature in juxtaposition with Northwest Coast boaters' accounts, I am trying to understand or map the social conventions that sometimes made—and continue to make—the space on board boats different worlds for men and women.

---

3 In *Power/Knowledge*, Michel Foucault writes: "A whole history remains to be written of spaces—which would at the same time be the history of powers— ... from the great strategies of geo-politics to the little tactics of the habitat" (quoted in Spain 1992, 1).

Floating Worlds

According to the well-known and highly respected boat designer Uffa Fox (1960), "In our vessel we are a little kingdom separated from the rest of the world and completely cut off" (134). A boat is a "floating world" (Maillart 1942, 75), "a small and complex universe" (Frankel 1990, 12). "A small yacht's cabin," writes Samuel Eliot Morison (1965), "is not only a home away from home and a floating camp; it is a little, closed-in world where you are free from all anxieties, problems and considerations except the primitive ones of keeping dry, warm and well fed. It is a little space walled off just for you and your ship-mates" (25). "Our world," writes Philip Davenport (1953) when describing his honeymoon voyage from Australia to England, "was something like a four-mile radius from the deck of the cutter. Everything else was another life" (55).

In *The Psychology of Sailing: The Sea's Effects on Mind and Body* (1987), Michael Stadler analyzes this sensation of existing in a small and closed-in world:

> *In many respects the situation at sea does not differ in principle from the situation in a prison or cloister. Sociologists have described such living conditions as 'total institutions'. There is no separation of the disparate areas of life which are found normally elsewhere: work, leisure and sleep. All activities are carried out within the same living space, with the same objective and under the same single authority—the ship's captain. (91)*

In accord with Morison's sentiments that "primitive" considerations take priority on the water, Stadler writes "the yachtsman finds himself in an elemental situation," so that all his work is directly concerned with his survival. This creates, Stadler concludes, "a special emphasis on action on board yachts. In contrast to other areas of life what matters here is ... what he [*sic*] is physically capable of" (92).

Stadler's emphasis on the boat as a space for action and strength is not my main interest here; however, given that the Western world conceives of sex difference in terms of simple binary oppositions (action = masculine, stasis = feminine; strength = masculine, weakness = feminine), clearly Stadler *does* construct the boat as a masculine space (and he is certainly not alone in his belief).[4] With the invention of motors, pulleys, steering wheels, and hydraulics, and given the fact that a small, limber person can scramble faster than her or his burly counterpart, one can easily argue against this particular prejudice. Katy Burke (1985)

---

4 The acceptance of boats as masculine spaces containing only active and strong men has economic impacts on women. For example, in the British Columbia fishery, women typically find themselves in jobs that are routine, monotonous, stationary, and seasonal (Guppy 213), in part because the work performed on boats is wrongly perceived as "too heavy" for women. In "Labouring on Shore" (1987), Neil Guppy discusses some of the underlying reasons why people are not "randomly" assigned work, and how lower paying "women's work" is created.

has written an entire book on "non-macho" sailing practices. Pat and John Samson (1970) write, "A girl can be as good a crew member as a man. What members of one sex lack in one respect, they make up in another" (103). A young Ella Maillart showed, in the 1920s, that a crew of girls could handle a boat well if the rigging was altered to suit the size of the operators. Their ten-ton French vessel was engineless, and "her cutter rig, with its very long boom, was too heavy for a crew of girls, so we altered her into a yawl" (71). The 1995 bid of an all-woman crew in the America's Cup poses another question mark after the assertion that action and physical power deserve special emphasis afloat.

What interests me more here is the widespread acknowledgement that a boat is a universe unto itself, a space cut off from society. It seems to me that this perception is utterly false. We do not leave our socialization or our experiences on the quay when we step across the gangplank. We bring them right on board, along with our stereotypes and biases. And given the cramped quarters and lack of privacy, the environment on board can soon become a pressure cooker of those elements, not an escape from them. The social interaction that takes place on board a boat *is* influenced by maritime tradition, but more significantly, that interaction is an exaggeration of the everyday hegemonies in place on land. Thus, the accounts of mariners speak to evaluating and deconstructing those power relations.

But if, as I argue, boats have been cut off from the ideologies of human society in myth but not in practice, their space *has* historically been a territory closed to the literal presence of women. In this respect, Stadler is correct in comparing the situation at sea to a prison or cloister. Extending this situation to the port, Ann Davison (1951) uses the term "monastic" to describe the masculine space of a French fishing port:

> I was used to working among men. In the days when my interest had been in horses it was far more a man's game than it is now; when I was flying, there were probably not more than a dozen women B-license [commercial] pilots in [England], but I had found no difficulty in penetrating and being accepted in either sphere of interest. Not so this time. A fishing port is almost monastic in its exclusive masculinity; a woman's place is in the home, in the net-making shops, in the fish curer's possibly, but certainly not aboard. (97)

The "quayside commentators," she writes, were astonished by her presence as she helped fix up an old yacht that she and her husband had bought to live aboard:

> The possibility of a woman aboard was never considered, in spite of the markedly feminine appearance of some of the garments [on our wash line]. If I came on deck with a bunch of scrapers and a can of varnish, the crowd positively surged

---

5 Burke's text is prefaced by the humorous but realistic comment: "If I hear one more man tell one more woman how to step from the boat to the dinghy (put your little foot right here, dear) I think I'll spit" (Burke acknowledgements, unpaginated).

forward. Mothers called to their children, "Look—thur's a woman down thur!"
I felt it was up to me to justify their excitement by turning cartwheels or hanging
upside down in the rigging and only refrained from doing so because I can neither
turn cartwheels nor hang upside down anywhere. (130)

Literature set at sea has had, until relatively recently, little to say about
women—although the absence of women as maritime writers is, of course, telling. Writing of what they believed a masculine endeavor, the authors of sea fiction avoided "feminine" style. Herman Melville said of *Moby-Dick:* "It is not a
piece of fine feminine Spitalfields silk—but it is of the horrible texture of a fabric
that should be woven of ships' cables & hawsers" (quoted in Kazin 1988, 22).
Bert Bender's (1988) analysis of the tradition of American sea fiction is entitled
Sea Brothers. Its twelve chapters include no primary texts by female writers.[6]

The most obvious female presence on the sea is written in the names of ves-
sels and reflected in the common use of "she" and "her" in reference to boats.
Walking past Vancouver's False Creek docks recently, I saw that the custom
of naming boats for women was still alive. The usual complement of female
Christian first names was painted across transoms and bows as were *Miss
Seabright, Miss Marl, April Lady, Loyal Lady, Alaska Queen II, Ladner Lass,
Seamaid,* and (surprise!) *Ms. Maxine.*

T. C. Lethbridge writes in *Boats and Boatmen* (1952):

... directly a vessel takes the water she becomes a living thing in the eyes of
seafarers. She has to be named like a human child and to be studied in her moods
as if she were a wife, or even a goddess. This curious relationship between man
and his creation is becoming less apparent year by year, but it is still there, even if it
is no longer on the surface of a seaman's mind. (63)

Many countries, Lethbridge adds, including Egypt, Mesopotamia, Wales,
Norway, Sweden, Denmark, England, Scotland, and France, had a Bronze Age
tradition of burying men in model boats; they buried men in actual ships by the
early Saxon period (80). It is not uncommon for men to speak of being married
to their boats and to compare the shapes of women and boats. Morison writes:

Maybe there is an even more subtle reason for our love of a yacht—the parallel
of a well-built hull with a fair woman's body. St.-John Perse suggests this in his
Sea Marks: "Slender are the vessels, and more slender still thy figure, O faithful
body of my beloved.... And what is this body itself but the image and form of

---

6 Bender notes that "many women" traveled at sea at the end of the nineteenth century, as liner
passengers and as companions to their husbands in the merchant trade, but "the frequency of female
participants" as supporting characters in sea fiction of the period, he writes, resulted largely from
the authors' efforts to placate romantic readers (102). Bender briefly discusses the "'what to do
with' their women [characters] once they had them aboard" problem for sea-voyage authors such
as Hallet, Norris, and London (151).

the ship?—boat, ship and votive model, even to its 'midships opening, built like a
vessel's frame, fashioned on her curves.... Shipbuilders of every era have used this
fashion to bind the keel to the play of knees and frames." (13)

In a more regional context, Archie Binns (1942) remembers the transition from
the steam engine to the gas engine on Puget Sound in the 1900s. As an adolescent he would "slip away to the boathouse in the cove and consider the launch
Gloria, brooding in the half darkness of her shed." He gazes "worshipfully"
at her "mysterious power ... between dark plush cushions," while to his nostrils comes "the strange, exciting perfume of gasoline which we had not smelled
anywhere else" (33). In our own time, the New York-produced journal *Motor
Boating & Sailing* (the best-known yachting magazine in the world) continues
to feature photographs of boats juxtaposed with women in bathing suits on
most covers (the occasional exception is made for male celebrities such as
Don Johnson).[7] Roland and Janice Smith (1990), co-founders of the liveaboard
Homaflote Association, acknowledge the metaphor of the boat as "the other
woman" (87). Margie Livingston (1980) describes the metaphor in more detail:

*Many of us [women] join the boating scene because our skippers have fallen in
love—with a boat. It is no coincidence that the vessels are named* Psyche, Juno,
Circe, Aphrodite, Mistress, *and no secret that the owners lavish time, attention,
and money on them. If we first mates are wise enough to welcome these ladies, not
to fight them but to join them, we enter into a ménage-à-trois in which everyone
comes out a winner. (83)*

Joan Skogan even shows, in *Voyages: At Sea with Strangers* (1992), a metaphorical connection between fishing gear and women's bodies:

*The ropes and meshes on a trawl are arranged in sections called the bosom, belly,
wings, and bridle, which means that while I am peering around the edge of my
door to see if the codend is showing on the ramp yet, I am wondering if all the
trawl fishermen I know—Polish, Russian, and Canadian—imagine their gear is
either a winged woman or an angel in harness. Maybe they give their nets names
I never hear, names of mothers, wives, sisters, or daughters, of lovers, movie stars,
hookers, saints. (135)*

Although boats are conceived of as having the bodies and personalities of
women, and are loved and even desired by men, the space within boats has been
vigorously protected as masculine territory. Until recently, mariners have commonly acknowledged a tradition of women being bad luck or taboo on board,
whether or not they themselves claimed to believe the superstition. This superstition continues to find occasional expression in popular culture but is explicit
in literature set in marine environments.[8] "The worst thing of all," admits B.C.

---

7 *Boating for Women*, a new magazine published by women, has recently entered the market.

fisherman John Daly in 1975, "was a woman on a fishing boat" (Iglauer 1988, 128). These superstitions are vague in nature and are usually offered with no explanation of the reasoning behind them (as is the case with all superstition); for example, Frank Carr (who sailed in the Baltic Sea with a crew of women in 1930) admits, "I did not approve in a general way of taking women to sea, this being considered by seamen to be unlucky" (quoted in Heaton 1966, 163). When man about town Ludwig Bemelmans buys a yacht in France in the 1900s and hires a captain, the old salt is quick to teach him that "boats are for men alone" and "the happiest boat is a boat without women on board" (Bemelmans 1987, 300). No explanations are offered, therefore making the superstition difficult to challenge or disprove.

In his chapter "Superstition and Ritual," Lethbridge argues that the taboo against women on boats was a pagan tradition, later blurred into Christian custom. Pagan ships were "shrines" to the female goddesses who protected them. In Roman Catholic countries, the protecting goddess was later translated into the Virgin Mary (75). The belief that women were unlucky on board was grounded in an assumption of the jealousy of the goddess; Lethbridge explains that:

> the ship was under the protection of a female goddess, who might well be jealous of the presence of another woman in her shrine. This belief that women are unlucky aboard ship has, of course, faded from the minds of the crews of passenger vessels, but it still remains in those of men in some fishing-boats and freighters (71).

The goddess was also jealous of the representatives of Christianity: "The belief that priests are unlucky has a similar origin. The priest is a devotee of a different God to the one who protects the ship. The ship's goddess might well be jealous of a man who serves another god" (74).

Fear of female jealousy is still offered as an excuse to keep women off boats—especially off working boats where the occupants earn a "family wage." Writing of the British Columbia towboat industry in 1981, Ken Drushka explains that it is the jealousy of wives that precludes the presence of women on board:

> The cook's job is the only job on board a tug that is sometimes filled by a woman. The towboating industry was and remains a male-dominated industry. This is not because women are unable to perform the tasks involved in towboating: over the years a number of them have worked with their husbands on owner-operated boats. Company-owned tugs, however, have limited the role of women to that of cooks, and even that is rare. The explanation offered for this situation is that a tug

---

8 For example, in an episode of the Canadian television series *Due South*, scripted by Paul Gross and R. B. Carney, the regular characters solve a mystery involving a ghost ship on the Great Lakes. A seaman's dialogue suggests women may be bad luck aboard ships. Interestingly enough, a parodic and swashbuckling female captain eventually leads the charge to capture the "bad guys" in this episode—so perhaps she is only bad luck for them.

is a very small vessel having a tight social order, and the presence of women crew members would produce discord on board. And, the argument continues, though a woman might be able to work successfully in this traditionally male environment, the wives at home would not tolerate it. (191 and 194)

It is no longer the goddess who is constructed as intolerant of the presence of women on board, but the wives at home. This belief is still very much in circulation in towboating. In an interview with Vicki Jensen (1995), towboat cook Mary Levesque says: "I don't think the acceptance of women has changed much in towing. You see, one of the big problems is that this fellow on the crew is married, and his wife is like the ordinary person on the street who knows nothing about sailing. O.K., I'm out there with her husband, and she's conjuring up all kinds of things going on" (5). The (alleged) disapproval of wives may be a factor in the limited presence of women working on the water, but the force behind that disapproval is the widespread belief that "normal," healthy men cannot control themselves in close proximity to women. Rather than learn to accept women as persons—not as sex objects—men limit the presence of women on board working vessels, keeping them out altogether or assigning them to the cook's position in the cabin (a space separated from the "real work" of men most of the time).[9] "Those few determined women who do run tugs or work on them," writes Jensen, "usually do so as part of a family business" (2). Betty Andrews, who works with Ron Robinson aboard the tug *Stalker* in the Queen Charlotte Islands (Haida Gwaii), can say with authority: "there aren't many tugs that will accept a woman.... We won't join any union because then we wouldn't be able to work together" (Jensen 3).

Superstition and taboo can be mapped not only by women's absence on board boats, but by the spaces men and women occupy near the water. Fishing communities in western Europe believed it was bad luck to meet a woman on the way to your boat: "Many fishermen would turn back if they met a priest, or a woman, or any animal which might be a witch in disguise. For the same reason, women must not step over nets or gear, thereby dedicating these to themselves and not to the goddess of the boat" (Lethbridge 90-91). Although boats were masculine territory forbidden to women, women did sometimes enter those spaces—although perhaps more from necessity than desire. Distressed by her long separation from her partner, Libby Beaman attained special permission from the president of the United States to accompany her husband to the Pribilof Islands in 1879. Her husband was to observe the seal harvest as a government representative; nothing about the trip resembled a cruise or vacation. When they sailed from San Francisco, the seamen were outraged; Beaman's 1987 memoir

9 In her novel *The Watery Part of the World* (1988), Gladys Hindmarch depicts women working as cooks and housekeepers aboard a British Columbia freight and passenger carrier. Her text is based upon her own experiences working on British Columbia ferries; it shows how hard and carefully these women work at their domestic labor and how territorial they are in protecting their own spheres of influence.

shows that the sailors were "a superstitious lot," feeling cursed that a woman was on board (9). She spent most of the voyage hidden below deck.

Beth Hill (1978) writes that historically sailors were so poorly paid that their wives were in danger of starving if they were left behind:

Just as the institution of "camp follower" is as old as the armies they accompanied, so it is reasonable to suspect that the stowaway female is as old as ships large enough to hide her. If her protector was of sufficiently high rank, she walked openly upon the decks. There are, of course, few records concerning stowaway women, but in 1589 printed orders to the Spanish captains of the vessels of the Armada explicitly prohibited women on board and threatened severe punishment for anyone disobeying the order, clear evidence that the custom of hiding women below decks was an ancient one. Like the rats who shared the stinking hold where she would hide, furtiveness was the passport of the stowaway woman. Sometimes these shadowy figures were only seen when they were dead. (25-26)

We see, then, that when women did enter the space on board, their territory was usually in the darkest and lowest place available. Even today a woman's space on board tends to be explicitly and rigidly confined to the interior of the boat's cabin.[10]

A woman traditionally enters a vessel through the sponsorship of a man who, in essence, acts as a bridge to bring her on board. Jeanne Baret, for example, the first known woman to circumnavigate the world (with the Bougainville expedition of 1763), was disguised as the valet of a scientist on the voyage (Hill 1978, 25). Jennifer Brown (1980) describes the experiences of an Orkney Islands girl who successfully disguised herself as a laborer on board a ship to follow her lover to Albany in 1806. Granuaile, a sixteenth-century Irish pirate who eventually commanded three galleons and two hundred men, began the profession by stowing away on her father's ship (Chambers 1979). The stowaway tradition continues into modern times. In *Gilbert Said* (Swain 1992), a collection of oral history from Alaska's Gilbert McLeod, the recorder includes a story by McLeod's wife, Carolyn, of how once, as a young girl, she "hid out in the fo'c'sle" of her father's fishing boat against his wishes: "Before Dad ever got back to Ketchikan, I had a thrill. Going back we ran into heavy seas and had to dump all the fish on deck overboard. I should have been scared, but I never was, on the boat with Dad or Gilbert. I love it all" (77). Carolyn's father, and later her husband, serve as her link into the space and experience she loves. In fact, most women who work on boats gain that position by having a husband who shares his space or a father who shared his knowledge of boats with her.[11] In the Pacific Northwest, the first known female captain (figure 7) gained

---

10 Note that women on tugs tend to be limited to the role of cook, and hence to the interior space of the galley.

11 Women who boat for pleasure—as I discuss later in this chapter—almost always do so because their husbands own boats and invite them aboard to make it a home.

her position through her husband, who shared his space and knowledge with her. She earned her master's and pilot's license in 1886. The mammoth *Lewis & Dryden's Marine History of the Northwest*, first published in 1895 and containing information on literally thousands of men and ships, records the existence of Captain Minnie Hill in this footnote:

Figure 7. Captain Minnie Hill, the first known female captain west of the Mississippi, who earned her master's and pilot's license in 1886 (unattributed photo from Wright 1895).

> *Capt. Minnie Hill, who enjoys the distinction of being the only steamboat captain of her sex west of the Mississippi River, was born in Albany, Or., in 1863. She commenced steamboating with her husband, Capt. Charles Hill,* on the Columbia River steamer Governor Newell. *The young lady mastered the details of steamboating with but little trouble and in due season received a regular license permitting her to take full charge of a steamer. She has been remarkably successful in her calling and has handled the* Governor Newell *for the past eight years, her husband running most of the time as engineer. (Wright 339)*

Burgess Cogill describes living aboard a 228-foot sailing schooner that visited Puget Sound in *When God Was an Atheist Sailor: Memories of a Childhood at Sea, 1902-1910* (1990). Because her father was the captain, she and her mother and sister were allowed into the space of a working cargo vessel; however, her mother and father had rigidly defined territories: "Mother's sphere seemed to cover us and our outbursts, which she dealt with directly. Father's sphere was the ship and its domain. She never interfered with his domain" (99). In Cogill's case, the sailors are described as "male mother hens" who enjoy the presence of small girls aboard. But generally, men are not too keen on the appearance of a woman in a man's traditional role within masculine space. As Drushka observes, husband and wife partners in towboating still function in the margins of the industry. Women are having relatively more success in Northwest Coast commercial fishing, where they occasionally work as partners on board with husbands or (rarely) operate their own vessels (Allison et al. 1989). In "Labouring at Sea" (1987), Neil Guppy points out that the B.C. fishing industry is "peculiarly dependent" on the work of women; but in "Labouring on Shore" (1987), he notes that women overwhelmingly contribute to the industry from shore.

In this century women have just begun to enter boats in the capacity of hired workers, without fathers or husbands to open the space for them. Betty Jacobsen's *A Girl Before the Mast* (1934) documents the skirmishes for space and power the author faced as a nineteen-year-old apprentice in 1933. Sailing with the barque *Parma* from Australia to England, Jacobsen wanted to experience the competitive "grain race" of sailing ships on that route. She had spent the first five years of her life on her Norwegian father's ships, but on this trip she did not have his protection. The captain assures Jacobsen she can be an apprentice, but "no woman will ever be a sailor" (4). When the cabin boy tells her "women at sea is bad luck," she writes: "This was 1933 and I thought that all such superstitious notions had gone" (5). But in fact, the crew of her ship is convinced the presence of a girl will make them lose the grain race (which, incidentally, they win in the end despite a late start). "I can always feel a deep resentment and hostility," she writes, and she is made to understand daily that if anything goes wrong it will be her fault: "This continued superstitious fear of bad luck from a woman's presence gets on one's nerves, until you begin to feel yourself that some misfortune may come" (147). The boys go so far as to discuss sabotage; one day when she is high up on the yardarm of the rigging she overhears their conversation: "They were suggesting going down to slack up the tops'l sheet that I was sitting on, and then I would probably have been killed. On calmer reflection I decided that they did not mean it for a moment and would never have done such a thing, but at the time I felt angry" (166). Segregated from the boys, Jacobsen has her own small cabin, which she notes is more comfortable than theirs (9). The crew would prefer her to stay in it: "I have to go very circumspectly about my ways, and apart from working hours I do not go on the main deck very often. I stay on the poop, where I am told I belong" (146). The boys particularly dislike her presence up in the rigging:

> They like to think they can do what I cannot do. They like to fight the sails by themselves, and to feel that here, at least, is something that a woman will never do.
> I don't blame them for their attitude, and I agree sadly that after all I am better not up there for the time being. But my time will come. I would be as strong as any of these boys now if I had had a chance to develop as they have had. (22-23)

More than sixty years have passed since Jacobsen resented her inequality in the spaces aboard and above the *Parma*. For Joan Skogan (1992), a Canadian participant in the Foreign Fisheries Observer Program, those issues remained fresh even at the end of the twentieth century. Placed aboard foreign vessels in the 200-mile fishing zone off the West Coast of Canada, her job was to observe and record the ship's take:

> When I begin work as the fishery observer on Provideniaa, I become the "foreign woman." No-one [sic] is permitted to be alone with me. Doors must be left open if I am present. In the factory below decks, the workers press their bodies

into the edge of the fish lines and never look up from the heading and gutting
machines when I pass behind them. The men I meet in the passageways stand
back against the bulkhead, holding themselves stiffly, turning their heads away,
until I walk by. (19)

Part of Skogan's otherness is caused by her nationality and the assumption on
board these eastern European vessels that a Western woman must be lazy and
spoiled. But she is also highly conscious of the assumptions the men will make
about her because of her female body:

She is alone on the boat deck. She can't remember where her cabin is and her
cheeks warm with shame and awkwardness when she looks up to the storm bridge
and sees a dark-haired man, probably the chief mate, watching her.
    Would you rather have had a man to work with you? she wants to ask him. I
know you'd rather not have a fishery observer at all, of course. Maybe a younger
woman? a thinner one? with longer hair and bigger breasts? one who smiles more,
who won't stand at the bridge window when she is exhausted, staring at the sea in
the dark? one who doesn't smoke as much as you do yourself?
    You don't understand, she would like to call up to him. I'm not like the others
they've told you about. I never complain about the cockroaches and the food. I
know my job. There won't be any trouble. You'll see. (17-18)

There won't be any trouble, she promises—a claim still made by many women
working in masculine territory, and still doubted. There appears to be only one
way to counter that doubt, both on work boats and pleasure craft: get your own
boat. Jensen (1995) and Allison et al. (1989) both demonstrate that, for females
trying to work in the commercial fishery, buying and operating their own vessel
is sometimes the only way to move out of the galley. Nancy Marshall, for
instance, comments: "I was fishing with a guy who only wanted me working in
the galley, so the only answer was for me to get my own boat" (Jensen 134). It
is much the same story with recreational boating. Virtually all traditional guides
for women boaters stress subordination; one or two admit that, for the "women
who love to sail, ... rare as cats who swim for pleasure," the *only* answer is to
"get your own boat and have done with it" rather than attempt the impossible
compromise of sharing the skipper's role (Morgan 1974, 6-7; her emphasis).[12] A
recent alternative has appeared in the San Juan Islands, Chesapeake Bay, Cape
Cod, Long Island Sound, and other recreational hot spots. Women's groups,
such as Womanship, Women for Sail, Sailing Women, Women at the Helm, and
The Phoenicians, have begun to offer boating experience and support in all-
female environments (Frankel 1990).

---

12 The only female captain I have discovered in cruising narratives (Muriel Wylie Blanchet) boated
with her children as a widow.

Women and Cruising Literature

Yachting and the modern idea of the home both originate in seventeenth-century Holland (Heaton 1966; Rybczynski 1986). By the 1670s Dutch admirals had established the fashion of lavishly furnishing naval vessels for purposes of entertainment. Soon after that records show that the Dutch East India Company owned a variety of yachts used by company officials for both business and pleasure (Heaton 28). During the same period on shore, the concept of home emerged. Home was not only the house but also the sense of satisfaction and contentment located there. Witold Rybczynski argues that Dutch women's insistence on cleanliness within the home and their requirement that visitors take off their shoes upon entering the house, created a new boundary between the public realm and the private home—a boundary that defined the home as "a separate, special place" (66) and a "feminine" space (72). When furnishings, pleasure, and at least some of the comforts of home arrived on certain vessels, the gender associated with the home was apparently less taboo on that class of boat; the first known account of a privately owned yacht includes mention of a woman aboard. Yachts had quickly become popular in Restoration England, and Samuel Pepys recorded sailing aboard Sir William Batten's *Charlotte*: "September 3rd, 1663, Boarded her early in the morning at Greenwich accompanied by Batten and Lady Batten, who, for pleasure were going to the Downs" (quoted in Heaton 1966, 32).

But although women may have been present on pleasure craft for more than three hundred years, no substantial body of literature exists to describe their experiences before the twentieth century. This lack of early cruising literature by women appears to result from of a number of factors. First, until the beginning of the twentieth century, one had to be wealthy to build and maintain a yacht and a crew of men to sail it. The class of people yachting before the twentieth century was therefore extremely limited. Modern pleasure craft are smaller, lighter, require less "manpower," and until relatively recently were affordable to the middle and even working classes. Second, before the use of the gasoline engine on pleasure craft, the cabins on board were smaller and more cramped to allow ample space on deck for sails, ropes, a swinging boom, and a crew to control the boat. Less cabin space translates into less comfort, and apparently less appeal to women. Finally, widespread interest in women's travel writing began in the Victorian period; after that time, women would be much more inclined to publish personal travel accounts.

In the twentieth century, women did not occupy the space on small craft as equal partners with men. This fact seems to remain true throughout the century; in 1990 Michael Frankel describes "the all too familiar, and less than equal partnership [of women] with their male counterparts in managing their floating homes" (90). Repeatedly—almost obsessively throughout the century—women are depicted as, and describe themselves as, "the crew," or even more commonly, "the mate." The term "mate," of course, is frequently a good-humored comment on the situation that brought the woman to sea: she married a man with a boat, or with an interest in boats, and therefore she boats. The husband is uniformly described as the captain, master, or skipper.[13] As his married mate, the wife becomes his second in command at sea; the result is that the woman is on the low end of the power hierarchy afloat. These titles reflect and reinforce the role-playing done by husband and wife and the separate spheres captain and mate occupy on the water; men are concerned with the outside world of the deck and the spaces beyond it, women with the interior world of the cabin. The captain controls movement, navigation, and communication (for example, operating the ship's radio and taking responsibility for customs interactions), whereas the mate's role on board—in parallel with her role as his mate in the home—is to support him and see to their comfort. Although she is required to help on deck from time to time, she knows she is within his territory at those moments. Her own power is located within the cabin, where (much like a traditional homemaker) she produces food and maintains the tools of comfort. Typically then, a woman's account of cruising is much concerned with the interior territory she occupies on board.

Early in her opening chapter of *A Yachtswoman's Cruises and Some Steamer Voyages* (1911), Maude Speed notes that she has "begun (woman-like) with the interior arrangements because so much of the pleasure of cruising depends on them, and with a little attention they can be made all right even in the smallest boat" (7-8, her parenthesis). This "little attention" involves making certain that "every comfort is packed into the small space that [the cabin] will hold" (90). Describing her cruises with "the Skipper" in the waters of England, Holland, and France, Speed's text combines personal memoir and ethnography and develops a thesis concerning women afloat. Explaining that small-boat cruising is hard work, she writes: "I do not think that many women as yet care sufficiently for the sport to face all this [hard work] for it, as one so seldom meets a woman who is really any help on board or the least bit enthusiastic over hard cruising" (10-11). "Hard cruising" involves a woman taking a turn at the tiller and suffering "black bruises from tumbling and knocking against the sharp edges of seats, &c., in the general plunging and pitching about" (12). But rough weather is not an everyday occurrence in pleasure boating, and more often the work on board is divided as follows: "While the Skipper was getting things ship-shape on deck, I was busy with chamois and dusters below drying up the inevitable leaks which always will squeeze through the skylight, chain-pipe, and other places in a wet thrash to windward" (22). Speed is frequently occupied with keeping the out-side *out*. The work that occurs below deck is clearly defined as her work, and the rare occasion for "the Skipper" to descend to her realm is written about as a special occurrence worth noting. She writes of paddling up a small creek in the dinghy and forgetting the time until she "heard the Skipper's voice in the

---

13 This construction remains alive and well today. In *Gently with the Tides* (1990), Michael Frankel writes: "In most instances the captain is a male and the mate a female. And therein lie a multitude of differences and sometimes conflicts" (86), and "I am not suggesting that we do away with the supreme role of boat captain as master of the vessel, and I do understand that with most couples the male is the traditional captain" (90).

distance shouting something about supper (bother that supper! it always brings one down to earth again with a run), and rowing back found that like a good man he had done *my work* and got the soup and chops ready cooked and the cloth laid" (55, my emphasis). Normally cooking is her role. "As to food," she writes, "I could fill a whole chapter with a list of things long experience has proved to be feasible" (4) on board. In fact, creating such chapters is precisely what the authors of more recent guidebooks for women boaters do.

Bringing their socialization on board, both sexes expect women and men to perform the same duties at sea that they traditionally accomplish on land—if in modified form. Nowhere is this assumption made more explicit than in cruising handbooks and manuals. Guides aimed at a male audience emphasize safety and navigation—the compass, lead and line, pilot books, sextant, anchoring, docking, rules of "the road," and marine radios (see Fox 1960, for example). They may explain how to select and purchase a boat. Handbooks for women place primary significance on the importance of making a boat a home and identify the galley as "the mainspring of a motor cruiser or yacht" (Wickham 1971, 9).

Enid Wolf's *A-Boating We Will Go: A Cruising Manual for Women* (1958) emphasizes boating as a family project. The woman boater here is referred to always as "the first mate" (perhaps threatening that there will be a second mate to supersede if she does not learn to boat), and her role on board is consistently a reflection of her traditional role in the patriarchal nuclear family. "The father is truly head of the house and master of his craft for each boating excursion," her text informs the reader; "every first mate feels this instinctively" (121). Before penning her manual, Wolf contacted 199 of the U.S. Power Squadrons for information on women's auxiliary groups, then she surveyed women from across the United States. If her text is an accurate reflection of the information she gathered, women boaters felt the most significant issues for females afloat included:

- having "a home study method for learning [nautical] terms as you (1) step aboard, (2) go below...."
- "the need for more stowage space"
- "cabin decor and conveniences"
- clothing
- bedding
- choosing a stove
- stocking the galley
- first-aid knowledge
- safety
- "good boating recipes"
- children aboard
- pets aboard
- guests aboard
- housekeeping at the end of the boating season and (the final section of the book):
- why the first mate should learn to handle the boat

Wolf's manual is an informal and sometimes silly book, written in an irritatingly offhand manner: "Now, you say, it's about time to take a look at my number-one job. What gives in the cooking and housekeeping departments?" (23). However, the work is significant because it records how gendered territories on board were carefully separated and how eager women were to know their space was "charted territory." One woman apparently wrote in a letter to the author:

> We've got a collection of handbooks, magazines, and pamphlets all over the house, but they deal in hull design, engines, fuel consumption.... All well and good, but where does a gal get a few pertinent facts about what to wear, where and how to keep the kids quiet during an eight-hour run, or what to take along in the ice chest? Now I understand we're going to have our own reference work. Swell! (Wolf 4)

Defining the boat as "the Skipper's home afloat" (272) and the woman's project there as "a new way of being a housewife and a mother" (8), Wolf's text amounts to a collection of strategies for following the ground rule that "the Skipper is number-one boss" (16).

Jane Kirstein and Mary Leonard's *Family Under Sail: A Handbook for First Mates* (1970) follows in the wake of Wolf's manual. Where Wolf's text locates itself mainly in Pacific Northwest waters, the American authors here boat in New England with their husbands (although Kirstein grew up on Puget Sound). They each "married boats" (20)—that is, married men who already owned boats—and they assert in their foreword that they "hope to work a sea change" (x) in wives reluctant to boat with their husbands.[14] Their strategy is to include the expected chapters on housekeeping aboard, children aboard, clothing, recipes, and "Woman's Role, or, What Every First Mate Should Know," and then to add sections on "The Rewards of Sailing" and "For Husbands Only: The Care and Training of First Mates." Their argument is that the space limitations on board dictate a utilitarian lifestyle; therefore, housekeeping is "light," clothing is "easy to care for," and meals are "sensible and simple" (17; *that's* the reward of sailing for women). This environment of lessened drudgery among the wheeling seagulls and blue water (94), they stress, should appeal to women. A guide closer to the truth would acknowledge that the mate spends a great deal of her vacation in the boat's cabin. George Sass (1990) describes his feeling about the cabin space when he lived alone on board:

---

14 This reluctance continues to be an issue. Between 1975 and 1990, Michael Frankel (1990) surveyed "more than 2,000" liveaboards about their lifestyle afloat. He writes: "The most prevalent source of conflict had something to do with the mate, and particularly the mate's lack of enthusiasm for 'messing around in boats.' Comments included: 'Can't get the wife to share the skipper's duties.' 'Mate refuses to live aboard.' 'Shorebound girlfriend.' 'Finding someone to go cruising with.' 'Wife just not interested'"(12).

But there was always this undeniable feeling that I was "below" when cooking, eating, or relaxing [in the cabin]. One literally and figuratively lost sight of what was going on outside ... it's a fact of life that being below on a typical sailboat is being down in an out-of-the-way, tunnel-like environment. (61)

Diane Taylor's *The Perfect Galley Book* (1983) admits: "There's no doubt that, on some boats at least, the cook feeling left out is a real problem" (28). But for Taylor this feeling is simply a result of poor boat design, not gendered roles; "the location of the galley" on some pleasure craft, she points out, makes some cooks feel "excluded from [cockpit and main saloon] conversation" (29). She overlooks the limiting nature of unshared domestic labor itself.

Once she is on board, Kirstein and Leonard write, "Every First Mate Should Know" that "the skipper is absolute boss. On a boat there can be no division of authority as there may be at home. Throughout history the navies of sea powers have operated under this principle. Mother, as hard as it may be, must cooperate" (64). "Mother," therefore, must bend not only under the burden of patriarchy, but also under the tradition of navies at sea.

One of these traditions is that the skipper or captain's power accords him the status of using the symbolically significant right-hand side of the boat: "According to marine protocol, the captain rates the right-hand position of everything on the boat: the bunk, the locker, even the green running lights, if he wants them for his very own. I find this procedure a handy way of remembering which is 'his' and 'hers' at times" (89). His authority is even discussed as one of the pleasures of cruising: "By tradition, the skipper is the only boss on a boat, and I like it that way. I am not a particularly submissive type, but it's restful to have someone else make all the decisions" (5). "All the decisions," it should be noted, are the decisions that occur topside; it is up to the mate to plan for and prepare meals and to take general responsibility for what goes on in the cabin. Women's presence below, they note, has led to significant improvements in boat design:

The galley has seen more changes in recent years than any other part of a boat's living arrangements, moving from its traditional stuffy hole in the forwardmost part of the boat ... because the first mate has replaced the paid hand at the stove and she wants to be where both the action and the ventilation are. (30)

Samuel Eliot Morison (1965) is in agreement, and he extends the effects of women on board throughout the interior of yachts:

The amenities of a yacht cabin have been vastly improved in recent years; and this I credit to the women. Sixty years ago no young lady thought of cruising except in a big yacht with paid hands, private stateroom and all that. But around 1912 girls began demanding to do everything their brothers did, and young wives refused to stay at home when their husbands went cruising. The male sex discovered that females not only helped navigate the yacht but kept her neat and clean below and made up bunks nicely with sheets, replacing the unseemly huddle of blankets that came apart in the night. The girls demanded better toilet facilities and got them,

soft watertight mattresses instead of the old "donkey's breakfast" that soaked up
water like a sponge, new and shiny cooking pots instead of castoffs from the home
kitchen, disposable paper plates, towels, and the like. (15)

In 1961 Beth Eberhart writes that the presence of women and families on West
Coast fishing trollers also resulted in changes in both comfort and safety afloat:

Each year more and more wives, and often whole families, go along for a
summer's outing. Trollers are improving accordingly. Two-way radios, fathom-
eters, automatic pilots, and electric gurdies make for greater safety, while inside
heads, showers, refrigerators, and cute little ranges, all white enamel, fool the
wives into thinking that housekeeping on a boat will be a cinch. (43)

Interior renovation appears to be one slim portion of the marine industries
in which women are leaders. In essays such as "Boat Interior Decorating"
(Lawrence 1974) and countless first mates' guides, women have long offered
advice on the topic. A feature in the *Seattle Post-Intelligencer* (Goodnow 1986)
suggests that women began to capitalize on that interest. Customizing yacht
interiors became a fast-growing market in the 1980s; wealthy boaters "want it
more like their home, with plump cushions." The piece acknowledges that "the
push for comfort and style has come from women [boat owners]," and quotes
client Carol Kessi: "I wanted the comforts I have at home." All of the designers
featured in the reading (Judy Bell, American International Design Corporation;
Ann Wightman and Kris Hotchkiss, Windrose Interiors; Sally Ferguson, Sally
J. Interiors; Judie Baker, Baker's Marine Interiors; and Carolann A. Surdyke &
Co. Inc.) are women who apparently profit by making boats into "homes" for
wealthy clients. For a few women, then, homemaking afloat has become an economic opportunity rather than a mate's duty.

In their final chapter, "For Husbands Only: The Care and Training of First
Mates," Kirstein and Leonard suggest that, although the skipper has all authority for making final decisions, husband and mate should try to negotiate on
some issues (for instance, to agree on an itinerary). Moreover, the skipper should
teach the interested mate a thing or two about seamanship so she can assist him
underway and feel useful. To reward a woman for her efforts at masculine tasks,
he should indulge her feminine desire to be clean and beautiful; understanding
"that a clean body and a clean head of hair lie close to every woman's heart—no
matter how salty a sailor she is" (227), he should get the woman to a port with
a shower occasionally (228).

American Morley Cooper agrees that "salt water cruising reaches its highest
point in enjoyment only when it becomes a family affair" (173), and he dedicates *The Cruising Yacht* (1945) "TO MADGE A fine sailorman and perfect
cruising companion, who has also mastered the difficult art of making of [*sic*]
a small yacht a home afloat" (v). Cooper's chapter "Your Family and Your
Boat" is punctuated by the telling headings: "Let Your Wife Handle the Boat,"
"Motivation by Flattery," "Ornamental Females," "Give Her a Real Galley,"

"Baths and Toilets," "Cabin Heating," and "The Feminine Touch Restrained." Issues dealing with comfort on board are categorized as belonging in the "Your Family" chapter. Cooper explains that the presence of women dictates changes to the masculine space on board: "If you expect her to cruise with you, you may have to make several changes, every one of which will definitely improve the boat and make it as livable as a floating home should be" (160). Once again we see that the space on board becomes constructed as home when the presence of a woman is added. But in "The Feminine Touch Restrained," Cooper advocates curtailing women's desire to go overboard in homemaking:

> *Women usually like to add a few touches to the decoration of the cabin. Mostly their ideas on this subject are good and will make the place more homey and livable. But you may have to use a little firmness here should the lady happen to run hogwild and attempt to convert the cabin into a seagoing boudoir. Generally, and ordinarily without the necessity of using force, she can be made to see that restraint must be practiced after a certain degree of softness has been attained in cabin decoration. (172)*

"Your floating home" (173), Cooper argues—and here his view differs from that in other guides—is neither an exclusively masculine nor exclusively feminine space; it has a "dual personality" (174):

> *In harbor your cruiser or auxiliary is, first and last, a home.... At sea your boat takes on its other personality, a sterner, more businesslike attitude, in which its softer, homey characteristics are submerged in the task at hand, which is to transport you over a possibly boisterous sea to another snug harbor. Now the center of interest is transferred from the comfortable cabin to the cockpit. (174)*

Which is to say that the primary or dominating space changes from inside to outside, from feminine to masculine. For this reason, Cooper argues that there must be *two* skippers alternating in command:

> *When you're lying in harbor and the center of interest is in the cabin and home-making, there must be a port captain in charge, and there can be but one choice for this appointment—the wife and mother. Whether you like it or not, skipper, she's going to run things in port, so you might as well make it official and save yourself a lot of fruitless effort.*
>
> *But when the time comes to get under way the port captain must gracefully step down and permit the sea captain to take command of his ship. How far she steps down will depend upon how much help she is in handling the boat. She may be demoted only to mate, she may descend further to a cabin-boy billet, or she may go all the way down to the bottom of the scale and become just a helpless female guest. But if she's wise she will know when to stop giving orders and begin taking them. After all, in a summer's cruise your ship is at sea only a fraction of the time it's in port—which is a tough break for the sea captain if he likes his authority. (174-75)*

With this division of command, in Cooper's scheme, comes the seemingly natural division of labor on board—men work on deck or in the cockpit, and women take the interior:

> *Care of the ship's gear, the engine, the dinghy, the riding lights, and the deck swabbing—these are, of course, the men's responsibility. The housekeeping and all below-deck chores are taken care of by the women-folks and there should be no overlapping of duties. Any other arrangement is unnatural and will soon lead to friction. (175)*

In *The Psychology of Sailing* (1987), Michael Stadler argues against an "inconsiderate division of labour [that] can bring the motivation to go sailing to absolute rock bottom" (78). Although "not everyone who feels like it can set himself up as skipper," "a flexible division of labour is quite feasible" and allows every member of the crew an opportunity to gain confidence and knowledge (78-79). Sailing crews, he insists, should exchange work or risk serious discontent. "Something similar can often be seen with typical 'family crews,'" he writes:

> *Dad spends the whole cruise at the chart table, Mum stands to the left of him in the galley attending to the needs of the family day in, day out.... It is just the same year after year, and then the head of the family wonders why his wife no longer has any real enthusiasm for sailing. (77)*

Ironically, in their desire to encourage family cruising and to give women more confidence in a traditionally male space, the authors of women's boating guidebooks encourage this "inconsiderate division of labour" through the "home afloat" metaphor. And although boating guides are a limited genre, their contents do seem to reflect accurately the attitudes of many pleasure boaters around the globe and throughout the twentieth century. A woman is just as likely to be constructed as a "mate" whether she is boating near England in 1929 (Graham 1950), Norway in 1932 (Heaton 1966, 167), Mozambique in the 1960s (Karlsson 1969), or off the coast of British Columbia in 1989 (Nicolls 1990).

All of the spatial issues described in guides surface repeatedly in personal accounts. The most common thread is the designation of the cabin as a woman's territory on board, and her initial dismay at—or ingenuity in expanding—the limited space there. When Frank Carr sailed the Baltic Sea in 1930 with a female crew, he writes: "They loved the neat way in which a large amount of accommodation had been worked into a comparatively small space below" (Heaton 163). When, in 1932, Dora Birtles joined the first party to sail from Australia to Singapore with some female crew members, the battles over space aboard their "floating home" (vii) were epic. "House-pride" (146) overwhelmed Ann Davison occasionally on board the *Reliance* in France (Davison 1951), and the "exigencies of space" limiting her wardrobe when she boated off the coast of Florida had a place in her account (Davison 1964, 22). Alina Karlsson put her foot down when her husband attempted to despoil "the appearance of the cabin" aboard their eighteen-foot *Symphony* off the east coast of Africa (Karlsson 152), and when American Emily Kimbrough (1958) boarded a barge to travel the English canal system, she exclaimed: "Now we were going to 'play house'" (260). Kimbrough felt quite strongly about her role "playing house" afloat; when another woman joined her party, she wrote: "I was discomfited at having been replaced [in the galley]. I had considered operation of the galley my prerogative.... I was now without portfolio" (162).

Repeatedly for women in worldwide cruising narratives, the options are the galley portfolio or no portfolio; out of a desire to participate in the voyage (or simply to spend time with their husbands), women submit to the role of "galley slave." Philip Davenport (1953) records that on his honeymoon cruise from Australia to England aboard a forty-six-foot sailing cutter he "escaped from helping [my new wife] Roz prepare the meal by pretending to be more occupied with the business of navigating and setting course than I really was" (155).[15] And: "While the rest of us [men] were yarning with Frank on deck Roz cleaned and tidied the cabin in preparation for our arrival in Montevideo" (170). This clear division of space and labor shows that although Maude Speed may have been half jesting in 1911 when she claimed "mutiny has never been encouraged on the skipper's boats, and the crew knows its place!" (89), men and women do know indeed who holds the power in the home afloat.

A number of women attempt to gain some degree of power by making themselves appealing. The pressure to act ornamental, to make oneself beautiful in a "feminine" sense, becomes a particular issue on the water, where sunburn, windburn, broken fingernails, and greasy hair are the norm. Speed writes:

> ... *smart blouses and elegant hats have to be left at home. The coiffure also harks back to primitive simplicity, one's complexion becomes like a haymaker's, and one's hands don't look exactly as if they had come straight from a manicure's [sic]! We must therefore all bid a temporary good-bye to vanity when we embark for a cruise! (14)*

In *Florida Junket: The Story of a Shoestring Cruise* (1964), Ann Davison describes how, near the end of the cruise, she becomes "aware of my clothes—my hair—the way make-up stood out on my sunburnt face like colour out of register in the Sunday supplements" (149). Speed hypothesizes that "a reason for the unpopularity of cruising with ladies may be found partly in the hopelessness of looking pretty in the way of dress. The effort to do so may be given up from

---

15 Sometimes the knife cuts both ways. In *North-West by North* (1935), Dora Birtles describes how the men on board regard the women as "almost pieces of luggage, incurable amateurs in sailing" (219). Therefore, like Davenport, these women did not feel "really responsible" (242) for participating in the space beyond their own gender-specific territory. As a result, "when a disagreement on nautical matters arose the women were all tacitly dumb" (114).

the beginning" (12-13). The authors of cruising guides for women disagree, or if they acknowledge the effort, they do not encourage giving up. The key to looking and feeling pretty, they write, is space. Space to stow a variety of practical—and a few impractical—clothes (guides include lists of garments), and space to shower so a woman can look and smell as she does at home. Kirstein and Leonard describe how to invent a shower, using little of the precious fresh water stored on board:

> Remove everything from the [tiny bathroom] that you don't want to get wet, including the toilet paper, then strip (you knew that already?) and fill the wash basin with half a teakettle of boiling water (reserve the other half). Add only enough cold water to the basin to avoid third-degree burns. Thoroughly wet a washcloth but don't squeeze it until it is suspended over the body at strategic points. (169-70)

The instructions continue, giving one the idea that a "shower" and the cleaning of the bathroom to follow could take hours. Within the confines of the cabin, finding, changing, and stowing clothes all take a great deal longer than they do in a house. By trying to appear and smell exactly as she does at home, the woman has to spend even more time in the cabin. Meanwhile, the skipper is on the deck in his old jeans, thoughtfully pulling at his three-days' beard.

In his *Gently with the Tides* (1990), Michael Frankel acknowledges that frequently for women, boating "is not a relief from the house but a duplication of household chores and frustrations" (86):

> To her, boating may not mean getting away from problems but rather shouldering a whole set of new ones: lack of labor-saving galley equipment, damaging exposure to her complexion or hair, hands becoming dry, cut, maybe blistered and fingernails broken, lack of privacy, the substitution of relatively crude facilities for the comforts at home. To her, boating may represent physical discomforts, possible injury to herself, her children, and/or her mate. (87)

Language is a related spatial issue on the water, for there is a language of seamanship to learn when one steps on board. Glossaries of terms appear regularly not only in women's cruising manuals, but also in women's personal accounts. Wolf's *A-Boating We Will Go* includes one entire chapter on the importance of learning the language. In the guides for women, learning this "foreign language" (Kirstein and Leonard 42) is described as a necessary initiation into accepting the power hierarchy on board: one learns the terms to be able to follow the skipper's commands. Kirstein and Leonard write: "If your boat seems a bit like a Marine Corps Boot Camp, with the skipper yelling like a drill sergeant and the water up to your knees, be joyful!" (42). Some women, of course, do not joyfully participate in such rituals on their vacations. Dora Birtles notes that she had come on board with her party "partly to escape the net of bondages being long-married implied, to find an individual freedom for a little time" (61). Birtles' account demonstrates that, although a woman can call the boat a "floating home" (vii), she is yet aware that it remains a territory lacking some of the pleasures she most values at home. One of these pleasures is non-hierarchical "woman's talk." When Birtles comes ashore to meet a Mrs. White and her daughter Ruth, a group of women gather and drink mango wine while seated under a rain shower beating on an iron roof:

> *The talk was a spate, it flowed out torrentially, questions stood out like boulders in it, answers and comments raced on, extended, swirled in explanation, reunited with the main stream again. It was exhausting, all our woman-knowledge, woman quickness ... this was afternoon tea-time at [Ruth's] home. Her laughter was the ceaseless high spattering of rain on big leaves, mango leaves. (100-01)*

Birtles describes this flowing, watery woman's talk (interesting imagery in contrast to *sea*man's language) as the natural result of combining a group of women in a civilized and quintessentially domestic environment: "We had a meal, a meal that women had made in a proper kitchen and served with refinement, poultry, potatoes, bread sauce, incomparable bread sauce, jelly, a paw-paw salad and little mince pies. Civilization breathed fragrantly from the little mince pies" (101).

The use of a technical and hierarchical language system on board, and the discouragement from using "women's talk" in the marine environment (on the boat, on the dock, over the radio), reinforces the notion that a woman is in male territory. Accounts written by both men and women commonly relate stressful or comical situations in which men impatiently attempt to teach resistant women nautical language. Usually the context for this tense or funny situation is that the "mate" feels so overburdened by her galley chores, or so insulted by what she perceives as snobbery in nautical rhetoric, that she initially refuses to learn it. "Kristin said I was babbling in a foreign language," writes Iain Lawrence (1997). He recounts, "She said I was using terms that went out with the sailing masters. 'It's pretentious,' she said." After Kristin begins to learn the jargon, he quizzes her from a book:

> *"Do you know what a hen frigate is?" I asked.*
> *"What?"*
> *I read from the book. "A vessel," I said, "where the...." I had to stop, I was laughing so hard. "... where the captain permits his wife to interfere with the running of the ship."*
> *"I don't think that's very funny," she said. (14)*

Later, when Kristin beckons for the salt shaker by growling for "Lot's wife," the author credits himself for initiating her into legitimate sailing society: "I handed her the salt shaker and smiled. My God, I thought, I'd created a master" (14). But his good-humored allusion to Frankenstein's monster makes this an ambiguous scene. Is Kristin now acceptable—or an aberration?

Women Boating the Northwest Coast

Along the Northwest Coast, pleasure craft and the marinas that materialized to cater to these small boats (see chapter one) offered a particular accessibility for women. For respectable women before the mid-nineteenth century—often wearing skirts, stockings, delicate shoes, and gloves—the movement between a pier and the deck of a steamer could seem very awkward indeed. Because of the tidal range along the coast—especially in the northernmost areas—a ship could not simply pull alongside a waiting pier and find its decks level with the pier. In the late nineteenth and early twentieth centuries, some destinations did not have piers at all; at other villages all vessels used the cannery wharf.[16] The farther one was from "the beaten track," the more chance there would be of creative measures designed to move people from ship to shore. For a man, wearing sturdy shoes and pants, these measures might be inconvenient. For a woman, they could be bizarre and terrifying. When Helen Judge McAllister, traveling to the Pribilof Islands with her husband in 1894, was "unloaded," she "was strapped in a chair, hoisted up by a yardarm and deposited in a boat made of sealion skins called a 'Bidora'. In the bottom of the Bidora were a number of sheep with their legs tied together. I sat down on one."[17] When Libby Beaman (1987) had arrived at the same location fifteen years earlier, she too had been unloaded into a small boat from her ship. She was accompanied ashore by local boys in a sailing skiff, and she writes: "I was terrified. There are some events for which a woman is not properly clothed, and this was one of them. My skirts blew out from me like a parasol and threatened to be torn from my waist" (69).

The most common "gauntlet" was the slimy or insubstantial ladder. British Columbia artist Emily Carr (1941) describes climbing one of these ladders—at low tide, in the dark—to a cannery wharf:

> "Couldn't I ... couldn't I crawl under the wharf round to the beach?" I begged.
> "It is not possible, go!..."
> I grasped the cold slimy rung. My feet slithered and scrunched on stranded things. Next rung ... the next and next ... endless horrible rungs, hissing and smells belching from under the wharf. These things were at least half tangible.

---

16 Although modern marinas offer much better access for women than did those of the past, the journey between boat, float, and wharf can cause some fear. I have many memories of slowly anchoring each toe as I traveled down steep ramps at marinas, government wharves, and provincial parks. Margaret Sharcott (1957) describes her experiences: "... there was a very old and steep wooden walk, its ancient cleats worn away and broken in places. At low tide it was almost perpendicular. Add a coating of ice and then try to climb it. I had always stepped on each cleat with a mental picture of me crashing the twenty feet to the bottom. I looked on that old ramp as my personal enemy" (104).

17 "Memoirs of the Pribilof Islands Nineteen Years on St. George and St. Paul Islands Alaska." Helen Judge McAllister papers (V.F. 476), Univ. of Washington Manuscripts and Archives, Seattle, 1945. 2.

Empty nothingness, behind, around; hanging in the void, clinging to slipperiness, was horrible—horrible beyond words! (93)

In *Cinderella Takes a Holiday* (1937), Rebie Harrington comments on the same theme, claiming that

I think the most heroic act I ever performed was when I mounted at least sixteen slimy [sic] covered, slippery, green rungs of the dock ladder at Kasaan. It was low tide and for that reason the ladder was excessively long. This seemed to be the only method of making a landing and I ... made the ascent in fear and much trembling, though I flatter myself that I managed to cover up the horrible fact. (29)

Descending the ladder for the trip back to the steamship was even worse:

Lying almost on my stomach, I managed one foot over the edge to the pier but found it utterly impossible to negotiate the other; so I called upon Linda to assist, which she did.

With the large handbag, which I carried over my arm, my movie camera festooned over my shoulders, a "still" camera in each pocket, I commenced the descent.... It seemed an endless journey; each rung was as slippery as jelly, and they were by no means close together, without doubt modelled for use of longshoremen and not for ladies from the outside world. (29-30)

Florence Lee Mallinson (1914) describes climbing a rope ladder to board the steamship *Meteor* in Seattle in 1913—with a crowd of boys looking up her skirt: "... and once more [I] climbed up a rope ladder on to deck, holding as tight as a leech. The boys were wearing the big smile that won't rub off" (189-90). By the time she gets to Nome, Alaska, she writes: "We had to climb up by ladder (I was getting used to ladders by this time)" (192), when those going ashore were asked to climb a tower. She did, however, find a surprise at the top of that tower:

We were put into a cage and were drawn to shore by cable power. Thus we were suspended in mid-air by a cable, and some hundred feet from the surging Bering Sea. Of course, we had to hold on to the rails, for it would be worth our lives to move lest we would tilt to one side and lose our balance. Talk about cold—umph! Whew! It went through like a driven nail, and I was numb in a few minutes. I was the only lady that was going. (192)

Having gained access to the large passenger ships, under some circumstances women found the space aboard segregated. For instance, in *An American Girl Abroad* (1872) Adeline Knox describes how carefully sailors and passengers of different classes occupy space on board for a church service in the Atlantic: "The sailors in their neat dress filed in and ranged themselves in one corner.... The passengers filled their usual seats, and a delegation from the steerage crept shyly into the unoccupied space" (22). Gender segregation was less an issue on tourist vessels catering to wealthy White travelers. On these ships, or "floating hotel[s]" (Speed 171), paid help cooked, cleaned, and occupied the lowest stations—socially and physically—on board. In 1911 Maude Speed (the same Maude Speed identified earlier in this chapter, who also traveled by pleasure craft with her husband) writes that off the coast of Sicily she

> ... once got round the chief engineer, and through his courtesy inspected the great engine-room, and penetrated to that awful region where half-naked men, looking demon-like and fantastic in the red glare, keep the life-blood beating in the heart of the [ship]....What a contrast their lives present to those of their fellow-creatures lolling in deck chairs high up over their heads! (245)

In turn-of-the-twentieth-century European steam tourism, segregation by race and class clearly existed, but it appears that some monied men and women had free run of the ship. On the Northwest Coast, where the tourist industry was new and the ships were sometimes inappropriate for tourism, steam travel was less luxurious. In 1889 E. Katharine Bates collects her memories of traveling throughout the world and writes that "the accommodation on board the Alaska Steamers [in 1888] leaves a great deal to be desired" (225); she complains that far too many passengers were crammed on board the Pacific Coast Steamship Company vessel the *George W. Elder* (see figure 1), and that dinners were poor and badly served.[18] But dinners *were* served, the (bare) services of homemaking were provided, and therefore women travelers were not isolated in the galley as they might be on board a small and private boat.[19]

On some steamers, women could be found on deck mixing with the locals. Emma Boyd (1909) writes that while traveling aboard the *Yosemite* between Victoria and Vancouver "here were a few ladies on board, but the majority of the passengers were miners from the Yukon, who looked wild and unkempt after their late hardships" (96-97). Perhaps because of the perceived danger of allowing women to interact with "rough" men, space on local commercial steamships (those not catering only to tourists) was segregated by gender as well as by class and race. Aboard vessels in the Union Steamship Company (a company serving logging camps, fish canneries, small communities along the B.C. coast, and some tourists), space was carefully segregated in design. For example, in 1908 the space aboard the *Cowichan* could be mapped as follows:

> Her first-class accommodation provided fifty-three berths in comfortable staterooms. The cabin area and lounges were finished in white English oak, with the

---

18 Steamship companies soon realized the profit to be made from catering exclusively to tourist-class passengers. See my discussions of the rise of steamship tourism (chapter one) and the romanticizing of Inside Passage luxury tourism in the twentieth century (chapters one and three).

19 By the 1930s Rebie Harrington describes Northwest Coast steam travel explicitly as a vacation from housework. In *Cinderella Takes a Holiday* (1937), a nightmare of "endless household tasks" inspires her to take her third Northwest Coast voyage.

dining saloon being panelled in rich mahogany. There was a smoking-room on the
upper deck aft of the pilothouse, and a ladies' lounge near the stern. Her maindeck
accommodation included a sizeable loggers' saloon and separate sections with deck
berths for Indian and Oriental cannery workers. (Rushton 1974, 52)

As early as 1910, women and men began to travel the Northwest Coast
in private, motorized pleasure craft. Conceptualizing their transportation as a
"houseboat" (Pyle and Pyle 1910) or as "floating apartments" (Kell 1911),
women of this period could step aboard a chartered boat such as the forty-eight-
foot *Restless* "equipped with every possible comfort and convenience for cruising in all weathers" (Kell 9). Such a boat would be used for a few days or weeks
by upper- or upper-middle-class charterers. Charters would include a professional host (generally the owner and operator of the vessel) and a crew. When
Joseph and Annie Pyle chartered the ninety-two-foot *Lotus* (see figures 4 and 5),
with space "equal to that of a commodious house" (13,295), the crew included
"an engineer to look after the machinery; a sailor to clean up, work the ship
when the skipper is off duty, and man the small boats; and a Japanese cook, with
his wife as housemaid and steward" (13,296). Unlike the accounts of steamship
travelers, these texts say nothing to hint that space on board is divided differ-
ently between the male and female paying guests; however, on board the *Lotus,*
a minority couple takes over the traditional women's work, with the female serving as housemaid. Their labor appears to make the leisure of the White female
guest possible. As small pleasure craft became more available and less expensive
on the Northwest Coast, couples began to buy their own boats and to cruise
without luxury and without hosts or servants. Middle-class and working-class
people acquired boats for recreation, and sometimes as homes. With the division
of labor on these boats came the division of space I have already discussed: the
male's territory is the deck, the outside; the female's is the cabin, the interior.

For the remainder of this chapter I examine how these spatial issues can be
mapped in six Northwest Coast boating narratives. I have selected published
accounts spanning the period from the 1920s to 1990 and reflecting the experiences of working-class, middle-class, and upper-class couples. The first three narratives I discuss (Pinkerton, Dawson, Sandwell) describe cruising for pleasure;
the latter three (Eberhart, Sharcott, Iglauer) are set within the spaces of fishing
boats. Eberhart's text describes a holiday with her husband on his fishing boat,
while Sharcott and Iglauer write about sharing the space on board with a husband as he is trying to fish commercially. Although vacationing and working in
the commercial fishing industry are vastly different projects, I would argue that
these women face similar spacial situations; their texts are linked by their efforts
to accomplish "women's work" in what is perceived as masculine territory.

The "cruising wives" succeed at creating a home afloat within the interiors
of boats. This success puts women more at ease in the marine environment. Yet
the creation of a home also seems to require the necessity of a homemaker and
therefore limits the woman's experiences of the world beyond the cabin space.
"Fishing wives" also perform women's work afloat, but they are less apt to

Figure 8. "The Yakima Points North" (photo from Pinkerton 1940).

conceive of any part of a working boat as a home. Working in a smaller space than would be available on a cruiser, and under harsher weather and economic conditions, these women—who are working as homemakers without a home, not as fishing partners—are not at home afloat.[20]

Three Pleasure Craft Accounts

In his foreword to the 1991 edition of Kathrene Pinkerton's *Three's a Crew* (1940), Charles Lillard writes that the text "remains our first cruiser's-eye view of the Northwest Coast. By the thousands, men and women in their boats have unknowingly followed the courses laid out by the *Triton's* captain, but the Skipper and his crew ploughed along in no one's wake" (12). Although short published accounts preceded Pinkerton's work, hers does indeed appear to be the first book-length narrative of cruising the Inside Passage from Puget Sound through Southeastern Alaska.

"The Pinks"—as Kathrene and Robert were called—were both productive but not well-known writers who had lived in the American Midwest, Canada, and California before buying the thirty-six-foot cruiser *Yakima* (figure 8) in Seattle in 1924. For the next seven years they traveled the Inside Passage with their young daughter, Bobs, first aboard the *Yakima* then later on the forty-three-foot *Triton*, which they rebuilt and lived aboard.

Three's a Crew describes how a family came to "live at home while we travel" (164)—that is, how they were able to bring the comfort and security of home with them as they moved through a remarkable and "wild" territory. Beginning

---

20 Women who own their own vessels, or who work—by choice—in partnership fishing alongside their husbands (not working just in the galley), are more likely to feel comfortable, or as if they "belong," afloat (Allison et al. 1989).

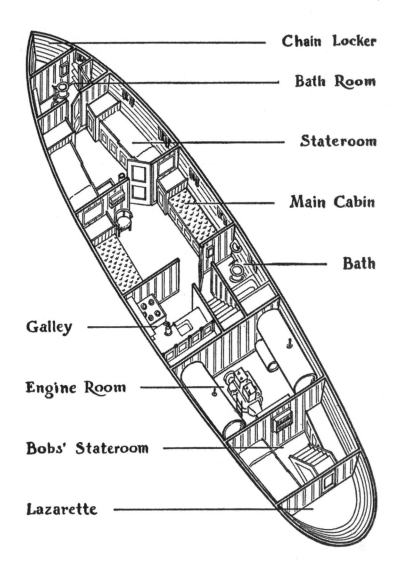

Chain Locker

Bath Room

Stateroom

Main Cabin

Bath

Galley

Engine Room

Bobs' Stateroom

Lazarette

Figure 9. Arrangement of space "below decks" in Pinkerton (1940).

with "a sense of being homeless" (24) in a strange boat that wandered without settling in one place, Pinkerton explains in detail how she created a "home afloat"—a term she uses throughout the book. Her account is full of detail regarding how to utilize space below deck: "Under the main cabin hatch were cases of butter, milk, jellies and canned meats. Behind the companionway steps were huge pushtop tins filled with preserved eggs. Canned goods, sugar and cereals crammed lockers under the berths" (113). It includes drawings of the layout of space on board (figure 9), and numerous passages about how space was improved upon over time:

I set up the portable sewing machine on the table in the cabin and made doll-size port curtains and pillow and berth covers. Not since we had left our log cabin had we had an outlet for home-making instincts. I selected china, painted food containers in matching colors, and added dashes of the blue and tile red [sic] of the china to the galley lockers. (205)

From the account and its illustrations, we see how Pinkerton "spent space as preciously as life's blood" (164), and how happy she was to participate in the creation of "our pocket home" (30). The Pinks considered hiring a crew to travel with them—it would have meant they could operate a larger boat and travel farther and into more remote waters (304), and Pinkerton herself felt it was a folly "for a woman to face the possibility of having to take the [steering] wheel ... in case of motor trouble" (219). After all, their close friends Betty and Stewart White had a hired crew and a Chinese cook aboard their boat, the *Simba* (279). But the Pinkertons settled for a crew of themselves, a "communal" "crew-family" (35) that worked hard to keep up when they cruised alongside the *Simba*:

On the Simba *life went on whether the owner was aboard or not. Boat work was done and dinner was ready. On the* Triton *cabins had to be put in order, berths made, breakfast dishes washed, lunches packed and the evening meal at least planned. Bobs and Robert and I divided jobs, ... but there were times when I felt breathless. (247)*

Despite her mention here of shared labor, there are few other descriptions of Robert working within the cabin. We tend to see Kathrene Pinkerton doing the laundry or explaining the "galley gadgets" (112) to another woman, while "the skippers brought out the charts and planned a few days of convoy cruising" (86). "Robert's name was entered as owner and master" (111) of their boats. "He had taken on the double job of captain and engineer, while I, as mate, had only to relieve him at the wheel and carry out orders" (25)—and, in the pattern of wives cruising in other regions of the world, to see to all the work done in the cabin. Discussing the importance of the wheelhouse on deck (the station from which to operate the boat while under way), Pinkerton writes: "When under way, it was our social center. We hadn't seen so much of Bobs since she had gone to school. She and I joined the skipper as soon as below deck tasks were finished in the morning" (34). The social center, then, is something the wife and daughter "rise" to, when their women's work is completed below. While under way, Pinkerton performs domestic work around the ill-placed engine: "A cook ranked lower than an engine and I had to adjust my activities to its needs. As I worked at the dresser [in the galley] the huge revolving flywheel threatened my calves and the rocker arms shot up and down beneath my chin" (15). Pinkerton portrays herself as enthusiastic to take on this makeshift role, lower than an engine; she is pleased to have found a way "in which travel and the routine of living could go on simultaneously" (34). She playfully mocks naval conventions of respect, writing that she "was always popping up, armed with a basting spoon or a fork, to salute a whale or a passing tug" (34). But at the same time, she feels she is only doing the work that comes naturally to her; "Bobs and I weren't under skipper's orders" (35).

However, in her chapters "Weather is as You Find It" and "Robert Goes Skipperish," Pinkerton describes how her husband was transformed into an arrogant and quick-tempered Bly when standing at the wheel.[21] In the chapter "Bobs is Instructed," she recounts a time when Robert was dissatisfied with her work; he is exasperated at her inexperience at reading the exterior environment, and he reminds her that the skipper's duties are more important than the mate's:

> It was my duty to check islands and rocks against the chart. I came back from a quick trip to the galley to find the scenery all jumbled.
> "This country leaps about so," I protested.
> "You can't take your eyes off it for a minute," Robert said in his most skipperish manner. "It's a lot more important to know where we are than to have apple pie for dinner." (88)

At other moments in the text Pinkerton acknowledges that her role on board gives her different priorities than Robert's, that below-deck tasks require skill and are sometimes "more important than navigation":

> The entree was to be my triumph—canned artichoke hearts stuffed with caviar, hardboiled egg whites stuffed with capers, tomato aspic and the whole garnished with ripe olives and julienne carrots which I hung in a wet bag on deck to be chilled by evaporation.
> All this magnificent preparation required time, and galley duties were more important than navigation. When we ran through the last of the flood in Whirlpool Rapids, I didn't even glance out of the porthole. I gave all my attention to keeping the party foods from landing on the floor. Later I ignored Robert's calls until his skipperish tone brought me above deck on the run. (189)

Whereas Robert's triumph might be a run through bad weather, hers is a carefully and skillfully prepared meal, made with limited resources in a confined space. Here, the magnificence of this project is not demeaned—Pinkerton gives it all of her attention until the tone of her husband's voice calls her to leave it. Because the cabin—and the labor accomplished there—is primarily Pinkerton's territory, when the Pinks decide to refit their boat as a liveaboard, she "spent [her] days selecting marine housekeeping equipment, galley stove, sink and pumps, electric light fixtures, upholstery and paint colors" (196). She has the "natural" authority to transform the interior space. Later—after much practice

---

21 Roland and Janice Smith (1990) describe this apparently common phenomenon: "Some men who are Dr. Jekyll ashore become Mr. Hyde on a boat. Men may be more competitive than women; a boat becomes a weapon, a means to victory over some rival—possibly over the crew who cannot be dominated at home.... Since women tend to sense such dangers, they may well balk at the dock" (87).

with the application of paint in the interior—Pinkerton is allowed to work on the outside of the boat: "When I had achieved a professional swing with a brush I dared work in public, on the outside of the *Triton*. Hull, decks, bright work and deck gear fell under my onslaught" (233).

Kathrene Pinkerton felt comfortable on board because she had made the boat a home. Her role as homemaker afloat gave her deep satisfaction, but it also pigeon-holed her in the galley space at times and garnered Robert's disdain and disrespect. His "skipperishness" when he stands at the helm is a sign of his power; it reflects both the history of masculine territory afloat and the status and values of the male head of the household at the time. Pinkerton's decision to name his attitude "acting skipperish"—a phrase that mocks naval hierarchy and Robert's pleasure in playing a pompous role—shows her awareness of gender-related power issues and her willingness to mock them.

Will Dawson's *Ahoy There!* (1955) offers a male perspective on couplehood, homemaking, and space issues while cruising local waters twenty years after the Pinks. Beginning in 1946, Dawson, a well-known voice on Vancouver-area talk radio, and his wife, Eileen, lived aboard their thirty-two-foot sailboat, *West Wind*. In the summers they cruised the Gulf Islands and occasionally continued upcoast; in the winters they moored at Vancouver and reconnected with family and friends. His account includes anecdotes, incidents, and descriptions of the day-to-day patterns of a couple's life afloat.

"Eileen took to the sea because I wanted to" (4), explains Dawson in his opening chapter; "Eileen made no objection to the suggestion that we shift from land to sea. 'There's nothing in particular that I want to do,' she said, 'so if you want us to live on a boat, let's try and find one'" (9). Looking back at the launch of their new lifestyle, Dawson recalls friends asking: "'Whatever did you buy [that boat] for?'" The couple replies: "'To be our home'" (1). But Dawson was apprehensive about the ability of a woman to feel at home afloat: "I believed that women and the sea don't mix. In general, that conclusion is, I think, correct. Most women prefer a home with cement foundations to one held to the sea-bed by a length of anchor rope" (6). Pinkerton and Dawson agree that females have an innate, "atavistic" need for connections to earth and for rootedness.[22]

Despite his initial doubts about women and the sea "mixing," in *Ahoy There!* Dawson describes Eileen as a woman entirely capable of bringing her homemaking skills to sea. Numerous times throughout his text Dawson describes how "normal" her role is afloat: "While I check the various working parts of the boat—sails, rigging, boom and gaff jaws, and the like—and fetch what is needed from ashore, Eileen washes up, sweeps, cleans, and polishes, much like any housewife ashore" (40). Eileen's ability to succeed at sea—proven to Dawson by her execution of the common duties of a housewife—appears to comfort her husband: "Throughout summer Eileen has made an occasional jar of jam and has canned an occasional tin of fish or berries. Now, as the decreasing arc of the sun warns of approaching winter, she busies herself like

---

22 See my discussion on women, ecofeminism, and *land*scape in chapter four.

any housewife in any suburb or on any farm" (200). In this division of labor, Dawson's territory is the deck, where he takes charge of the "working" parts of the boat; Eileen "busies herself" in the galley.

In fact, Eileen does more than busy herself. Although Dawson claims "meals [afloat] are no different from meals ashore" (3), virtually all women who describe cooking at sea give lengthy descriptions about how difficult it is to store, prepare, and serve food. Margaret Sharcott (1957) writes: "I always think it is more difficult to make a sandwich on a rolling boat than it is to prepare a full-course meal at home" (94). Eileen's work in the galley keeps her pre-occupied in the interior of the boat; for instance: "Eileen had bread dough rising and so could not join me when, after breakfast, I rowed to the reef" (102). Her "housework" also enables Dawson to produce the manuscript for his book: "Eileen set about preparing dinner while I sat down and wrote" (199). Even the assistance she gives him on deck is illustrated by a metaphor for homemaking: "she unclips the halyards, and folds and lashes the sails with the unconcern of a woman taking in the washing" (229). The subtext of Dawson's descriptions of his wife is that, although women and the sea do not *generally* mix, Eileen is an exception to the rule because of her unique willingness to perform "normal" housewife chores (such as canning) in a marine setting and her ability to transform the "real work" of sailing (unclipping the halyards) into a domestic chore. In fact, when compared to other wives at sea, Eileen's role is the rule rather than an exception to it. This domestic role is gently belittled by Dawson (labeled as "busying herself"), but is subtly praised at the same time; between the lines he seems in awe of the uninhibited grace of his wife, who folds and lashes sails with "the unconcern of a woman taking in the washing." The underlying message of the text is that women and the sea *can* mix, if women know their place in the galley and conceive of their work on deck as an extension of their domestic responsibilities.

The space on board the *West Wind* is divided into both inside/outside and left/right territories. The right is the traditional domain of the most powerful person on board (Kirstein and Leonard 1970). Dawson writes that in fair weather "we frequently fish, Eileen from the port [left] side, I from the starb'd [right], positions which match the fairly even distribution of the ship below into Eileen's half and mine" (40). The use of that space reflects their roles on board. Dawson's side houses the navigational equipment and his writing materials, and he believes their bed linens should stay on the side designated for Eileen's "exclusive use":

All the many lockers on Eileen's side are for her exclusive use, and all the lockers on mine are supposed to be for me; but I keep finding oddments of linen neatly stowed where my writing materials are kept. One section of locker Eileen does not, however, make any attempt to usurp. This is the inviolable space kept for navigational equipment. (21)

Dawson has a traditional conception of the *West Wind* itself, reminiscent of the tradition I discussed earlier of endowing a ship with feminine characteristics:

West Wind is a sturdy boat, a thing of beauty and comfort, of grace and utility. But she is also much more than that. She *is a* partner *in all our enterprises,* accepting *our whims without* demure *and meeting whatever we ask* her *to meet with* ready eagerness, *alive with a spirit of cheerfulness. (21, my emphasis)*

When he writes "she is one of us" (21), "our partner, ... our calling-card ... an advertisement of us" (31), and that "her trimness" appeals, Dawson is playing with the boat-as-wife metaphor. Historically, this metaphor reinforced the notion that a boat is a feminine character (desired and controlled by men) and that the space on board a boat is closed to women (for fear of offending the protecting goddess). Dawson's textual construction of the *West Wind* shows that this metaphor was still alive in his mind and suggests the origins of his belief that women and the sea don't mix.

Dawson is genuinely glad to have Eileen on board with him; he writes that "to my thinking a man who has a cheerful and capable woman as his partner to help plot and follow a course, whether afloat or ashore, will enjoy his cruise far more than he who sails alone" (225). Note that here, at the very conclusion of *Ahoy There!,* Dawson depicts himself as appreciating Eileen's nautical capabilities; or perhaps he is only speaking figuratively. He mentions occasionally in the text that they both read charts and agree upon destinations (40, 56). But the strongest impressions we have of Eileen's experiences afloat are of darning, ironing, sewing, and baking, and of her fear of Natives—"'There aren't any Indians here now—are there?'" (111). In the rare moments when Eileen is depicted as powerful and active, those qualities are undercut by a reminder of her femininity. For instance, when Eileen and another woman must row a skiff very near rapids, Dawson writes:

I wondered, as I watched them, when and where was fashioned the myth that women's nerves are not so strong as men's. Those two very feminine women were chatting and chuckling in that cranky little boat, with a crazy sea streaking by two oars' lengths away, as undisturbed as if they were sitting, legs tucked up, on a chesterfield ashore. (63)

His impulse to describe their act of rowing with an image of sitting on a couch, "tucked up" and immobile (perhaps gossiping?), suggests that Dawson can only perceive and depict his wife through images of domesticity and homemaking. This is the secret of Eileen's success when "women and the sea don't [generally] mix." If Eileen did attempt to enter the "inviolable space" (21) beyond domesticity, to move into the territory of the male/right/outside/navigator, then Dawson had no place for such boat rocking in his text. More recent accounts of couplehood afloat by male authors suggest that Dawson's narrative remains an accurate description of gendered roles on the water. For example, Jess Webb's *Going North* (1985) shows that his wife, Carroll, only takes the wheel to relieve him (31), then "turns the helm over to me and goes below to do the dishes" (32) on a typical run. She is frequently constructed as the stereotypical housewife of the 1950s, "frying fish for supper" (71), canning food (88), going grocery shopping (98), doing their laundry (124), baking (131), and fixing snacks (104). Meanwhile, the author is occupied with fixing the engine (84) or "stand[s] on the deck of my own little ship in a far place ... a realization of long held dreams" (99).

Recent cruising literature by women illustrates the point that, despite updates in boat design, and regardless of social class, men and women continue to occupy separate territories and perform a gendered division of labor on the water. Agnete Sandwell's essay "The Care and Feeding of Yachtsmen in B.C. Waters" appears at the back of a privately published book, *North of Anian: The Collected Journals of Gabrielle III Cruises in British Columbia Coastal Waters 1978-1989* (Nicolls 1990).[23] As the title suggests, the book includes journal entries and photographs from twelve years of cruising aboard the sailing yacht *Gabrielle III*, owned and operated (among other racing yachts) by Sandwell's husband, Dick. In his preface to the book, Dick Sandwell explains that he selected the title *North of Anian* to "project the romance" of Northwest Coast geography (vii). The agenda aboard the *Gabrielle III*, he writes, was to follow in the wake of explorers Cook, Dixon, Portlock, Barkley, Meares, Galiano, Valdes, Vancouver, Marchand, and others; "research and planning took place in winter time, fulfillment in the summers" (ix). The book recording this project is accredited to Nan Nicolls, "the principal journalist and photographer" (x) aboard. Apparently Nicolls was a family friend, one of many guests who regularly contributed to the writing of the ship's journals; each year she prepared an album from the journal entries. Nicolls stands out in the preface as a female not relegated to parentheses; Dick Sandwell writes: "Among my regular shipmates were and still are Glen Hyatt (and Jean), Mike Bell, Harry Bell-Irving (and Theo)" (ix). Skipper Sandwell's "first mate" (6) and three daughters sometimes accompanied the *Gabrielle III* beyond the Royal Vancouver Yacht Club.

"The Care and Feeding of Yachtsmen" is not part of the day-to-day journal narrative; the essay is separated from the main body of the book's text—suggesting its subject has a marginal place in the task of "project[ing] the romance" of travel or "Northwest Coast geography." It is written as a guide in the spirit of cruising manuals for women, yet it is obviously aimed at an elite class of women—women who are less used to imposed spatial limitations in their kitchens, if they cook much at all. Placed after the bulk of the text, this essay speaks of a geography nonetheless—although not the sublime vistas through which the vessel passes.

Sandwell's title and her opening sentence—"seeing to the galley is the easiest task of all" (310)—give the reader a strong sense of her territory and function on board the *Gabrielle III*. "The pleasure the planner and cook feels is great," she writes, "when the meal is above what was expected, and when it takes place seated at a table, rarely missing any of the comforts of home" (310). How she

---

23 "Anian" was a cartographers' label for a hypothetical Arctic region. The Northwest Passage, or "Strait of Anian," was believed to offer a northern route linking the Pacific and Atlantic Oceans.

delivers meals "as invitingly as at home" from a small "doll house kitchen" is her area of expertise (311).[24]

Like other women's boating narratives and guides, Sandwell's essay begins by describing the galley space and fixtures; she explains how inventive one must be to make creative use of limited space: "We would like our fridge and freezer to be bigger so we could keep white wine iced for lunch, but as this cannot be, we invented a way of resting a few bottles on top of frozen food and leaving them there for about one hour before the meal" (310-11).

In her section "Fine Dining Afloat" (a title without irony), Sandwell discusses those topics so common to women's cruising manuals and accounts: stowage and meal planning; "For a summer cruise I make a menu plan for at least one to two weeks" (312). The crew do indeed "dine" on this yacht; where recipes in Kirstein and Leonard (1970) and Wolf (1958) favor heavy doses of condensed cream of mushroom soup, dehydrated onion flakes, and hamburger, on the *Gabrielle III* Sandwell can serve "a fine roast beef dinner" (311). Snacks go far beyond stale biscuits: "We often bring cantaloupe onboard, either for breakfast or for lunch with prosciutto ham, or as dessert with Port" (313).

Because she writes that she likes "to have breakfast made and served before we cast off" (313), breakfast appears to be her responsibility alone, and "breakfast is often a chore to prepare" (314). But Sandwell does have some help with dining responsibilities:

> *When we have dessert, an apple pie cooked at home and heated onboard, served with cheddar cheese or 'creme fraiche' as in France, is always well received. Chocolate mousse in small china pots is prepared specially by Lolita, our housekeeper ... using a recipe given to her by Chef Jacques Pepin. (313)*

Housekeeper Lolita also prepares main courses: "One of Lolita's quiches from home, such as a quiche lorraine, is easy and disappears quickly" (314). The implication, of course, is that it is easy for *Sandwell*—not necessarily for Lolita. Although Sandwell clearly has less labor to perform in the galley than did Kathrene Pinkerton or Eileen Dawson, it remains her domain of expertise.

Other women do work in the galley. Daughter Barbie makes a fine creamed spinach, and Nan Nicolls "does have a magic touch with Yorkshires [puddings]" (315). Men function in the galley to signal when the red wine should be opened (314) and to carve the meat. Carving the meat seems to fall within the domain of masculine territory because it is a task men sometimes perform on land; here, it is performed on the navigation table, a place symbolically associated with the space outside the galley: "The ablest and most willing man offers to carve, and a roast or a baked ham is lifted out of the oven and placed on the navigation table, which has been dutifully covered with a terry cloth" (314).

---

24 Sandwell's "doll house" metaphor echoes Kimbrough's (1958) description of "playing house" afloat. Together they suggest woman's role on the water is akin to child's play, in contrast to man's work.

Sandwell makes no mention of her experiences beyond the galley, except to describe a shopping trip in Sweden to purchase bakeware. In the journals comprising the main section of the book, we most often see her (described by guests) as happy in the galley: "At 19:00 Agnete stood contentedly slicing some large and juicy mandarin oranges (to ward off scurvy??). The ham sent aromatic waves into the cockpit" (23). The mock chivalry of yachting manners also appears to have led the skipper into the galley to make a cup of tea occasionally; Nicolls records that "Like a spotlight, the sun poured into Agnete's bunk. The time was 08:00 and the Skipper, *very* pristine in all-white clothes, presented the ladies with morning tea" (178, Nicolls' emphasis).

In the 1980s Agnete Sandwell may well have been an active participant in the spaces beyond the interior of the *Gabrielle III*. But whether she was or not, her territory to write about, her acknowledged expertise, is limited to the galley in this text. Her social class allows her to acquire and use the best galley gadgets available, to buy the highest quality foods, and occasionally to rely upon the labor of a servant. But as a woman, as first mate, Agnete Sandwell regularly undergoes "the Skipper's inspection" (315), to which she submits playfully. "The Care and Feeding of Yachtsmen" suggests that gendered spaces can be as clearly mapped upon elite yachts as they are upon the family cruisers of the lower classes and that the gendered division of space has remained little changed since the initiation of Northwest Coast family cruising in the 1920s.

Three Work Boat Accounts

"Home was the place for me" (95), writes Beth Eberhart in *A Crew of Two* (1961), a collection of twenty-three chapters and numerous charcoal sketches by the author. Comprised of material created between 1946 and 1961, Eberhart's book is the story of a "homeless" (12) period in her life, a period just after the Second World War, when her husband moved her to Southeast Alaska. The American couple lived in a "wanigan"—a five-room house on log floats—but spent a great deal of one summer on a fishing troller. The narrative is her reflection on the past, written after Eberhart is no longer afloat, having finally acquired the house and stability she always wanted (in Washington State).

When Vady and Beth Eberhart traveled to Alaska, they had already been married for twenty years. A military family, "we moved on an average of once a year.... Each time my home-loving roots protested loudly as we jerked them up for another transplanting" (10). Her "root" metaphor echoes once again the ideology that women are uniquely tied to the earth and are "naturally" better suited to shore life than to travel on water. Their children grown, Eberhart longs for a permanent home and a chance to work on her painting skills. But her husband, who had served in the coast guard in Alaska, has other plans. He wants to try his luck at commercial fishing.

Vady buys a boat without telling his wife, then takes her down to the docks to observe a young couple living aboard a typical fishing boat of the era—a vessel with much less available living space than any cruiser or sailboat. Unaware that she will soon be in their shoes, she exclaims: "'Imagine living on a little boat like that! So crowded, no place to take a bath, or wash, nothing to look at but water and sky and more boats.... No boats for me!'" (25). But Eberhart has little choice in the matter. At first she goes along with Vady for short fishing trips. Her most serious concerns are her fear of water and the lack of space in the tiny cabin of the troller:

> To say there was room for us is stretching a point. We pivoted on each other's elbows, walked on each other's feet, and the bunk was as hard to get out of as a fish trap. I marveled every morning when, after a terrific struggle, we were ready for the day each dressed in his own clothes. (44)

When Vady asks "'Isn't this swell?'" she doubts she can last the entire fishing season in the cramped and dark cabin of the boat:

> "It's so small ..." I began doubtfully. "I don't see how we'll manage a whole season."
> "Small!" he echoed. "What would you do with any more room? We have everything we need right here."
> To Vady there's no such thing as cramped quarters. Small places may be "cozy" or "snug" but never cramped. Should I tell him that to me it was like living in a cave? That every time I took a deep breath I felt as if I was robbing his lungs to fill my own? (46)

Space is *the* issue on the minds of the fishing wives she crosses paths with afloat. A discussion of space breaks the ice when she and a young woman from the *Ruth* meet:

> "Your boat is awfully nice," she said. "It has so much room. Ours is a lot smaller, real crowded with the three of us, and of course I have to have Jimmy's diapers drying overhead all the time."
> She thought our boat was large! This bird cage! (100-01)

The only female she meets who likes life on the water is a nontraditional woman; she explains to Eberhart: "'I love it. But of course I'm not the home-maker type like you, and I don't much care how I look'" (152). "'I just don't like it, being on the boat'" (151), Eberhart admits to this woman; she "longed for home" (145), and the "bird cage" was emphatically not a home. Although she is "the homemaker type" like Kathrene Pinkerton, Eileen Dawson, and other women on pleasure craft, Eberhart appears too intimidated by the tiny space of the fishing boat and by its strangeness to attempt to transform it into any sort of home. Had she had such an impulse, her duties assisting her husband would keep her from executing them. Because she cannot, or will not, create a home on board their vessel, she constantly longs for her home on shore and never feels comfortable on the water.

Eberhart writes that her two main activities afloat were to keep the logbook and to "captain" the boat when Vady was occupied with fishing. "It was one of my duties to keep a fishing log," she writes. "When we caught a fish I'd jot down the time of day, spoon used, and the stage of the tide. This log proved valuable. It was by referring to it that Vady discovered the possibilities of our [fishing] 'hole'" (187). When she begins the log, Vady criticizes her for including anecdotal material and for not adopting strictly nautical language: "'That's no way to make entries,' he said scornfully. 'You have to keep the tides, winds and barometer readings under their proper headings. Put it away until later'" (30).[25] His tone brings to mind Robert Pinkerton's "skipperishness," which Kathrene Pinkerton undercuts with satire. Eberhart responds by updating that day's entry with even more colloquial language and anecdotal material; between the lines, like Pinkerton, she is mocking his authority: "8:15 P.M. Home. Big salmon got away. Caught one red snapper. Motor stalled as we were coming in. Crank slipped. Asked V if he was hurt. When he yelled, 'No, of course not!' I saw the bloody hole where the crank had knocked out a front tooth" (30). But Vady is determined that the couple use nautical terminology when speaking about his troller, the *Emblem*:

> "Betsy," Vady said reprovingly, "please learn to speak in more nautical terms. She's beamy, not wide. There's a bunk, no beds. I think you'll find the galley adequate. There's no kitchen."
> "Aye, aye, Cap," I said, giving him a proper salute. (41)

Eberhart works on learning the new language: "I got out our copy of *Knight's Modern Seamanship* to 'salt' my vocabulary" (47). But she prefers her everyday vocabulary from home:

> "Let's take a look at the map, pick out a tie-up for tomorrow night, write up the diary, and get to bed."
> Vady grabbed his head in both hands. "Babe! What kind of talk is that? Chart, anchorage, log, sack down—remember?" (53)

Her invented dialogue here may be an exaggeration of the rows the couple had over nautical terminology, but it does clearly illustrate the resistance she felt to internalizing this "foreign" language and the naval traditions of authority inherent in it. She has a husband eager to teach it to her, but she does not want to be his pupil, does not want him (or her audience) to believe she could become "fluent" in offshore ways.

---

25 Vady's comment is also strikingly similar to Robert Pinkerton's "jeering" response to Kathrene Pinkerton's personal log (see chapter three).

Eberhart's second job is to act as "captain," although she questions the title:

From the beginning my place was in the pilothouse. "You may as well learn to steer," Vady said. "It saves a fisherman a lot of time if he doesn't have to watch where he's going and steer from the cockpit. From now on you're the captain, I'm the crew." (44)

But, as she notes, "being the captain in this case didn't signify that I was in command. The crew was the law" (47). When Vady reminds her that all she has to do is steer the boat, she thinks: "Oh yes, I steered the boat! I also prepared most of the meals, polished [fishing] spoons, washed our clothes, and tried unsuccessfully to keep the galley clean, all under conditions that wouldn't be tolerated in any home" (184). Perhaps worst of all was the lack of hygiene; "'You can't keep clean on a boat,'" she tells another woman "'That's one of the things I don't like about it'" (152).

The other serious drawback to living on the *Emblem,* another reason for her to long for her "real" home, is the lack of opportunity for Eberhart to work on her paintings. By this time she had sold cover art to *The Alaska Sportsman* magazine, was giving painting lessons, and wanted to take the more creative part of her life seriously. The cramped space and her duties on board conflicted with her plans. Regarding her attempts to paint at sea, she writes that "Occasionally, struck by the beauty all around us, I'd make a quick, wobbly sketch, with my pad balanced on the wheel, while I kept a sharp lookout for kelp, logs, and other boats and watched the tips of four poles" (184). These halfhearted attempts were not nearly enough to satisfy her. When Eberhart suggests to her husband that she stay home in the wanigan while he goes out for the longest and farthest fishing trip of the season, Vady makes it clear that her work is a "vice" if it conflicts with his own plans and her homemaking:

"If your painting means more to you than I do, by all means paint. You have to make your own choice in these matters, live your own life."

"Do you mean I have to give up painting or you?'

"No, of course not. I can fish alone and you can paint all summer long if you want to, but I can tell you right now that it isn't going to help our marriage. You're not a career woman, you're a homemaker. A hobby is a fine thing for a pastime, but if you let it take on undue importance it becomes a vice, just as everything else that's overdone." (72)

Although Vady never seems to catch on to the notion, the problem is that she (and Vady) can indeed only conceive of Eberhart as a homemaker. The notion might not be a problem ashore, but on board the *Emblem* she has no home to make. The marine environment, she feels, is "no place for a woman" (81). There, she thinks she is unsuccessful at the one job she does well (homemaking). Untrained to work on a fishing boat, she believes she is a failure as Vady's helper; therefore she "longed for home and our former quiet life, when I went on the water only when I wanted to" (145).

Eberhart does accompany her husband on the long trip. But when Vady foolishly keeps them out in bad weather and they lose power in a storm, Eberhart catches the next float plane back to the wanigan as soon as they make it to a port. "'I want to go h-o-m-e,' I wailed, laughing and crying at the same time. 'Then go,' Vady said. 'I've got to clean those fish'" (278). She is not sure whether she and Vady will ever be together on the boat again:

> But such thoughts didn't fill all my time. Being at home was a delight. How could anyone complain of the monotony of housework? Just to be able to move around freely was pleasure enough, but to sleep in a bed that stood solid all night! Tide, weather, wind—at last they had no importance. (283)

When Vady returns two weeks later, he apologizes and promises "now we'll have what you want" (284). Eberhart, never at home afloat, eventually gets her home on shore; she considers Vady's decision to put the nautical life behind him a sign of his love:

> Sometimes on stormy evenings when our house trembles from a gusty blast whistling down the gap from Mount Rainier, Vady says, "I'm glad we're not bucking this southeaster around Cape Chacon tonight!"
> In his devious way my husband is telling me that he loves me. (9)

In this way, Eberhart exemplifies Will Dawson's generalization about women: that they "prefer a home with cement foundations to one held to the sea-bed by a length of anchor rope" (6). Her narrative acts as a passionate argument for what she perceives as the feminine need "to sleep in a bed that stood solid all night," to have the comparative spaciousness of a house and the safety of a structure indifferent to storms. The comfort she feels in such a house—which she cannot replicate on a boat—is what makes her feel at home.

Unlike Eberhart, who essentially gains her home by mutiny, the young wife Margaret Sharcott labors simply to cope on the water. In *Troller's Holiday* (1957), she describes her first holiday in five years after marrying a fisherman and moving to the village of Kyuquot on the west coast of Vancouver Island. With her husband, Stan, their thirteen-month-old baby, David, and dog, Skipper, Sharcott circumnavigates Vancouver Island in the winter of 1954—first aboard the couple's thirty-foot *Sea Lion*, then aboard the larger *Thornton Isle,* which Stan purchases en route.

Although Sharcott occasionally assisted with fishing before David's birth, she is more used to waiting at home than traveling. After the couple embarks on their voyage in bad weather, she imagines the perspective of a fisherman's wife in an old fishing village:

> In the dark of night his wife sat waiting at home, hearing the wind adding its voice to the roar of the waves breaking outside the cove. She would see the gusts of wind ripple the water in front of her home to a solid black. The moan of the sea increased as the wind-driven waves crashed over the barely submerged rocks

and splashed against the feet of the wind-twisted trees on the barrier islands. Fear choked her. Had her man arrived safely or had the wind risen before he crossed the dreaded Nahwhitti Bar? She could have no way of knowing. (18)

The perspective is undoubtedly one she does not have to work hard to invent in her mind.

The purpose of their holiday is to show their new baby to family in the towns of Duncan and Courtenay. Despite her struggles with seasickness, Sharcott writes that someday she would like to cruise upcoast in the summer:

I thought how much I should like to make that trip to distant Alaska, stopping at tiny fishing villages along the way, taking our time as we journeyed slowly northward in our troller. The trip would cost little in actual expense. Its only drawback lies in the fact that fine travelling weather is also fine trolling weather. (44)

But *Troller's Holiday* is much more about coping than about vacationing. Unlike Eberhart, who explicitly articulates her dislike of the cramped spaces and drudgery on board and challenges her husband's power there (ultimately by abandoning ship), Sharcott humbly accepts her subordinate role and tries to make the best of it. For instance, when Stan heads the boat out into bad weather even though she has asked him not to, she writes that she "didn't want to [go], but the skipper's word is law on a boat, so all I could do was protest weakly, and beg that we might turn back if it was rough when we got outside the harbour. I stowed everything movable in the cabin" (184). This quotation suggests that Sharcott has little say in how the craft is navigated; when her protests have no effect, she moves down to the cabin of the boat—the space where she has more control. In her account, Sharcott never operates the boat, plots a course, or assists with any of Stan's work on deck; her world afloat is the small cabin, where she accomplishes the same duties she would at home, only under much more difficult circumstances:

David was whimpering with the motion of the boat, so I moved from my perch in the doorway where I had sat to watch the wallowing sea. I knew I must move now if I was going to do it easily. It is not a simple thing to climb down a companionway and cross the cabin with a year-old baby in your arms when there is a sea running. Each of those steps is a hazard. You can slip and fall; you can bang into the lockers on your way while your hands are too occupied holding the baby to use them to steady yourself. It must be now if I was going to get to the bunk.

I stumbled the half-dozen steps and laid David down. As I tried to loosen his snowsuit, I knew my seasick pill wasn't going to be much help. (23-24)

Describing homemaking in an extremely limited space while traveling in swells, she writes:

I unhooked the table that folded against a cupboard, doubling at its door, to reach
David something to eat. As I stood, feet apart to keep my balance while the Sea
Lion lurched, I found the can of milk and the butter. From the bread-box I took
a loaf of bread. David wouldn't get much of a meal now but he would have his
supper when we arrived at Comox. I gave him the slice of buttered bread and
the glass of canned milk and water. I always think it is more difficult to make a
sandwich on a rolling boat than it is to prepare a full-course meal at home. (94)

The lack of stowage space and limited supply of fresh water does change one
of her domestic tasks for the better; they keep few dishes on board, and the
"luxury" of hot-water rinsing is omitted from her dishwashing chore:

To boat-dwellers, dish-washing is never a major task as it is to housewives. You use
as few dishes as possible; no saucers under the coffee mugs, no bread-and-butter
plates. David had eaten his cereal from the pan it was made in. This economy is
not just laziness but shortage of water. (43)

This water shortage comes from the lack of space for large water tanks, a
common circumstance on board all boats.

Sharcott's text moves beyond her domestic experiences afloat when she writes
about local history (which she researched by writing to the British Columbia
Provincial Archives for information and by reading library books mailed to her
home community) and offers impressions of people near the wharves. Of Alert
Bay she writes:

We slowly wandered back toward the wharf, passing groups of clean, well-dressed
Indian children in sweaters and overalls, middle-aged Indian matrons in fur coats
and tiny hats. Loggers in neatly-pressed slacks and imitation Indian sweaters,
Indian or white fishermen in rough tweed pants and sloppy fisherman's shoes,
white and Indian teen-agers giggling together, a Chinese store proprietor in a
business suit. (69)

Her work becomes political when she supports discrimination against "the
hated Japanese fisherman" (126-27) and out-of-province job-seekers at the
Duncan Bay paper mill (88).

As a writer, Sharcott is uncharacteristically lyrical when she briefly describes
her childhood on Hornby Island and comments on nature and the landscape; in
chapter four I show how these passages suggest where she is most "at home."
But generally, *Troller's Holiday* shows once again the clear mapping of gender
roles onto the built environment of the boat. When Stan buys a new vessel (that
is, an old one that has been at the dock for a year and a half), Sharcott immediately moves to the cabin to clean the filthy storage space and the grease and
the maggots in the domestic space: "I spent most of one day scrubbing with
disinfectant, detergent and hot water. The floor was coated with grease and dirt
that only succumbed to a strong kitchen cleanser. I lined the lockers with layers

of newspaper.... On a boat every inch of space must be utilized" (153). The division of space and of responsibilities shapes her constructions of the marine environment. For example, a protected slough is significant because it allows her to wash and dry diapers: "Now [that] we were harboured in the slough for a week or two," she writes, "I could settle down to a routine of 'housekeeping'. Baby's washing could be done regularly and hung out on the stern to dry" (101). Her description of open-sea gulf trollers is highly "feminine" in that it conforms to the expected perspective of her gender; she appraises the vessel wholly by its domestic space, not its design or the features on the deck:

> Some of these gulf trollers are so small that living aboard them looks decidedly uncomfortable, even to one who has grown used to cramped quarters. The fo'c'sle is so low that the occupant cannot stand upright but must sit down, lie down or stoop over his stove as he prepares a meal. Some of these tiny craft don't have good stoves, just a miniature affair with two stove holes and no oven. (106)

There is nothing "wrong" with Sharcott's sensitivity to interior spaces, but her narrative demonstrates that she is never entirely comfortable afloat. I would argue that her discomfort results from her lack of knowledge (and power) in the world above the deck. Whereas women traveling aboard pleasure craft could gain some sense of power and control by feminizing the cabin of the boat and excelling at homemaking there, Sharcott (like Eberhart) appears to have no comfortable territory on the fishing boat and no abilities or special talents that are respected. Unlike Eberhart, she is not strong willed enough or angry enough to rebel or to question her lack of power. While Stan is the stoic skipper, Sharcott describes herself as frequently seasick (a problem much worsened by being below deck; see Stadler 1987), constantly worried, and sometimes beside herself with genuine fear. She "frets" about what to do if Stan is washed overboard. In bad weather she thinks "of drowning in that icy water.... I put my arm around David and lay, tense with fear" (26). At times she "dreaded the thoughts of the rest of the trip" and "buried my head in the pillow and cried" with anxiety and fright (53). She explains her discomfort by writing "I'm not a good sailor" (95); yet it seems that she is never given the chance to learn a sailor's duties or gain a sailor's ease on deck. Had Stan taught her how to handle the boat if he fell overboard or how to judge weather conditions—that is, had he shared the knowledge and power that went with his territory—Sharcott might have conceived of herself as a better sailor. Unlike Eberhart, who staunchly and consistently resists being on the water, Sharcott has disclosed a desire to boat to Alaska some day. Vacationing by sea—during good weather, under less frightening conditions—appeals to her. Perhaps she had the potential to be much more of a sailor.

Ironically, Sharcott concludes by encouraging others to travel the coast by boat. "You are your own captain," she exclaims. "We lived a water gypsy's life ... with all its thrills and freedom" (221). But a few pages earlier, in a moment that seems more honest and reflective, she concludes that "Our journey was nearing an end now. Within a day or two we should be home. I dreamed happily of our own little house, with its space for David to play, a washing machine to lighten my chores" (203). Given the division of space, labor, and power on board, the washing machine—not the boat—probably offered her more tangible freedom.

Perhaps because she embarks on couplehood afloat with more maturity and self-assurance, Edith Iglauer is more enthusiastic about her experiences aboard a working boat in *Fishing with John* (1988). A journalist, she was on assignment with John Daly in 1975 aboard his commercial troller in British Columbia when she fell in love with him and his "way of life" and decided to stay. When the couple shares the space aboard his *MoreKelp*, Iglauer undergoes a sea change; she describes how this positive transformation is reflected in her visage:

> John suddenly swooped from his perch on the steering seat, seized the square mirror from its slot behind the sink, and held it up to my face. "Look at yourself!" he exclaimed. "Look at yourself in the mirror and tell me whether you think this fishing life with me agrees with you or not."
>
> I looked from his beaming face into the mirror and saw, as if for the first time, the sunburned face, brown eyes, white hair, and freckles of a woman I was familiar with, all right, but the glowing look was new. I turned back with astonishment to John, who was still holding the mirror up to my face. "Is that really me?" I said, and covered my face with my hands. He took my hands away and looked at me.
>
> "I guess I've come to stay," I said. (187)

Daly allows Iglauer into his space on the *MoreKelp* despite his awareness of the superstition that, in his words, "the worst thing of all ... was a woman on a fishing boat" (128). But in her romantic account, there is always an undercurrent of tension because of Iglauer's awareness that this boat is *John's* space, and "I was afraid of being a nuisance by getting in the way" (32). "What? Where?" she cries again and again as Daly barks instructions (36-37), until she admits:

> "Nothing that has to be done on this boat comes naturally to me," I said unhappily. "I don't think I can do any of the things you really need."
>
> "Like what?"
>
> "Oh, cleaning fish, or making up gear or jumping off the boat and tying it up to docks when you bring it in, and I'm not very good at steering. I don't understand compasses and charts, and I can't do anything *mechanical*."
>
> "You'll learn. You'll learn," he said. He leaned over and took one of my hands in both of his. "All my fishing life, I've dreamed of having someone like you with mental protein between the ears as a permanent partner on my boat. I've fished alone most of my life, so I don't need help there." (37-38)

Iglauer is more than a guest afloat, but clearly the boat remains Daly's—not theirs—by definition and the partner Daly has dreamed of is one who will support him without interfering with his role as the one who actually fishes. All of the things that do not "come naturally" to Iglauer (working with gear, fish, ropes, steering, charts, and the compass) are chores to be acted out within the most masculine territory of the vessel. Anthropologists Charlene Allison et al. point out in *Winds of Change: Women in Northwest Commercial Fishing* (1989) that wives often contribute in family fishery ventures but are much less frequently involved in the actual harvesting of fish (160). They note that wives "sporadically move into their husband's work space [on board]. The wives may serve as companions or occasionally emergency replacement-crew members, or they may work as crew members more or less regularly" (162). But they are rarely owners and captains, moving freely on deck. In Allison et al. we see many portraits of women supporting men in the fishery from a position in the cabin, or from the home on land. With the advent of mechanized fishing, women can be physically capable of the work, but the stigma against them remains in place. Only one woman in the study owned and operated her own fishing vessel and she had been divorced several times because, she said, her husbands could not handle her level of involvement. In contrast, Iglauer is wanted and valued on the *MoreKelp* and she has a significant role: "By silent agreement, I gradually took over all the traditional female household chores—especially cooking and laundry. It was what I knew how to do, and I wanted to be useful" (89).

Iglauer is not traveling the coast by boat because she chose a life on the water. She came to interview Daly, and she stayed to be near him; her text concludes: "When John died ... [I] could not continue alone in the fishing life. There are women who do, but I had been an observer, not a participant; it was fishing with John that I loved so much" (305). Perhaps it is not surprising, then, that as a boat traveler Iglauer is not interested (as other women in the fishery may be) in moving into her captain's work space. Throughout *Fishing with John* (1988), Iglauer describes herself as nearly incompetent in the marine environment. This strong woman had raised two children, survived on her own in New York City, and made a name for herself as a journalist in Europe and the Arctic. Yet in this account, she describes everything that Daly does easily and gracefully as extra hard for her because she is slight and female: "We walked up the beach in single file, past an old fish boat on its side above the high-tide mark, and over some logs that John stepped across easily but that I had to scramble up and down" (146); the fishing poles "were too heavy for me" (303). Because *Fishing with John* serves as a eulogy to the late Daly, I suspect that Iglauer paints her physical struggles with a heavy brush, a rhetorical device to make Daly appear masculine, powerful, and in control (in contrast to herself). As a result, her writing tends to depict the marine environment as particularly hostile to women.

Like Kathrene Pinkerton, Eileen Dawson, Agnete Sandwell, Beth Eberhart, and Margaret Sharcott, Edith Iglauer accomplishes most of her work afloat in the interior space of the boat. Like Pinkerton, she takes great pleasure in being useful, efficient, and domestic; when her work below is done, she comes into the open to observe the scenery or the work her husband has accomplished outside:

I finished my housework: the breakfast dishes washed and put away, the toast crumbs brushed into a dustpan held to the edge of the stove, and a light sweep of the floor with the broom. I rubbed three brass-and-copper lures with a rag with Brasso until they shone so brightly that I did not think any fish could resist their appeal on John's lines. I visited the cockpit to admire two small springs and six large cohos that John had caught. (279)

Perhaps because taboos, rituals, and the distinct division of space and labor are most explicit on working boats, Iglauer (like Eberhart and Sharcott) refers to her work as "housework" but resists constructing the fishing boat as a home afloat. Since the Industrial Revolution, and before the recent popularity of the notion of the "home office," the workplace and the home have been conceived of as opposites; because fishing boats are work sites, women may resist labeling them as homes. Women on fishing boats undoubtedly dislike having their accounts compared with those of pleasure boaters.[26] However, when it comes to issues of gender and space, the similarities should not be overlooked. Whether traveling the Northwest Coast on a fishing boat or a pleasure craft, and regardless of social class, women generally remain unequal partners in the project afloat and only gain a toehold in the male space of the boat by performing the domestic work of the home. Many men, and some women, continue to assume that women make natural "mates" (second in command) both at home and at sea, and men depend upon women's unpaid labor in those spaces. The following advertisement in the "men to women" personals section (not the employment section) of the Vancouver newspaper the *Georgia Straight* illustrates that romance, not a wage, is the expected compensation for this mate's work:[27]

FIRST MATE wanted for world sailing trip aboard 40 ft. ketch. Your skipper is also 40, NS, educated writer. Phone 4318

The advertisement was followed months later by a corresponding ad in the "women to men" personals section of the same paper:[28]

MEDICAL MATE

Looking for univ. educated sailboat skipper, nonsmoker, ready to share rather than command. I'm 51, energetic, like music, golf, cooking, Xcountry skiing, & time with friends and family. Need to live out of city, presently on Vancouver Island. Phone, write 9387, c/o G.S.

This mate's emphasis that she is seeking a skipper "ready to share rather than command" underscores the continuing relevancy of the gendered politics of space and power in ordinary women's lives.

---

26 Iglauer, for instance, discusses the fisherman's belief that tourists are an abomination (126).

27 24 February to 3 March 1995 issue, p. 52.

28 21 to 28 July 1995 issue, p. 60.

Performing domestic labor while cruising appears to deeply satisfy women who revel in feminine ideals of homemaking. But at the same time, the acceptance of a mate's duties undercuts a woman's ability to move beyond the confining space of the galley. As the works of Jensen (1995), Allison et al. (1989), Blanchet (1961), and Morgan (1974) suggest, one way out of the gendered space and gendered role-playing of the galley is to invest in a boat of one's own. This conclusion is supported by domesticity theorists; Cynthia Rock et al. (1980) write that "For many women, escape from restrictive roles has meant moving out to live alone and taking exclusive control of their living environments, often for the first time" (93).

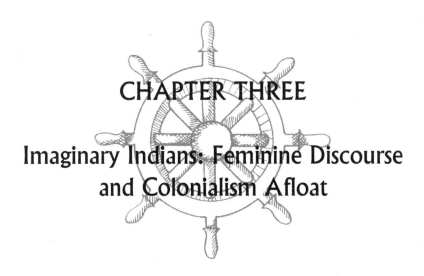

CHAPTER THREE

Imaginary Indians: Feminine Discourse
and Colonialism Afloat

A white-shell beach. A white-shell beach sounds different to me than other beaches: hushed, muted, found on the quiet sides of islands, in the protected wrinkles of coves. No slurp or squelch of mud, nor clatter of small stones raked back and forth with surf. The clickings and tickings of barnacle-covered rock are absent. Perhaps beaches have languages; maybe the smooth-edged discourse of midden whispers along the Northwest Coast. Layers of broken and buffed clam shell turn the water green near Bedwell Harbour, stick to the soles of my feet at Montague. I spent many summers boating between the white-shell beaches before I knew they were middens—layers of stone tools and antler, bone, and tooth artifacts embedded in and preserved by the calcium-rich shells. Their presence acts as an archive of Native culture along the Northwest Coast.[1] As steamships slid south past these midden sites in the late nineteenth century, the tourists on board tabulated lists of "curios" they had purchased on their voyage to Alaska: baskets, knives, and other objects (see chapter four). The middens did not speak to tourists; the travelers, rehearsed in the rhetoric of barter, bought history and took it home as evidence of their contact with the "other," with the "disappearing" primitive past,[2] with people they could only imagine.

White women who traveled this region by boat in the late nineteenth and early twentieth centuries may not have been fluent in the language of midden, but they knew the discourse of a woman's place: the home. They had also internalized the discourse of colonialism, which they read in popular travel literature, and their accounts (from the 1860s to the 1930s) can be read within a context of late colonialism on the Northwest Coast. Their conviction that travelers were part

---

1 For an introduction to Northwest Coast midden excavation, see Koppel (1985).

2 Significant discussions on the myth of the disappearing Indian in British Columbia include Crosby (1991), Fulford (1993), Hume (1988), and Francis (1992).

of a movement to report and to civilize, to bring the morals and manners of the homeland, the mother country, to "uncivilized" places and aboriginal peoples influenced the language they used in their accounts. Travel for women, as Doris Jedamski (1995) writes, "then meant: leaving the sheltered home to slip into a provisional one for the journey" (19, 21). It should not really surprise the careful reader, then, that "home" is an important undercurrent in these accounts.

The well-documented Victorian "cult of home" had specific effects on these early boat travelers' accounts, especially noticeable in the way they wrote about Native women. In this chapter, I focus on the images that women boat travelers of the period imagined, recycled, and passed along to their readers, and on the ways that the discursive pressures of feminine discourse[3] shaped these images. In this respect I am reading travelers' accounts with the sensibility one would bring to a contemporary reading of ethnography, a field that James Clifford (1986) describes as "always caught up in the invention, not the representation, of cultures" (2). Reading travel accounts in this way is by no means new; Johannes Fabian (1983) points out that ethnography "acquired its scientific and academic status by climbing on the shoulders of adventurers and using their travelogues, which for centuries had been the appropriate literary genre in which to report knowledge of the Other" (87). The accounts I examine here function as "cultural filter[s] that [distort] 'reality' into an image that is more consistent with European preconceptions and purposes," part of a process that culminates when "the image becomes more real than 'reality'" (Fisher 1977, 73).[4] In this case, the cultural filter is also a gendered filter.

Since the late 1980s, there has been an explosion of interest in anthologies of women's travel writing and travel guides for Western women,[5] and the narratives of European women traveling to Asia and Africa are enjoying recent popularity and re-publication. This body of work has begun to receive intense attention from scholars of language, history, and geography, but so far virtually nothing has been written about gender and tourism along the Northwest Coast. In 1884, 1,650 passengers traveled aboard the ships of "the major steamship company" to the newly purchased Alaska; by 1889, the number had jumped to 5,432 (Cole 1985). Many of these tourists published diaries of their voyages, but I am not aware of any critical studies of this literature.

In this exploration of femininity and colonialism along the Northwest Coast, I am interested in how, over time, these constructions of Native women gradually became less derisive and how changing modes of water transportation

3 The term "feminine discourse" refers not simply to women's writing, but to writing that specifically illustrates the awareness or internalization of contemporaneous definitions of the "feminine."

4 With *The Imaginary Indian* (1992), Daniel Francis set a precedent for studying "the images of Native people that White Canadians manufactured, believed in, feared, despised, admired, taught their children" (5).

5 For example, Aitken (1987), Birkett (1989), Robinson (1990), White (1991), Zepatos (1992, 1994), McCarthy (1992), Morris (1993), Davies and Jansz (1993), Frawley (1994), Lawrence (1994), Mullen (1994), Schriber (1995), and the *Virago* series for women travelers.

influenced travelers' perceptions of "Indians." Initially, feminine discourse led White women to depict Native women as facsimile or counterfeit ladies, implicitly contrasting and emphasizing the writers' own impeccable and authentic femininity. In more recent accounts, feminine discourse allows White women the space to question their preconceptions of Natives and to reconsider their own position in the Native world through which they moved. Literary theory on the significance of feminine discourse within the larger frame of colonial British travel writing offers a good place to begin this exploration.

Theorizing Colonial Women's Travel Writing

In "First Impressions: Rhetorical Strategies in Travel Writing by Victorian Women," Eva-Marie Kröller (1990) identifies ways in which the tropes that women writers share with their male peers can be "used with different intention and to different effect" (88). This rhetorical complexity, she writes, leads to the multiple personae and multiple voices of Victorian women travelers that frustrates feminist readers. The same accounts that show evidence of strength, independence, and sensuality also demonstrate "the women's insistence on propriety, their conservative politics and sense of racial superiority, and ... their apparent lack of pride in their own achievements" (88). Doris Jedamski (1995) observes the same contradictions in early twentieth-century accounts by women traveling the Malay Archipelago. "Displaying a clear colonial and racial attitude at one moment," she writes, "they then become progressive and emancipatory the next" (2). Kröller analyzes the narratives of Isabella Bird and Mary Kingsley, showing how Kingsley's "typically self-deprecatory style" (95) ironically undercuts her implicit approval of colonial possession in West Africa, and how Bird's trope of sexual penetration to describe her arrival in Japan "suggests that her insistence on her own freedom did not necessarily imply a refusal to collude in the oppressive business of imperialism" (91).

The same year that Kröller's article appeared, Shirley Foster published similar ideas in *Across New Worlds: Nineteenth-Century Women Travellers and Their Writings*. She identifies the ambiguous position of female travelers, who must adopt "the 'masculine' virtues of strength, initiative and decisiveness while retaining the less aggressive qualities considered appropriate for their own sex" (11). One common result of this ambiguity is that "women travel writers have to substitute self-effacement or self-mockery for more aggressive or positive assertiveness in order to demonstrate a true femininity" (19). This self-deprecating tone is frequently established when a female travel writer begins her text by apologizing or appealing for leniency toward the deficiencies in her work, "in contrast to the prefaces appended to the works of most male travelers which positively burst with confident self-assertion" (20). I believe that when women traveled by boat, they were under even greater pressure to adopt an apologetic tone; as I described in chapter two, women were still "taboo" aboard ships. G. de Montauban romanticizes this expectation for apology in the popular nineteenth-century novel *The Cruise of a Woman Hater* (1887). When a woman unexpectedly appears on board, a male passenger is perplexed and irritated, not only by her presence, but specifically by her unapologetic discourse: "Now, this was not at all the kind of language Jerves had expected to hear. There was no apology for being on board, no excuses, no call for his sympathy, no demand for his forbearance. Her manner, indeed, almost seemed a trifle haughty" (44).

Foster concludes that it is possible to detect "a distinctive and overtly feminine voice" in women's travel accounts of the nineteenth century, recognizable by both a self-effacing tone and the treatment of topics not generally explored in depth in male travel writing:

> These include the appearance, costume and manners of women; details of domestic life such as household management and culinary habits; behaviour towards children; marriage customs and female status; the importance of "space" in the physical environment.... The woman writer often represents foreigners sympathetically, as individuals with whom she tries to identify rather than as symbols of an alien "otherness." (24)

Foster draws attention to much earlier works, such as Elizabeth Rigby's article "Lady Travellers" (1845), which acknowledge the special nature and value of women travelers' accounts. She concludes that, although the written style and topic choices that mark women's travel texts are not constant, they are clear enough to invite a definition of a sense of gendered discourse.

With *Discourses of Difference*, Sara Mills (1991) takes up that invitation by theorizing a discourse of femininity within a colonial context; she writes that "there are various discursive pressures on women writers which encourage them to write in particular ways. That is not to say that all women write in the same way, but rather that there are pressures which they either resist, negotiate or simply give in to" (99). These discursive constraints on both the production and reception of texts, Mills tells us, create a feminine discourse in travel writing of the British high imperial period (1850-1930) that is identifiable by its ambivalent position. Female narrators of this period use the dominant writing techniques of colonialism (such as "othering"[6]), yet at the same time they are prohibited from fully adopting them because of the narrators' position within patriarchal culture. For example, a woman could not construct herself as an authority on race (or, for that matter, as an authority on anything beyond the realm of the home—and even in the home the patriarch had final authority[7]) without calling her own femininity into question:

---

6 In typical colonial discourse, a narrator may "other" a race to assert the superiority of the race of the writer and readers. The othered race is frequently perceived as living in "the past." Travel writers can other a race by concentrating on "strange" smells, "filthy" villages, or "mysterious" and "uncivilized" customs. Such narrative strategies can legitimize authoritarian and discriminatory forms of government. Septima Collis (1890), for instance, writes of Native Alaskans: "If I was the government of the United States, I would put the Indians under such discipline that their quarters should be subject to inspection" (49).

7 See, for example, J. W. Kirton, *Happy Homes, and How to Make Them* (1870).

... women's texts are not supposed to be 'scientific' and authoritative, but rather, supposed to be amateurish. This problematic positioning of these texts often leads to the writing being prefaced with a disclaimer which denies any scientific, literary or other merit; this occurs very frequently with women's travel writing in the nineteenth century. (S. Mills 83)

Mills supports Foster's idea that colonial women travel writers use humor, self-effacement, and an emphasis on personal relationships in their writing. She also writes that, as a result, their texts can then operate within colonial discourse *and* serve to criticize it from its own margins. These writers are not exempt from racism nor from participation in imperialism, Mills points out (98), but feminine discourse additionally creates the opportunity for women to feel "affiliated" with Natives (99). That is, their accounts draw attention to their interaction with Natives not as representatives of the colonizing race (as in male-authored accounts) but as individuals. Mills argues that what she calls feminine discourse constitutes a challenge to male Orientalism—a challenge overlooked by Edward Said (1978) in his study of Orientalism.[8]

Mills rightly points out that there are many discourses at work in the whole of the colonial situation: "Each colonial relation develops narrative and descriptive techniques particular to its setting and history" (87). In the American Pacific Northwest, for example, Robert Cantwell (1972), Richard Maxwell Brown (1986), and David Laskin (1997) theorize that rainfall has been used as the primary descriptor in constructions of regional topography and identity. Historians on both sides of the Canada-U.S. border, including Gillian Creese and Veronica Strong-Boag (1992), Jean Barman (1991), Karen J. Blair (1988), and Carlos Schwantes (1989), offer more complex analyses of connections between local setting, history, and historiography. They all suggest that a preoccupation with "rugged" topography and with White, masculinist frontier life (in response to that topography) has shaped not only the regional colonial situation but also regional history and identity. One result of this preoccupation is a lack of knowledge about pre-contact Native culture generally and Native women's lives particularly.

Tourists who visited the region were preoccupied with a desire for contact with "authentic" representatives of a primitive past; at the same time, domestic ideology made female tourists especially interested in the spiritual and moral conformity of Natives. Lacking written history of Native culture, women boat tourists relied heavily on contemporaneous codes of femininity from home to depict and judge aboriginal women.

---

8 Mills' argument is supported by other feminist theorists of postcolonial studies. For instance, Deborah Gordon (1988) suggests Said's work is "inadvertently masculinist" 94); Julia Emberley (1993) writes:

The process of "othering" which takes place within the colonial epistemic formation of Orientalist knowledge, is not, however, without a certain gender specificity. For Said, I would argue, the construction of a de-centered colonial subject is based largely on Western or European standards of masculinity, masquerading as transparent and universal representations of the colonial experience. (7)

Contacts

The ancestors of the peoples called "Indians" or "Siwash" in tourist accounts arrived on the Northwest Coast at least twelve thousand years ago. The Salish people were established at what is now called Cattle Point in north Puget Sound by 1300 B.C.E. Barry Gough (1984) writes that in 1835, forty percent of the Native population in the area now called Canada lived within the British Columbia region. At the time of Columbus, "in all of North America and Mexico, 30 per cent of the two million Indians lived on the Pacific coast on 6 percent of the continent's land area. Except perhaps for California, the place of greatest Indian population density in North America was the Northwest Coast" (Gough 9).

In *Land Use, Environment, and Social Change: The Shaping of Island County, Washington* (1980), Richard White argues that "Far from being creatures of their environment, these people had shaped their world and made it what it was when whites first arrived" (26). For example, he writes, Native communities set fires to extend berry grounds and hunted selectively to shape the populations of certain animals. Communities lived in alternating summer and winter residences in relative plenty; salmon runs and quantities of other fish, sea and land mammals, and a variety of plants were the bases of a subsistence economy that demanded intense labor during summer months. Neighboring coastal peoples and inland sub-Arctic peoples had established trade long before White contact. When trade for pelts began by sea in the eighteenth century, and when the land-based fur trade commenced on the coast in 1831, Euro-Canadian traders entered a system that already understood and appreciated trade (Klein 1980, 96).

Trade drew world attention to the Northwest Coast as a region promising resources and opportunity. By the time the women I consider in this chapter arrived on the coast and described it and its Native population, colonialism was significantly affecting regional culture and landscape; the area was already what Mary Louise Pratt (1992) calls a "contact zone,"—a social space "where disparate cultures meet, clash, and grapple with each other, often in highly asymmetrical relations of domination and subordination" (4). By the middle of the nineteenth century, Governor James Douglas had determined that economics and colonial politics would dominate local topography. Missionaries and federal policymakers in what is now the province of British Columbia were affecting local culture, as well; in *The West Beyond the West* (1991), Jean Barman writes that they "sought to reorder the three fundamental components of natives' lives: their relationship with the land, their unique social structures, and the way they educated their young" (158). Similar changes were happening in Washington Territory, and soon after, Alaska. Epidemics altered and even obliterated Native communities; women traveling the coast by steamer in the late nineteenth century saw a quickly declining race, and tourists traveling in the early and mid-twentieth century believed that the Indian had all but vanished.

The authors of the accounts I analyze frequently depict Native people as lazy; Native women are described as loitering on piers waiting to sell souvenirs. In reality, away from tourist sites, Native women worked in a variety of ways. In his study of Native labor in British Columbia between 1858 and 1930, Rolf Knight (1978) suggests that after contact the roles of Native women changed less than did those of men (33). Native women comprised the bulk of B.C. cannery labor in the 1870s, 1880s, and 1890s, worked in cottage industries (for example, knitted the Cowichan sweaters introduced at missions in the 1860s) and domestic labor, tended potato gardens, backpacked eighty pounds of freight—standard weight for Native women to carry "over narrow trails, up hills and down, over roots, muck and rock" (143)—, migrated with their husbands and families from the British Columbia coast to work in Washington Territory sawmills in the 1870s, and "paddled canoes for their husbands or relatives in seal hunting" (216).[9] The strength and flexibility of Native women after contact is illustrated by Knight's description of their work on the water:

> *Gillnetting by oar and sail demanded able bodied, healthy men—and sometimes women. At least some Indian women worked with their husbands and other relatives, usually as boat pullers [see figure 2]. This presumably occurred when a man could not get another fishing partner or when he wanted to retain the total catch returns in the family. It is unknown how numerous Indian fisherwomen and boat pullers were but it was sufficiently frequent for canning companies to stipulate that advance payments would not be made to women boat pullers. There were also Indian women working with their husbands in early hand seining operations.... Indian women often helped crew the mosquito fleet of handline trollers, cod boats, and halibut hunting canoes which took fish both for subsistence purposes and offered surpluses for sale until well into the 1930s. (80)*

Pre-contact activities of women in Northwest Coast First Nations appear to have focused on the preparation and storage of food, but some oral histories indicate grandmothers or other female ancestors who were skilled at fishing and hunting, even though taboos associated with menstruation could prohibit women from hunting or handling fish nets (see Klein 1980, 93; Cooper 1992-93, 47). Carol Cooper theorizes that, because women controlled the production and distribution of food and other economic resources among the Nisga'a and Tsimshian, they "received recognition for the skilled management of resources, because the surplus they produced became the basis of trade and generated wealth for distribution in the potlatch" (45). The presence of White fur traders, she argues, did not have a negative impact on the status of the women of these specific native groups, but offered further opportunities for women to create wealth and enhance their status: "On the northern Pacific coast, amassing wealth through successful exploitation of resources and trade was an equally if not more important means to prestige and public power than warfare. Significantly, these were activities in which Nishga [*sic*] and Tsimshian women could readily engage" (49). Some Native women participated in trade by controlling resources, by setting prices, and by getting into canoes and engaging

---

9 Knight does not consider the significant labor of post-contact prostitution.

in trade themselves. Nisga'a, Tsimshian, and Haida women were known as excellent canoeists, commonly receiving instruction from the age of six (Cooper 47); it was not uncommon for women to paddle hundreds of miles to trade.[10]

Because coastal Native ideologies and languages differ from my own, I hesitate to blithely claim that these women were "at home afloat" in a way that can be easily compared with the experiences of White women at sea. As members of maritime cultures, Native women were undoubtedly more comfortable and more skilled on the water than were any of the women I consider in this project. It is also true that their roles on land sometimes followed them offshore, and that their trade afloat affected their status in society (Mrs. Tom, whom I discuss later in this chapter, is an example). British Columbian painter and writer Emily Carr (1941) describes being taken to the Haida Gwaii/Queen Charlotte Islands village of Yan by a Native woman early in the twentieth century:

An Indian woman came down to the bank carrying a heavy not-walking-age child. A slim girl of twelve was with her. She carried a paddle and going to a light canoe that was high on the sand, she began to drag it towards the sea.

The woman put the baby into the canoe and she and the girl grunted and shunted the canoe into the water, then they beckoned to me. (59)

Carr hesitates to enter the canoe with the woman and her children; she had expected a Native man to take her to Yan.

Pointing to the bow seat, the woman commanded, "Sit down."

I got in and sat.

The woman waded out holding the canoe and easing it about in the sand until it was afloat. Then she got in and clamped the child between her knees. Her paddle worked without noise among the waves. The wind filled the flour sack beautiful as if it had been a silk sail.

The canoe took the water as a beaver launches himself--with a silent scoot.

The straight young girl with black hair and eyes and the lank print dress that clung to her childish shape, held the sail rope and humoured the whimsical little canoe. The sack now bulged with wind as tight as once it had bulged with flour. The woman's paddle advised the canoe just how to cut each wave. (60)

This passage demonstrates that, from one White woman's perspective, Native women are competent mariners who bring their domestic roles afloat. But what did this Native woman herself think? How different was her concept of "home" from that of Euro-Canadians of the same period and from mine now? Explicating White Victorian attitudes toward home, family, and sex difference tells us something about what missionaries attempted to teach Native peoples

---

10 Some Northwest Coast tourist accounts, such as Winthrop's (1862), comment on the dominant roles Native wives played when Native couples bartered with travelers.

along the coast,[11] but does not reveal the ideologies of Native women on the water. The history of Native women before contact remains vague to academics like myself because, as Knight points out, "comparatively few Indian women were interviewed in the classic ethnohistorical accounts" (25). Because Native cultures were oral, and because Native women have not belonged to a leisure class, Native women after contact did not produce diaries or written accounts of their voyages[12] to be compared with those of White women. The study of Native women and the marine environment remains to be done, and done by someone thoroughly educated on the subject of Native oral history.

Regardless of the Sacajewea or Pocahontas stereotype for Native women in North America, descriptions of Native coastal women by European men do not focus on their beauty or strength. Sylvia Van Kirk (1980) and Jennifer Brown (1980) have shown how valuable Native women were in the lives of overland fur traders in early Canadian history. However, men visiting the Northwest Coast in ships to trade for furs were less interested in domestic companions or guides. Their depictions of Native women draw attention to the "filthy" look of their painted faces and oily hair and to their sexual availability, and these constructions extended beyond fur-trade rhetoric. In "Construction of the Imaginary Indian," Marcia Crosby (1991) comments on the widespread stereotype of the Native woman as bad-smelling, promiscuous, and drunk. For some White men, young Indian women seem exotic and attractive; after a paragraph describing a mixed-blood girl's blushing face, Theodore Winthrop, a traveler in Washington Territory in 1853, says simply: "Indian maids are pretty; Indian dames are hags. Only high civilization keeps its women beautiful to the last" (15). Such a construction draws attention to the writer's own power, masculinity, "good taste," and absolute right to judge, and is one that many women boat travelers on the Northwest Coast share—although not for the same reasons. Winthrop's comment that high civilization *keeps* women beautiful to the last hints at the difference. Nineteenth-century women travelers who did not keep themselves beautiful, who did not adopt a pose of certain and steady femininity in their writing, were commonly received as either liars or untrustworthy eccentrics (see S. Mills 121).

---

11 For example, Native people were counseled to stop living in communal houses and to set up individual homes with nuclear families. In the Victorian period, the homes of England were "the brightest spots in the world, and ... the foretaste of the home above" (Kirton dedication page), justifying the authority of the father. Debates about the importance of the Victorian ideal of home remain with us today; the current outcry for a "return to family values" in the United States and Canada emphasizes that wives, husbands, and children must relearn their traditional place in the home.

12 As Julie Cruikshank et al. (1990) point out, female elders in the North did and continue to

Counterfeit Ladies

Eliza Ruhamah Scidmore's *Alaska, Its Southern Coast and the Sitkan Archipelago* (1885) is the product of an American woman traveling the coast as a passenger on working steamships in 1883, 1884, and 1885. Her account generally resists the expectations for Victorian feminine discourse. She never apologizes for herself and she writes authoritatively about history. She gives details regarding the experiences and influences of explorers and pioneers, and she has researched the process of Alaska changing hands from Russia to the United States, the development of fish cannery operations, the educational system, the international politics of the fur-seal harvest, and rules of navigation. Scidmore rarely writes about herself as a woman, except to note that she thinks she is the "first woman" to visit some of these places and to downplay any attention drawn by her sex. When a male passenger comments on her presence, she depicts herself and another female passenger as taking danger lightly—definitely not the "shrinking lady":

> *"You ladies are very brave to venture up in such a place. If you only knew the risks you are running—the dangers you are in!" And the pioneer's voice had a tone of the deepest concern as he said it.*
>
> *We received this with some laughter, and expressed entire confidence in the captain and pilot, who had penetrated glacial fastnesses [sic] and unknown waters before. (132-33)*

Using penetration—which Kröller (1990) identifies as a typical trope of masculine colonial discourse—Scidmore acknowledges the capability of a professional without feigning helplessness. An early writer and editor for *National Geographic,* Scidmore was the first woman on the National Geographic Society's board of managers (Lillard 1992, 158). Her confident and factual style would have been more acceptable than feminine discourse to the quasi-scientific magazine.

The pioneer's emphasis on the danger of boat travel up the Northwest Coast was not, however, an overstatement. Steamer passage up the coast was still risky in the 1880s, and the mid-1870s saw the highest loss of life and property at sea off the Northwest Coast of all time (Wright 223). Some steamers, such as the *George S. Wright* (figure 1), simply disappeared between Alaska and Portland. Other wrecks, such as that of the *Pacific* in November 1875, generated horrifying accounts:

> *[The crew] succeeding in getting one [lifeboat] over the side, in which several of the women were placed, but, before it could clear the steamer, the boat capsized and all were drowned. A baby, which a Mrs. Parsons carried in her arms, was crushed to death before its mother entered the boat. (Wright 225-26)*

One of the paddle-wheel steamers on which Scidmore traveled, the *Ancon* (figure 10), was later wrecked (Wright 371).

Figure 10. Scidmore traveled aboard the *Ancon* (unattributed photo from Wright 1895).

Because Scidmore toured on working boats, opportunities for her to get off the deck and into the villages were rare. Near the village of Karta off Clarence Strait, she writes that "The inexorable law of ship's duty only permits it to linger at a harbor for the time necessary to load or unload cargo, or for the time specified in the mail contract" (267). Her perceptions of the landscape and people, then, are shaped by the commercial schedule of the steamer, and she meets Native people used to the comings and goings of steamer passengers in their villages. Her area of contact is sometimes enlarged when she has the opportunity to travel in a skiff:

> *For another perfect summer afternoon the* Ancon *lay at the wharf in Kasa-an Bay, and in the mellow, Indian summer sunshine, we roamed the beach, buying the last remaining baskets, bracelets, pipes, and spoons of the Indians, and pulling hard at the amateur's oar we trailed across the bay in small boats to watch the [Native] fishermen cast and draw the net. (267)*

In the next chapter I consider the effect of steamship travel on Scidmore's depiction of nature; here, I would like to point out her construction of Native people as the creators of cultural artifacts (she calls them "curios") worth possessing herself, and as people worth going out of her way to watch. However, Scidmore's subjectivity as a woman does not, as Mills' and Foster's work on British women travelers may suggest we should expect, "align" her with Native people. In fact, the conventions of feminine discourse appear to lead Scidmore to focus on the differences between Native and White women. When describing Native women, Scidmore switches into a feminine discourse (identifiable primarily by her attention to "women's topics" such as women's age, weight, appearance, and morality) that is not evident in the bulk of her account. She does not, in contrast, use these codes of appearance to depict the captain of the ship.

Scidmore's construction of Native women is highly concerned with social position. She is interested in the status of coastal Native women compared to those on the plains, recording that the former have "a good many rights up here that [their] sisters of the western plains know not" (37). She connects coastal women's status with water travel and trade:

> Woman's rights, and her sphere and influence, have reached a development among the Sitkans, that would astonish the suffrage leaders of Wyoming and Washington Territory. They are all keen, sharp traders, and if the women object to the final price offered for their furs at the Sitka stores, they get into their canoes, and paddle up to Juneau, or down to Wrangell, and even across the border to the British trading posts. They take no account of time or travel, and a journey of a thousand miles is justified to them, if they only get another yard of calico in exchange for their furs. (182)

In her text generally, Scidmore resists the sentimentalizing, self-deprecatory, and overtly moralizing tone that characterizes feminine discourse of the nineteenth century, and she adopts the language of the male imperial adventurer when she tells us that she "feels quite like an explorer penetrating unknown lands" (3). But although she resists feminine discourse throughout most of her travelogue, she adopts it when writing explicitly about Native women. Her construction of one particular Native woman illustrates this point.

"Mrs. Tom," an aboriginal woman who imported baskets for trade from the Yakutats, was a character many tourists observed in Sitka. Douglas Cole (1985) writes that she "operated a regular shipping service between the two towns, initially using a large canoe, later her own little schooner" (99). Mrs. Tom, Scidmore tells her reader, "is the reputed possessor of $10,000, accumulated by her own energy and shrewdness" in trading. "Even savage people bow down to wealth," she writes. When Scidmore visits Mrs. Tom, she has this to report:

> She is a plump matron, fat, fair, and forty in fact, and her house is a model of neatness and order. On gala occasions she arrays herself in her best velvet dress, her bonnet with the red feather, a prodigious necktie and breastpin, and then, with two silver rings on every finger, and nine silver bracelets on each arm, she is the envy of all the other ladies of Siwash ["native"] town. (176-77)

Her use of feminine discourse here—focusing on Mrs. Tom's neat home and velvet dress, and on the envy of the other Native women Scidmore mockingly calls "ladies"—creates an ambiguous and absurd portrait of the Native women of Sitka, whom she considers (as she states on the same page) to be "savage people." Scidmore's perception that Natives are held back from "upward progress" because of "their want of all moral sense or instincts" is clear in this text (233). Mrs. Tom is caricatured as a woman who does not know the difference between elegance and gaudiness; she is wealthy but too crude to understand that two silver rings on each finger is unladylike. Scidmore enhances Mrs. Tom's perceived coarseness by reporting unconfirmed gossip that Mrs. Tom bought a young male slave, then married him. Shown the respected trader Mrs. Tom, a reader could be left vaguely admiring a Native woman decked out in Western apparel, but aware that her lack of morality and feminine subtlety makes her only a facsimile of a "real" woman.

In *A Woman's Trip to Alaska* (1890), eastern American Septima Collis also employs many of the self-conscious constructs of feminine discourse to describe her voyage generally and Native women specifically. Collis recounts a twelve-day voyage in May and June of 1890. Her narrative switches back and forth between past and present tense and takes the form of chronological letters or journal entries directed at her daughter,

Figure 11. Septima Collis, as shown in the frontispiece to *A Woman's Trip to Alaska* (1890).

Amelia, left at home. She includes sketches and snapshots "kodak'd by the author" and by others, and her main concern appears to be "explain[ing] how this delightful excursion can be enjoyed without the slightest fatigue or discomfort" (unpaginated preface). The account opens with a studio photo of herself, a middle-aged woman in a tightly fitted black dress with puffed sleeves (figure 11). She wears gloves, carries a case for field glasses over her shoulder, and holds a pen in her right hand and a small book in her left; we can see immediately that this will be a text influenced by posture and posing.

Her work—addressed to "my country-women"—begins with a preface detailing the limitations imposed upon her by her female readers, whom she believes would be uninterested in history and science; she acknowledges she could never compete with the existing works on such topics. Her characteristically feminine apology reads:

In the following pages I have not made even a pretence of writing a scientific or historical work. It is not of special interest to those for whom I write [i.e., women] to know the exact pressure to the square inch which propels the seas of ice as they furrow their way from the Arctic regions through the mountain gorges down to the softening influences of the Japanese Stream, nor to trace the vicissitudes of Alaska from the voyages of Captain Cook down to the purchase by Mr. Seward in 1867, nor yet to familiarize themselves with the ethnology of the various tribes of Indians who inhabit the Aleutian Islands. All this has been done better than I could ever hope to do it. My sole object is to put on paper, for the benefit of others, the impressions made upon me by the voyage, and to explain how this delightful excursion can be enjoyed without the slightest fatigue or discomfort, and at a trifling expense. I want them to know, as I know, that the ship is a yacht, of which the Captain is the host, the passengers his guests, and the object of the cruise the pursuit of pleasure; and if I succeed in inducing my country-women to follow my example and postpone Paris and London, Rome and Vienna, the Rhine and the Alps, to some future day, they will always have reason to be grateful to me, and I shall always have reason to be satisfied with my effort. (unpaginated)

Collis comments directly and in a self-effacing tone on the influence of gender on her traveling behavior: "Womanlike, I was mentally packing my trunk for the next few hours with the many things which I felt sure would be indispensable to my comfort" (1). She tells women readers what they should pack for such a voyage, and tries to capture the romantic imagination of her daughter and all female readers by confiding:

Entre nous, *I have heard of and seen more than one friendship, commencing on an Alaskan trip, which has ripened into mutual pledges "for good or for bad, for better, for worse," and especially of one wealthy and much-travelled Benedict who ... fell a victim in Alaskan waters to female charms, in furs and ulster.* (193)

Feminine discourse, at home in the realm of the private, the indoors, is used to describe her (and her husband's) curiosity toward the interior of their ship, the *Queen*: "Of course our curiosity was excited to visit all parts of *the floating home* that was to furnish us with all the comforts which exacting tourists demand" (45, my emphasis). "At home afloat" for Collis does not simply convey a sense of ease or comfort but a sense of being pampered. Collis is speaking from another class and from a different boating experience than Scidmore (on what she calls a "yacht" rather than a working steamer), but despite this difference they both rely on feminine discourse to construct aboriginal women.

Collis notices that Native families are at ease in what she haughtily calls "roving habitations"; clearly, she does not approve of the migratory or "homeless" lifestyle of Natives. In port at Seattle, she comments ironically on the "'dugouts,' occupied by Indians as roving habitations. It was curious and instructive to see the wonderful economy of space practiced by these people; a whole family in a single boat" (51). Here she uses the phrase "wonderful economy" to mimic the discourse of homemaking literature. She goes on to describe how the animals and people share eating utensils and describes "two little ugly children who had better never been born" (52). She concludes: "I don't know where they were going [in their canoe], as the hop-picking does not take place until fall, but probably they had come down to trade their fish or their furs for flour and groceries. At all events that is what I was told, and if it is not exactly true it does not make much matter" (52). The cause of the Native family's voyage "does not make much matter" in her account because—as she states in her preface—she believes that her female audience is not interested in ethnology and because she thinks Natives are so far from her own class that they do not deserve the effort of accurate depiction.

Collis' attitude leads to an ambiguous portrait of Natives on the Northwest Coast, quite similar to the ambiguity present in some Northwest Coast missionaries' accounts. "The missionary," Robin Fisher (1977) points out, "could never deny the humanity of the Indians, for that would be to deny their capacity for salvation" (93). Nevertheless, Natives had to be constructed as heathens, barbarians, and savages to legitimate the presence of the missionaries. Collis' construction of Natives focuses upon their "poor souls whose darkness may never be dispelled by the enlightenment of education and civilization" (127). Like many upper- and middle-class women of her time, Collis gains a sense of power by directing help toward those she perceives as beneath herself. Ironically, Collis, a Jew—"I am not a Christian woman; my faith is that of the chosen people" (119)—, emphatically praises the work of the Presbyterian missions: "... hereafter no man, nor woman either, shall outdo me in words of praise and thanks for the glorious Godlike work which is being performed by the good people who are rescuing the lives, the bodies, and the souls of these poor creatures from the physical and moral deaths they are dying" (119).

Christian charity was a cornerstone of Victorian feminine discourse; it was, of course, also a significant element in colonial discourse. In London, the 1837 House of Commons Committee of Aborigines agreed on the national duty "to carry civilization and humanity, peace and good government, and, *above all the knowledge of the true god, to the uttermost ends of the earth*" (quoted in Gough 1984, 17; my emphasis). Barry Gough (1984) writes that, in general, Victorian tourists believed "concern for law, order, and industry would bring the 'savage' *from infancy to a civilized maturity*" (34; my emphasis). It is not surprising, then, that many nineteenth-century women travelers—sometimes called "maternal imperialists" (Chaudhuri and Strobel 1992, 9)—describe colonialism through metaphors of motherhood and care giving and legitimize their presence in the colonial project by their sex. That Collis redirects attention from her own otherness (as a Jew) to praise the Christianization of Alaska intimates the power and appeal of both imperialist and feminine discourses and underscores the dominance of Christian ideology in both colonial and patriarchal world views. To criticize the Christian missionary enterprise would have amplified Collis' own position as a "heathen" Jew in anti-Semitic times. Although she chooses to make one reference to her "other" religion, she appears compelled to adopt the discourse typical of Christian charity, thereby amplifying her feminine role in the colonial project in the Northwest Coast region.

Yielding to the pressure of nineteenth-century feminine discourse, Collis cannot depict Native women without judging their manners against her own feminine habits. In her account, aboriginal women are "stretched upon the ground like as many seals" (185) and are "repulsive" (170) because of their smell. She describes a group of Sitkan women squatting in the shadow of a house as "counterfeiting with their olive skins, bright black eyes, and showy colors the Italian peasants" (100). "Mrs. Thom"—apparently the same Sitkan woman who appeared in Scidmore's popular account—is exposed here as a counterfeit as well: "her Royal Highness,"[13] as Collis dubs her, "is said to be worth $100,000[14] (though we saw little evidence of any such luxurious wealth)" (104-5). She ironically calls the woman's home a palace, then judges it unworthy of special attention: "The palace itself, like all the houses in the row, had one large room and a small annex in the rear, the customary fire in the center, and her regal couch was not only a quite comfortable bedstead, but the bedding blankets, and sheets were all neat and clean" (106). In apparent reference and contradiction to Scidmore's description of Mrs. Tom as "fat, fair, and forty in fact" (Scidmore 176), Collis mimics the alliteration and points out "she is very fat, of course not very fair, and much over forty" (105), and she includes an image of "Princess Thom," who appears to beg (figure 12). I think that in her allusions to Scidmore's account, Collis is not so much updating us on Mrs. Tom five years later as drawing attention to what she perceives as Scidmore's lack of feminine discourse, her lack of attention to the important *un*femininity of coastal Native women. When paired with Scidmore's travelogue, Collis' almost appears directly competitive— she desires, perhaps, to be read as a more genteel author writing to a higher-class (and hence more feminine) audience of female readers.

Such unflattering constructions of Native women may have been typical among female travelers of the period, but they were not inevitable. The journals of Caroline Leighton (1884), who lived and traveled in the Puget Sound region from 1865 to 1879 (Buerge 1995), stand in contrast to the narratives of Scidmore and Collis. A woman educated in the sciences who worked at the beginning of the Civil War to educate African-American refugees fleeing the South, Leighton's experiences made her less inclined to exoticize or other the aboriginal and Chinese people she met. Although her work was published nearly contemporaneously with Scidmore's (1885) and Collis' (1890), Leighton does not construct Native women as "counterfeits." Instead, she is more likely to comment without irony or mockery on how much more helpless European

---

13 Collis is not unique in ironically bestowing titles of monarchy upon Native people. Thoedore Winthrop did the same in *The Canoe and the Saddle* (1862). Fanny Stevenson (1915), wife of the novelist Robert Louis Stevenson, writes that when traveling by cargo boat in the South Pacific she made friends with a Native couple: "So began our friendship with Nan Tok and his wife (my husband always called them the 'baron and baroness')" (6).

14 Note that her attributed worth has increased tenfold.

PRINCESS THOM.
(*Kodak'd by Miss M. D. Beach.*)

Figure 12. Collis' depiction of "Princess Thom" with Native baskets in the foreground (1890).

women seem than "Indian crones." She writes: "when I compare them [Native women] with civilized women of the same age, who are generally helpless, I see that they have a great advantage over them" (Leighton, 1995, 102).[15]

Although Collis and Scidmore are very different writers, their depictions of Native women have something in common. Both authors depict and to some extent applaud Native women as counterfeit White women. Collis represents Native women as odd, sometimes interesting, and laughable in their manners—thus calling the reader's attention to Collis' own "normalcy" as a woman.[16] For Scidmore, the Native woman is admirable in her social freedoms, yet her "want of all moral sense" makes her less than a real woman. These constructions are not simply the result of a general Eurocentricity among nineteenth-century travelers along the coast; they are also the result of the discursive pressures of the Victorian cult of the home on women travelers.

15 Leighton's work brings to mind Emily Carr's. As residents of the region (Leighton south of the border, and Carr north), neither appear preoccupied with the "crude" mannerisms or speech of the locals (as were European and eastern American tourists), and both write of Native and Chinese people with respect.

16 Jedamski (1995) notes that Emily Innes did much the same with her 1885 account of Malaysian travel: "she apparently felt the need to degrade and humiliate the Other in order to maintain a minimum of self-esteem. The dress issue served as a means to stage-manage her superiority" (40).

The Victorian Cult of the Home

Victorian ideals of womanhood were derived from Enlightenment theorists and spread far beyond the geographical and historical boundaries of "the home islands" (Gough 1984, 213) of Great Britain; as upper-class Americans, Collis and Scidmore would have been highly aware of the expectations detailed in etiquette books, manuals on domestic economy, educational tracts, sermons, popular poems, novels, and travel accounts. These ideals worked from (relatively new) assumptions regarding the biological weaknesses of women. When Nina Auerbach (1982) refers to the "familiar cult of the home" (125), she is describing not only a culture that conceived of sexual difference in terms of strict opposites (men were intellectual, active, and strong; women were emotional, passive, and fragile), but also an intricate system of symbols. C. Willett Cunnington (1935), lamenting that Victorian women's merits were "apt to be overlooked" (v), writes that "The 19th century woman, whose economic position was still largely dependent on her powers of sex-attraction, made a virtue of necessity, and in her hands modesty became a fine art" (5-6). His comments on the symbolism of fashion and physique help us understand the cult status of femininity at the time:

> Symbolism is an unconscious way of expressing hidden thoughts, and is most used, of course, when conventions forbid more outspoken methods; ... all through the Victorian era, symbols were abundantly employed by women.
>
> The small hand, and therefore the tight glove, indicated that the owner was above having to do manual work; the huge crinole signified that the wearer occupied a large space in the social world; the trailing skirt that she did not belong to the "walking classes," and the stiff corset proved that she was a woman of unbending rectitude.
>
> May we not also read in the small waist a mute appeal for the support of the masculine arm? (20-21)

Lest we think Cunnington was exaggerating, Joan Perkins writes much more recently in her book *Victorian Women* (1993):

> Women spent their leisure time in a variety of pursuits, depending on the kind of person each was, but women of all social classes were preoccupied with dress. In the upper and middle classes the variety and complexity of their clothes showed rank and position. Every cap, bow, streamer, ruffle, fringe, bustle, glove and other elaboration signalled some difference in status. It was said that jewellery was "a badge that women wore like a sergeant-major's stripes or field marshal's baton". (93)

Given this widely acknowledged system of symbols, it is not, therefore, unreasonable to assume that Collis' depiction of Native women as "seals," and Scidmore's portrait of Mrs. Tom wearing inappropriate jewelry, are meant to give very precise indications of the failure of Native women to meet the standards of "true womanhood." Such descriptions of Native women have definite implications for their status and morality. Perhaps because this system was so widespread and thoroughly absorbed by upper- and upper-middle-class White women in Victorian society on both sides of the Atlantic, and because (unlike Caroline Leighton and Emily Carr) Scidmore and Collis had no experience with non-White peers,[17] they fail to resist conceiving of or imagining "other" women in any other way.

Robin Sheets (1988) explains that the location of the Victorian ideal of womanhood was the home:

> Woman's mission was to begin the moral regeneration of society by displaying the principles of Christianity in all her daily activities; her sphere was the home, a shelter for her own innocence and a sanctuary for her husband when he returned from the brutally competitive world of commerce. Within the domestic sphere, she could exercise her influence, a moral and spiritual force so strong that it was said to obviate the need for political power. (864)

This mission, and the emphasis on the home, is commonly referred to in the United States as "the Cult of True Womanhood." When she traveled, the Victorian woman packed her Christian charity—"the most popular alternative to vacuity" for middle-class Victorian women (Vicinus 1972, xi)—and her moral and spiritual force and brought them with her from home. Mills writes that British women of the high imperial period were expected to concern themselves with "the spiritual and moral well-being" of others (94); this concern for Native populations extended from their role at home with their children. The pressure to address the moral and spiritual well-being of aboriginals appears to have traveled not just to Asia and Africa but also to the Northwest Coast; it was an important factor that led Eliza Scidmore and Septima Collis to construct Native women as counterfeit ladies, as something other than real women. Neither Collis nor Scidmore "affiliates" herself with Native women nor seriously challenges the othering aspect of colonial discourse.

---

17 Scidmore, who wrote a number of travel books regarding her tours of such places as Java and Japan, certainly had opportunities for meeting non-White women. Perhaps remaining a "tourist" kept her from gaining the perspective Leighton found.

At Home in the Company of Strangers

Passengers aboard sailing ships and steamers spent most of their time in their rooms or on the high decks of the vessels. Along the Northwest Coast, cloud cover, rain, and fog frequently hid the landscape and the presence of Native people. If local scenery and local inhabitants could be seen clearly, they were viewed from a physical perspective that cultivated rhetorical distancing. Collis comments on the lack of opportunity, when traveling by steamship, to stop in one place. She writes that because the weather can sometimes obscure the view, "I therefore hope the day is near at hand when it will not be necessary to remain on board the steamer and make the complete circuit of the coast whether it be fair or foul, but that you will be enabled to do it by easy stages" (53). Describing a typical day of touring, Collis shows us how—given her perspective from a deck—it was easier to imagine the region than to actually see it: "Making myself comfortable on the very uppermost deck, clad in an ordinary cloth walking-dress, with a little astrakhan jacket over my shoulders, I just sat and revelled in this monotony of constant change, and let my fancy wander through a score of delicious flights of imagery" (72). Unlike women such as Mary Kingsley and Isabella Bird, who were traveling at roughly the same time in Africa and Asia and who walked, rode horses, or paddled small canoes, women traveling the Northwest Coast were not daily surrounded with Native people unless they were missionaries. Unlike White males (such as Ezra Meeker and Theodore Winthrop; see chapter one) who traveled in small rowboats, they had little opportunity or cause to speak with Natives to obtain food or directions or shelter; such things were provided for them through the ship. Steamship tourists spoke with Natives to barter for curios, or when they entered a Native house out of curiosity, but they had little reason to work to understand First Nations cultures, to gain the trust of individuals, or to communicate beyond the language of commerce. When they took an excursion ashore, they were accompanied by a party from the society of the ship.

This society on board made colonial women feel at home afloat. Sophia Cracroft puts it succinctly when she describes how she and her aunt, Lady Jane Franklin (introduced and discussed in chapter one of this book), felt on leaving the United States frontier society and boarding a British ship in February 1861:

> I cannot tell you how really at home we felt in that ship from the first. We were once more among our own people only, after many months of residence with Americans. There was the thorough English character of the cabin—the repose of Sunday which in a ship of war is so real—officers & men in their tidiest coats & brightest gold lace—and lastly, the morning service after divisions. (D.B. Smith 1974, 2; her emphasis)

Here, order and ritual put the women at ease; they understand the purpose and symbolism of such activities, and they appreciate their station in a world where men in gold lace protect women. American women take similar comforts. When

Helen Judge McAllister[18] traveled to the Pribilof Islands and stayed there from 1894 to 1913 while her husband acted as a government agent, she records that she retained her sense of humor when the ship she arrived on unloaded her like cargo:

> *The morning we landed was calm and clear. The* Brunswick *came to anchor about one half mile from the village landing. I was strapped in a chair, hoisted up by a yardarm and deposited in a boat made of sealion skins called a "Bidora". In the bottom of the Bidora were a number of sheep with their legs tied together. I sat down on one and I remember saying, "This is the first time that I have been warm since I left San Francisco." (2)*

But her greatest pleasure occurred when women traveling by ship stopped to teach her about the changes in fashion and to take part in familiar social activities. "I was so delighted to see these girls," she writes in her account, "for they were the first white women I had seen since Mrs. Clark (the wife of one of our Government officers) left me over a year before" (13). She notes how they "got me up to date with regard to the changes in styles," and that "We were very gay that summer, dinner parties aboard the Cutters, buckboard rides, hunting and dancing on shore in the evenings" (14).

Even in this small excerpt from McAllister's account, we can see evidence of feminine discourse: "I was so delighted" and "very gay." In *Language and Woman's Place* (1975), Robin Lakoff shows how even in contemporary American usage, certain adjectives (such as "delightful") are largely confined to women's speech and writing. If men use words such as "adorable" and "divine," it is usually because they are speaking with sarcasm. Because men are listened to with more attention, women learn to pack their sentences with "meaningless" words ("so" and "very") for emphasis. As Lakoff points out, these words are not meaningless but indicate the relationship between the speaker and her audience, between the speaker and her topic (9). McAllister also records her pleasure in fashion and romance (figure 13) aboard the cutters and on shore; romance is not at all an uncommon topic in women's travel accounts set on the Northwest Coast. I have already discussed Collis' comment that *"Entre nous,* I have heard of and seen more than one friendship, commencing on an Alaskan trip, which has ripened into mutual pledges ... and especially of one wealthy and much-travelled Benedict who ... fell a victim in Alaskan waters to female charms, in furs and ulster" (193). In Agnes Herbert's (1909) account of big-game hunting while traveling up the coast, she concludes by revealing that her ultimate trophy is her newly found mate (256). By 1939, the University of Washington was advertising its summer-school cruise aboard the steamship *Yukon* with the following copy: "Alaska's Inside Passage—a thousand-mile ocean lane so subtle in its witchery that it has become "The Lovers' Lane of the Seven Seas"—brings

---

18 "Memoirs of the Pribilof Islands Nineteen Years on St. George and St. Paul Islands Alaska." Helen Judge McAllister papers (V.F. 476), Univ. of Washington Manuscripts and Archives, Seattle,

Figure 13. A budding on-deck romance, as promoted in a 1939 cruise information brochure, University of Washington summer school program.

you never-ending, ever-changing scenery-as-you-sail."[19] The promotional flyer is headed by a sketch of fashionable young women posed before totem poles and includes a snapshot illustrating a budding on-deck romance. The accompanying copy promises "many breath-taking thrills" and views of towering mountains which "thrust their snow-mantled peaks into the sky." The only credit course offered on the cruise is Anthropology 111-b, "Indians of the Pacific Northwest," but the brochure promises "to bring you still more happy hours aboard ship, as you lazily watch scenery from a deck chair, talk to friends, play deck games, or dance to the music of the ship's orchestra." Perhaps the well-respected professor Viola Garfield was able to get her students off their deck chairs and out of the arms of their dance partners in her anthropology class that summer. I would argue that as long as her students remained on board, their view of the landscape and culture of the Northwest Coast would remain distanced and obscured not only by the height of the deck and the clouds and rain of local weather but by the fog of their own comfortable society.

Society in the nineteenth century, and in 1939, and today, remains "obsessively concerned" with woman's physical appearance (MacCannell and MacCannell

19 University of Washington Summer School cruise information brochure, for 25 July-5 August 1939. Viola E. Garfield Collection, Univ. of Washington Manuscripts and Archives, Seattle.

1987, 235) and grants her limited power through her femininity. "Femininity," as Susan Brownmiller (1984) writes, is still "a romantic sentiment, a nostalgic tradition of imposed limitations" (14). One of those limitations, as I have explored in this chapter, is discursive, and it significantly affects the way women see and construct one another.

A Sea Change

Agnes Herbert's 1909 account, *Two Dianas in Alaska,* signals a significant transition in female boat tourists' constructions of "imaginary Indians" along the Northwest Coast. She describes traveling from England to Seattle and then up the coast to Kodiak by steamer to hunt. No doubt Herbert's extreme class-consciousness leads to her general depiction of coastal Natives as "low-grade," unintelligent, and perpetually smelling of fish (38). Like many of her peers, she believed the consumption of too much fish led to lassitude and a deterioration of the intellect; therefore the Northwest Coast Native compared poorly with the aboriginal of the prairies and most unfavorably with the European. Her Natives are not individuals but representatives of a backward race; their presence in her account serves to justify the virtue of a class system in which Herbert is poised near the very apex of society. In this sense, Herbert's imaginary Indians function much like the most common Indian figures in fiction; Gordon Johnston (1987) points out that in fiction, over time, "Indian figures have been interesting, not in themselves, but as symbolic referents in a discourse about European civilization's virtues and vices" (50).

Herbert's depiction of Native peoples is significant to my project in that it shows an effect of moving from the deck of a steamer into a smaller boat—in this case a *bidarka*. Herbert must make this change to have access to game. She writes:

> *The greatest hardship on the voyage was the cramp in our limbs, a natural result from the awkward position a* bidarka *mariner must take up. The same little sinister Innuit paddled my craft daily, and at first I thought he was the ugliest living creature I had ever come across, but after glueing my eyes for days to the nape of his short neck, ringed round with creases, and catching a glimpse of his countenance as he half turned to the paddle, I got so used to this vision of hideousness that almost he seemed to climb to a pinnacle of ugliness, and tumble over to a Looking-Glass topsy-turvy world which returned him revivified and passable. (166-67)*

Herbert's removal from the home-like and relatively comfortable deck of the ship, where she and her party play cricket (37), may have been a "great hardship" on her limbs, but it seems to have uncramped a small corner of her mind. Functioning on the same level with a Native man in his *bidarka* for a stretch of time makes him appear "passable" to her; Collis' Natives, by contrast, are not even human. Herbert's stint in a small boat—which she claims to have become proficient in paddling—may have led her to grow slightly more generous in her constructions of Native women, whom she perceives as excellent mariners. "The Siwash ... women," she records, "do a great part of the work of paddling, and are very difficult indeed to tell from their lords and masters" (37). "The paddler seems one with the craft, the rhythm, the balance, and the easy grace is so perfect" (39). She notices that canoes headed across the Georgia Strait, carrying families to work the Fraser River for the salmon harvest, contain "the father of the family asleep, and the mother, the grandmother, and the daughters doing all the paddling amidships" (39). As do Meeker, Carr, and Scidmore, Herbert admires the power Native women hold through their maritime skill; she perceives paddling as an art, not as menial labor.

Herbert's account is an odd mix of feminine and anti-feminine discourse. She opens her work with the sentence: "My last book, which was the record of a shooting trip in Somaliland, has just been returned to me by a lady to whom I gave a copy, as she said she 'didn't like so much killing'" (11). Herbert disdains and distances herself from the woman's feminine emotionalism; regarding her project to hunt, she states: "We went to Alaska to shoot, and—we shot" (11). She is unapologetic to the tender-hearted reader she would bruise with her grisly descriptions. However, by the end of her account, she sentimentally emphasizes that this "Diana" was incomplete before gaining the love of the leader of the expedition:

> *Were the most wondrous trophies in all the world worth the price of so great a loneliness?*
> *The handle of the door turned, and the Leader of the expedition that was stood in the doorway. His eyes were smiling, smiling.*
> *Perhaps, perhaps, I'm not so very lonely after all. (256)*

Herbert visited the Northwest Coast and Kodiak at a time when Native people were perceived as "part of the scenery"; although the aboriginal population was declining rapidly, Native families and fishers were a common sight to the coastal traveler. Fifteen years later, when Kathrene Pinkerton (whose account I analyze in greater detail in the "pleasure craft account" section of chapter two and "an atavistic female instinct" section of chapter four) began cruising the coast, Native population levels had reached their historical low point. Popularized by photographer Edward S. Curtis, the myth of "the vanishing race" or "the disappearing Indian" also had a powerful hold on the imaginations of many White North Americans by this time (see Crosby 1991; Fulford 1993; Francis 1992; Hume 1988). This myth, in combination with an evolution in boat transportation for women and changing feminine discourse, led to the beginning of an identifiable "affiliation" with Natives in women boaters' accounts.

Kathrene Pinkerton's (1940) account of learning how to live "at home afloat" between 1924 and 1931—first aboard the thirty-six-foot cruiser *Yakima* (figure 8), then remodeling and living aboard the larger *Triton* (figure 9)—is made up of "impressions which had no place" in the collaborative research and writing she was doing with her husband. To finance their life on the water, the American couple wrote articles and novels. Pinkerton explains:

Robert had suggested I write facts and figures indexed under different headings—
fishing, logging, country, and boats. Finally when I became so fascinated by
impressions which had no place under these headings or in the ship's log, I began a
volume of my own. Robert jeered. [...]
 "Just write down facts I might forget," he said.
 One evening, in a carping spirit, he flipped over the pages of what I called
my personal log. Then he settled himself more comfortably, adjusted the light and
began to read. When I was ready for bed he was still reading.
 "This is stuff you'll always be glad to have," he said. "It doesn't make any
difference if you never use it. You've put the fun of two summers in words." (150)

Robert initially dismisses Pinkerton's desire to record memories that do not
fit neatly into useful categories, but later he understands the value of her discourse and perspective which, she frequently points out (see chapter two), are
very different from his male viewpoint. A Native woman she identifies as "Mrs.
Hunt"—described as very large and very friendly and unable to speak a word of
English—is one of these memories.

Tsukwani, or Francine Hunt (figure 14), was the second wife of George
Hunt, field assistant to the renowned ethnographer Franz Boas. According to
Ira Jacknis (1991), George Hunt was raised as a Native but "had not inherited
any Kwakiutl crests or ceremonial prerogatives. Instead, he gained most of his
[Native] privileges, and not a little ethnographic data, from his two Kwakiutl
wives, along with their expanding web of relatives" (181). George Hunt married
Francine in the second decade of the twentieth century, after the death of his first
wife. Both women supplied him with recipes he collected, "and from Francine
he learned much sacred material" (Jacknis 181).[20]

Pinkerton describes meeting Francine Hunt near Fort Rupert, on northern
Vancouver Island:

She motioned me to sit beside her while she wove clams on three long sticks. The
two outer sticks were thrust through the bodies or pillows of the clams, while
the necks were interlaced around the center stick. One clam was strung on top
of another. The plaiting was so beautifully regular that the finished product, a
braid of clams two feet long and six inches wide, looked like an elaborate piece
of knitting.
 I tried it but my plaited clams had great holes where I'd dropped clam stitches.
We squatted there together, plaiting, smoking and stopping occasionally to eat
a roasted clam. Talk was not necessary to establish a feeling of friendship and
understanding. (172-73)

---

20 Francine Hunt's image continues to be used in constructions of coastal Native culture, appear-
ing, for example, in the *Chiefly Feasts* exhibit of Kwakiutl culture sponsored by the American
Museum of Natural History. The exhibit toured New York, Victoria, San Francisco, Washington,
D.C., and Seattle from February 1992 to October 1994.

Figure 14. Tsukwani, or Francine Hunt, with her husband George in Fort Rupert, 1930 (J. B. Scott; photo courtesy of the American Museum of Natural History #32734).

What Pinkerton describes as an "understanding" between herself and Mrs. Hunt is probably largely the imagining of a tourist, made all the more romantic by Pinkerton's frequent warning that "Soon all this [culture] will be forgotten" (175).[21] Pinkerton's regular use of adjectives such as "sad," "lost," "decrepit," "torn," and "broken" (131) to describe the Native villages they visit as they journey between Puget Sound and Glacier Bay plays neatly into the myth of the disappearing Indian; as Marcia Crosby (1991) and Gordon Johnston (1987, 52) argue, we should recognize this kind of construction and resist the myth it supports—for indeed, Native people are "our" contemporaries, not symbols of the past. But Pinkerton's account does mark an important shift; she uses feminine discourse in a way that seeks to braid together the experiences of White and Native women, not to contrast herself against the perceived unfemininity or inadequacy of Native women.

---

21 Pinkerton's depiction of the moments she shared with Mrs. Hunt brings to mind Emily Carr's "dumb talk"—wordless understanding—in *Klee Wyck* (1941, 10). Carr too was strongly influenced by the myth of the disappearing Indian. However, unlike Pinkerton, Carr was a resident of the Northwest Coast and she reached this "understanding" not simply from a handful of visits with Natives but from long-lasting friendships with Natives such as "Sophie," to whom she dedicates *Klee Wyck*.

Pinkerton constructs her connections with specific Native women as experiences that challenge her complacency and cause her to rethink assumptions; in her account, this effect is described using a "typically feminine" domestic scene such as "weaving" smoked clams or discussing the most delicious recipe for crab. In a second example, she and her daughter, Bobs, eat hot boiled crab with aboriginal Mrs. Cadwallader and her children; White Mr. Cadwallader refuses to join them:

> *"He eats only at a table at regular meals," his wife said, as though explaining a quaint custom. "White men cool their crabs to lose the flavor and then put on mayonnaise to make up for the flavor they have lost. He says it's civilized to do it that way."*
>
> *I felt as sorry for him as she did. Elaborations had never seemed quite so idiotic. As I started on the second crab of my morning snack I seemed to remember some other self in a comment on the native's irregular meal hours. "It's either a feast or a famine, and they eat when game is caught." Now having sloughed layers of [white] tradition, I wondered vaguely why this had seemed so reprehensible. (176)*

In reading accounts of women who traveled by boat all over the world, I have found that women frequently depict themselves as hungry for communication with other females. These travelers are aware that women talk about different subjects than men. Pinkerton writes: "our talk ranged through women's topics—marriage, children, families, and, inevitably, recipes" (176). Women are aware that they can speak in ways that differ from masculine discourse. In *North-West by North: A Journal of a Voyage* (1935), Dora Birtles describes stopping at a South Pacific island in 1932 and her delight in the company and conversation of local White women:

> *The talk was a spate, it flowed out torrentially, questions stood out like boulders in it, answers and comments raced on, extended, swirled in explanation, reunited with the main stream. It was exhausting, all our woman-knowledge, woman quickness. [Ruth's] laughter was the ceaseless high spattering of rain on big leaves, mango leaves.*
>
> *We had a meal, a meal that women had made in a proper kitchen and served with refinement, poultry, potatoes, bread sauce, incomparable bread sauce, jelly, a paw-paw salad and little mince pies. Civilization breathed fragrantly from the little mince pies. (100-01)*

Like Pinkerton, Mrs. Hunt, and Mrs. Cadwallader, these White women also believe they share an "understanding" based on female domesticity. But Birtles does not share similar conversations or "understandings" with the Native women she meets. What sets Pinkerton apart here is that she learns not to seek a taste of European civilization in her meals and conversations with Native women, and she does not criticize or mock Native women for offering something different.

Figure 15. Muriel Wylie Blanchet in the wheelhouse of the *Caprice*. Photo courtesy of Janet Blanchet.

Discursively, Pinkerton is ambivalent. She oversimplifies and misrepresents Native women when she weaves them tidily into a narrative about White and Native common understanding. On the one hand she values traditional Native culture; when she hears that missionaries had tried to stop George Hunt from visiting elder Native women and writing a cookbook of Native recipes, she protests: "But this is valuable!" and "Don't let anyone stop you" (175). On the other hand she is confused about "the strange mingling of two cultures" (136) on the coast. She admits, "There is a difference of opinion as to what the white man has accomplished for the coast Indian. We heard both sides" (131). Her account is not free of racism, and she might be less interested in Native women if she did not perceive them as the last of a dying race and unthreatening to herself and her family. Regardless of this ambiguity, Pinkerton's *Three's a Crew* marks a point in the accounts of women traveling the Northwest Coast by boat where narrators *did* affiliate themselves with Native women and challenge the jeers of men who had no discursive category for such impressions.

Muriel Wylie Blanchet's (figure 15) *The Curve of Time* (1961) uses feminine discourse to explore Native culture and expose herself as the other within that world. Her book is prefaced with an emphasis that she has not written a story or a logbook: "it is just an account" (7) of the summer cruises she took as a widow with five children from their home in Victoria, up the Sunshine Coast in the 1920s and 1930s. Her emphasis that this is "just an account" seems less an apology than an appeal for readers to take this book on its own terms—to drop our expectations for history or precise factual accuracy and accept the teasing fantasy she introduces among her family's memories. Because she did not write her account until the late 1950s, there are fewer or more subtle limitations placed upon women's travel discourse; we are less apt than Victorian readers to question her identity or honesty if she is not preoccupied with morals and manners.

The Curve of Time deals with motherhood and being a mother at sea, and as the title suggests, it is also a rambling exploration into time. As she describes the family's travels aboard the twenty-five-foot cruiser *Caprice,* Blanchet recycles the myth of the vanishing Native. She writes: "we had made up our minds to spend part of the summer among the old villages with the big community houses, and try to recapture something of a Past [*sic*] that will soon be gone forever" (66). As she and her children near the villages, "we felt we were living in a different age—had perhaps lived there before ... perhaps dimly remembered it all" (66). Playing the role of the adventurer, she ignores notices and padlocks and invades winter villages while the Native inhabitants are away. "We played with their old boxes-for-the-dead," she writes, "trying to see if we could fit in" (77). Blanchet wants to believe she can be Indian, or at one point in time was Indian.

Throughout her account Blanchet refers back to the logbooks of male explorers, drawing attention to the way that she and they explore the same sites but with different priorities. For instance, George Vancouver was primarily concerned with charting the coast to increase England's claim to the region following the Nootka Sound incident. Blanchet's main project is the health, education, and happiness of her children. Unlike Captain Vancouver, "Capi" Blanchet and her children play and dream, and her account challenges the form of the traditional exploration log by consciously including fantasy and stories told to her children. Here she tries to imagine Native women on a hill beyond an uninhabited village:

> *It was harder to imagine the women. Perhaps they were shyer. I could only catch glimpses of them; they would never let me get very close. But later, on a sunny knoll on a bluff beyond the village, I surprised a group of the old ones. They were sitting there teasing wool with their crooked old fingers, their grey heads bent as they worked and gossiped—warming their old bones in the last hours of the sun. Then a squirrel scolded above my head; I started, and it was all spoiled.... And all around me, perhaps, the old women held their breath until this strange woman had gone. (78)*

Unlike Pinkerton's construction, which plaits together the White and Native women's common understanding, Blanchet's construction recognizes that she is a stranger, an outsider perhaps to be scolded. Through her imagination or intuition, she faces the knowledge that "I did not understand ... or never knew" Native culture (79), and that her White family "were just visitors" (103) in this place.

Blanchet, like Pinkerton, is ambiguous in depicting Native culture and her affiliation with it. She portrays that world as romantic and gentle, dangerous and horrifying. Native people in her account are less than real both because she visits only their uninhabited villages and because she constructs aboriginal people as limited to the past. This latter element is not especially unique in ethnography or literature. In *Time and the Other: How Anthropology Makes its Object,* Johannes Fabian (1983) criticizes the persistent and systematic tendency of ethnographers to place their referents in a time other than that of the producer of the discourse (31). One assigns conquered populations a different space (a reservation) and a different time (the past), and this ideology has political consequences:

> Neither political Space nor political Time are natural resources. They are ideologically construed instruments of power. Most critics of imperialism are prepared to admit this with regard to Space. It has long been recognized that imperialist claims to the right of occupying "empty," under-used, underdeveloped space for the common good of mankind should be taken for what they really are: a monstrous lie perpetuated for the benefit of one part of humanity, for a few societies of that part, and, in the end, for one part of these societies, its dominant classes. But by and large, we remain under the spell of an equally mendacious fiction: that interpersonal, intergroup, indeed, international Time is "public Time"—there to be occupied, measured, and allotted by the powers that be. (144)

When Blanchet constructs Native people as the embodiment of "the Past" [sic], she refuses to allow that these very real people are her contemporaries, alive and working in the summer fishery while she is fantasizing about them from their winter villages.

Margery Fee (1987) writes that in Canadian literature White narrators are often gripped by a strong desire to know more about the past, and they rely on identification with Natives to pursue this desire. Fee writes that Euro-Canadians typically appropriate Native culture to move from outsider to insider, from observer to participant, immigrant to "native" (16). I find Blanchet's account remarkable because at times it stops and questions this easy movement from outsider to insider and because it demonstrates how feminine discourse had changed from the turn of the century. While Scidmore and Collis use feminine discourse to label Native women as counterfeit, Blanchet uses it to expose the possibility that *she* is the fake, the counterfeit in this particular world. The space for this realization is opened up for her partly because boat transportation had changed by the 1920s (allowing White women closer access to Native culture), partly because the myth of the disappearing Indian made it safe for her and others to value that culture, and partly because feminine discourse itself had evolved away from a limited focus on morals and manners.

Looking at women boat tourists' constructions of Native women in the context of feminine discourse is a slippery project. A great deal has been written about the Victorian ideals of home and womanhood and about the specific discursive pressures working upon women at that time. But since the early twentieth century, it has become—many of us would argue, fortunately—more and more difficult to define the "feminine" and hence "feminine discourse." In *Gender Trouble: Feminism and the Subversion of Identity* (1990), poststructuralist Judith Butler shows that:

The very subject of woman is no longer understood in stable or abiding terms. There is a great deal of material that not only questions the viability of "the subject" as the ultimate candidate for representation or, indeed, liberation, but there is very little agreement after all on what it is that constitutes, or ought to constitute, the category of women. (1)

As Susan Brownmiller (1984) writes in *Femininity*, the romantic nostalgia of imposed limitations upon women is alive and well—especially in the advertising world. But feminism has developed a political language about gender that "refuses the fixed and transhistorical definitions of masculinity and femininity" (Kaplan 1986, 6). It becomes, then, difficult for me as a feminist to essentialize about what makes twentieth-century women's travel accounts clearly "feminine" in their discourse. However, to look at their constructions of Native women and *not* understand that they are the result of gendered perceptions and gendered language is to miss a significant level of their meaning.

While critics of the Victorian travel accounts of British women in Africa and Asia have found that feminine discourse afforded writers a means to question or transcend racism (by allowing White women to connect with Natives as individuals rather than as representatives of their race), my reading suggests that this was not the case along the Northwest Coast in the nineteenth century. Here, the feminine discourse of travelers, combined with the distancing effect of local steamship travel, led to the othering of Native women as "counterfeit" ladies. Not until well into the twentieth century, when forms of marine tourism evolved (allowing longer, closer contact) and feminine discourse moved away from its limiting focus on Christian morals and the cult of the home, would such "affiliations" even begin to be explored by female boat tourists in a Northwest Coast setting.

CHAPTER FOUR

"Getting Our Dresses Wet": Women, Girls, and the Natural Environment

Every few years my father threatens to sell *Klunk*, our boat. It costs too much to run it, he says, with gasoline so expensive. He does not want to stop boating; he just wants a smaller, faster, more economical vessel. Besides, he argues, my sister and I aren't home much to go out in the boat any more. I meet my father's threats to sell our *Klunk* with indignation and horror, because it is not just *a boat* to my mind: laden with memories, it represents years of family history. Although its function is to provide transportation, our boat is itself an important site—much like a family home.

As an academic, I see that my impulse to compare our boat to a home appears odd. Like a home, our boat has been a stable psychic and physical space—enduring cosmetic changes and the occasional mechanical update over the past thirty years. Its interior is essentially private, reserved for our family and those we choose to invite on board. It is a "homescape," providing stimulation, security, and identity (see Porteous 1990, 107), and it has its routines and its familiarity. Within academic discussions about the contemporary concept of home, home is fundamentally defined as "not away." Yet *Klunk*'s purpose is to take us away. Yi-Fu Tuan writes in *Topophilia* (1974) that "'Home' is a meaningless word apart from 'journey'" (102); J. Douglas Porteous (1990) notes "geographers have pointed out that a fundamental dialectic in human life is home/journey, what traditional geographers referred to as man moving and man at rest" (107).[1] Within the framework of these definitions, the pleasure craft becomes problematic—for, as a floating home, our boat is simultaneously home and away. To complicate matters, our boat disrupts another "fundamental dialectic in human life": that is, the home/nature polarity.

---

1 Porteous adds here: "This is a false dialectic. The true antinomy ... is between home and 'away'" (107).

The function of home as the opposing and defining polarity in relation to *both* travel and nature makes some sense in Western ideology. A consistent element in nature writing, from the grandfather of the genre (Gilbert White) to the present, has been "the search for a lost pastoral haven, for a home in an inhospitable and threatening world" (Finch and Elder 1990, 20). A touchstone idea for nature writers is the idea of a return to nature and the restoration of a previously harmonious relationship between "man" and nature. Some nature writers and critics of nature writing use a Christian model of restoration; Thomas Lyon (1991), for example, argues that the point of nature writing is to critique how "we continue to live a wrong way of life" (6) and to restore a relationship with the environment such as the one before "the Fall," when Adam and Eve were evicted from Eden and forced to wander in search of a compromised home beyond its gate. Other nature writers evoke non-Western religion and myth as paths that can lead humanity back to a garden home, saving us from the hopelessness and homelessness of modernity.

The homeless condition of modern "man" has been well articulated; he is "placeless, constantly in flux" and wandering in "a world whose inhabitants are frequently rootless and often, in the sense of community membership, homeless too" (Porteous 9). This "rootless" condition of modern "man" (a metaphor suggesting both movement and disconnection from the earth) links both travel and nature as "away from home." But I think gender is overlooked here. Travel is an activity that has been relatively and historically closed to women (see Morris 1992). Moreover, discussions of home that focus only on exile, homeland, and alienation completely overlook how a large percentage of women continue to experience the idea of home—through domestic labor. To stretch the metaphor, women are frequently not only rooted, but root-bound in the ideology of the home. In a consideration of homes and journeys, Patricia Mills (1987) suggests that man's thirst for travel and mobility can only be understood in juxtaposition to woman's immobility. Discussing the mythological voyage of Odysseus away from his wife, Penelope—who remains at home and devoted to him—Mills writes:

> If Penelope were to journey with a crew of women ... Odysseus' journey would have neither source nor goal, neither origin nor telos. Thus, the quest of male recognition, the journey through alienation to a return, requires that woman not experience the journey. (190)

These ideological polarities of modern life are not my main concern, but they are an important context for this work. As I have shown, women boat travelers repeatedly return to an impulse—once they enter the masculine space of the boat—to define themselves as "at home afloat." This sense of being at home while simultaneously away—in a watery "wilderness" of sorts along the Northwest Coast—is my point of departure. In this chapter, I explore the contradictions and patterns that can arise as a result of experiencing the natural world as a female "at home afloat." Bringing her gender-specific role on board with her, a woman may travel through seascape and wilderness, but her experience in it can be limited significantly to the confines of the galley (see chapter two). Nevertheless, women boaters *do* emerge from below the decks. In this chapter I analyze what they see then and how they ascribe meaning to the natural environment, understanding that the longstanding associations between woman and nature, and woman and home, have important implications in this exploration.

Home/Nature/Woman

Because our boat was my strongest link to the natural environment, and because I thought of the boat as an extension of my family home, I was initially baffled by writers and philosophers who describe a "home versus nature" polarity. Richard Nelson's *The Island Within* (1989), a sensitive and poetic account of his experiences visiting the unspoiled ecosystem of an unnamed island in Haida Strait, articulates this separation between home and nature. His account, in particular, challenged me to consider the implications of gender in the home/nature dichotomy.

Traveling many times to the Northwest Coast island to camp, hunt, and meditate, Nelson writes that his "heart is torn between the island and home" (59). Describing the split he perceives between home and nature, he writes:

> It gives me such pleasure to be here with this woman and child, the crux of human love that sustains me as surely as food and air. But deep inside, I feel an ache, an emptiness.... Sometimes I feel torn between a desire to give more of myself to the island and a need to give it less, torn between two compelling loves, unable to imagine living without them both, struggling to find a balance that allows both to flourish.... I ponder these conflicting absolutes, and wonder again about the accident of being born to a culture that separates nature and home. (123)

On the island he feels "burdened by the shapeless desire that brings me here. Yet each day at home I long for the island" (163); this agonizing imbalance may stem from "a deeper need—to keep the wild, natural world clearly separated from that which is tamed, subdued, and controlled" (190). Traveling in a skiff one evening with his wife and son, Nelson voices once again this "deeper need" to separate distinctly home and nature:

> Homebound on the smooth waters of Haida Strait. Late evening sun distends above the sea horizon. The boat slices across reflections of purple sky, as if we'll soar across the mainland's snowy peaks and continue toward the newly risen moon.
>
> Ethan nestles among the mounds of rolled sleeping bags, lost in a young fisherman's dreams. Nita's cold hand curls inside mine. She looks ahead, toward the lights of town, anticipating her cozy little house. I turn and watch longingly behind. (143)

This passage connotes the tension between two individuals: one drawn toward civilization, culture, comfort, home; the other pulled in the opposite direction toward wilderness, freedom, danger, nature. On a more symbolic level, it illustrates Nelson's own ambivalence: which direction shall he ultimately choose for his life? This ambivalence—the longing to be a part of nature (the guilt of leaving his home and family behind), and the longing to go home (the sense that he is missing, dismissing nature if he chooses home)—saturates his experiences of the natural environment and of home.

While "man" has been struggling with a sense of alienation, a result of his perceived separation from home and separation from nature (leaving him caught, as Nelson describes, between the two), "woman" conversely struggles against her conflation with, rather than separation from, both home and nature. In *Woman and Nature: The Roaring Inside Her* (1978), Susan Griffin outlines the history of Western patriarchal thought regarding woman and nature. Showing how woman has been associated with nature, the emotional, the material, and the particular, and how man has been associated with culture, the rational, the nonmaterial, and the abstract, Griffin questions the false polarities that have allowed traits associated with man to be systematically privileged. In *Nature, Culture and Gender* (1980), Carol MacCormack examines these widely accepted dualisms, which, by the twentieth century, made the link between nature and femaleness seem "quite logical for us now" (6). Tracing the woman-as-nature association back to the eighteenth century, MacCormack describes some of the effects of that association:

> *We allocate honour and prestige to people of science and industry who excel in understanding and controlling the powerful domain of nature. We also honour people who overcome animal urges, curbing these urges in accordance with moral codes. When women are defined as "natural" a high prestige or even moral "goodness" is attached to men's domination over women, analogous to the "goodness" of human domination of natural energy sources. (6)*

Carolyn Merchant carries this idea further when she argues in *The Death of Nature* (1980) that the dualism placing nature and woman on one side and culture and man on the other "is a key factor in Western civilization's advance at the expense of nature" (143). While Merchant emphasizes the significance of language as an indication of how a culture values nature,[2] Mary Daly, in *Gyn/Ecology* (1978), promotes new uses of language to resist and deconstruct the "patriarchal myth and language" (9) that lead to the destruction of nature and the destruction of women.

In 1974, Françoise d'Eaubonne (trans. 1980) introduced the term "ecofeminism" (or, *eco-feminisme* in the original) into conversations about ecological

---

2 Merchant writes: "Because language contains a culture within itself, when language changes, a culture is changing in important ways. By examining changes in descriptions of nature, we can then perceive something of the changes in cultural values" (4).

politics. In the decades since then, many ecofeminists and their critics have grappled with definitions of the term and with the negative and positive aspects of ecofeminist philosophies. [3] Victoria Davion (1994) gets to the heart of the matter when she writes that:

> *Whatever else their disagreements, ecofeminists agree that the domination of nature by human beings comes from a patriarchal world view, the same world view that justifies the domination of women. Because both dominations come from the same world view, a movement to stop devaluing nature should, by demands of consistency, include a movement against the domination of women. (10)*

Ecofeminist thinking is significant to my project in two ways. First, it is that same world view (a view that is, of course, held by both men and women) that has, to a large degree, made women "naturally" responsible for homemaking and domestic labor on shore and at sea. That responsibility has had a significant effect on women's experiences in nature. In *Made From This Earth: American Women and Nature* (1993), Vera Norwood demonstrates how the ideology of the home shaped women's nature writing: "Focusing on the environment, making it one's familiar home, has been key to woman's appreciation of nature" (xviii). From 1850 to 1970, she writes, the defining feature of women's nature writing

> *... is the act of homing in on one spot, living with it through the seasons until the rocks, flowers, trees, insects, birds, deer, panthers, and coyotes are family. Enfolded within women's family, carrying the emotional weight of home, American flora and fauna are due the same consideration as human members of the household. (52)*

Because my project is a study of travel narratives, the writers are not always able to "home in" on one spot; as tourists, they move through shifting scenes and usually cannot, for instance, describe how seasons or years alter a landscape or a seascape. Nevertheless, the ideology of the home finds its way into these accounts when women "home in" on a particular feature of the environment that brings home to mind (for example, in the repeated and detailed attention given to flowers). In a rare mention of women in relation to water, Norwood notes how limited their participation has been: "Clearly, when women went into the ocean, they carried with them the responsibilities of home. They were not explorers, but wives and mothers who kept their priorities straight even under water" (165). This ideology of the home shows itself when women traveling

---

3 See for example *Reweaving the World* (Diamond and Orenstein 1990), *Rethinking Ecofeminist Politics* (Biehl 1991), *Woman and Nature: Literary Reconceptualizations* (Devine 1992), *Feminism and the Mastery of Nature* (Plumwood 1993), *Ecological Feminism* (Warren 1994), *Ecofeminist Theory: A Bibliography* (Nordquist 1994), and *Literature, Nature, and Other: Ecofeminist Critiques* (Murphy 1995).

the Northwest Coast carefully include images of home in descriptions of "wilderness" environments. In *The Cruise of the U.S. Steamer "Rush"* (1889), for instance, Isabel Shepard describes "the clear, pale-green sea-water, through which I could see the white bottom, with here and there patches of moss and sea-weed. A short distance away was the *Rush*, a little piece of home in that lone landscape" (198). Shepard's attention to the nearness and comfort of home in a foreign and wild environment is part of a larger pattern in many women's travel accounts of the region.

Ecofeminism and the deconstruction of the woman-as-nature association is significant to my project on a second and more subtle level. Ecofeminism asks, why is woman associated with nature, and what is the effect? I want to refine that question by considering the slippage that comes with the term "nature." "Nature" can denote the external world in its entirety, but the word "earth" is frequently substituted in texts that consider woman's relationship to nature: consider *Sisters of the Earth* (Anderson 1991) and *Made From This Earth* (Norwood 1993). Earth, in these instances, is no doubt meant to signify the planet or even to allude to Gaia. But earth, of course, also means areas of land, distinguishable from water or air; more specifically, it is cultivable soil. In that easy slippage from "nature" to "land" or "soil" is an important point. Woman has not only been associated with nature; her perceived familiar terrain is soil. As a society, we feel comfortable placing her there.[4] So my question becomes: Given woman's association with the *land*, how does that association influence her participation in, and descriptions of, marine environments?

When I began reading for this project, I expected to find an abundance of women's descriptions of the sea and of their relationship with waterscapes. What I have learned is that the sea remains an unfamiliar "landscape" for many women. Because women have not, until recently, been allowed to go to sea as active participants, the element remains largely beyond their experience. Literature about the sea is overwhelmingly male-authored; there is no female Odysseus or Ishmael. In the last decade of the twentieth century, the American Littoral Society published *The Seaside Reader* (Bennett 1992) with twenty-six selections—only one authored by a woman.[5] Bert Bender's 1988 study of American stories set at sea includes no primary texts by female authors. Melody Graulich's (1996) essay on nineteenth-century "women's sea literature" points out that this body of literature "does contrast with male tradition"; she writes that the difference is marked by female authors' focus on the shore, islands, and reefs—rather than on the sea itself (206).

Women who have beaten the odds and work at sea dwell on their connections to the land. Joan Skogan (1992), for instance, writes: "I never yearn for home when I am at sea, but the land sometimes reaches out for me, insisting

---

4 Annette Kolodny has written about the significance of metaphors regarding woman and land in *The Lay of the Land* (1975) and *The Land Before Her* (1984).

5 The single selection from a woman is "Winds Blowing Seaward" by Rachel Carson, who is undoubtedly the greatest exception to my argument that women, to date, tend not to write about

that I remember" (133). Gladys Hindmarch (*The Watery Part of the World* 1988), who worked as a cook and messgirl for Northland Navigation in British Columbia, shows how important land is through her character Jan's seascape aesthetic. In a rare moment when Jan is not peeling potatoes, scouring the floor, or defending herself from male workers attempting to sit on her lap, she stands on deck and admires

> ... *streams [of silt] in the water: wide bands of browny-green fanning out from the Fraser River amongst bluer, non-river strips of ocean water. I love that, ... seeing the Fraser mud in the ocean....The mud here, good soil, is washed down from the interior, from places like Osoyoos and Summerland and Kamloops, brought down by the Thompson and Similkameen to flow into the Fraser to form part of the delta or to settle in the inlet or to drift out to the Gulf.*
>
> *I feel like it's part of me and I want to merge with it, to swim among the particles in the ocean of everchanging water and light. (140)*

Jan's desire is to merge not with the briny salt water but with the near-shore water close to her home, where salt water mixes and melds with fresh water and soil.

Despite the obvious connection women's bodies share with lunar and tidal cycles, salt-water imagery and seascape are not standard elements in women's literature. Instead, female novelists, poets, and critics who use salt-water imagery tend to be radical and experimental writers; their subject is frequently women who extend themselves beyond boundaries (often feminists, proto-feminists, and lesbians).[6] Their telling and their style also challenge how dominant culture tells its stories. French feminist critic Hélène Cixous experiments this way, emphasizing the significance of the mother's womb: "It is within this space that Cixous's speaking subject is free to move from one subject position to another, or to merge oceanically with the world" (Moi 1985, 117). Canadian poet Daphne Marlatt (1991) prefaces *Salvage*, her unconventional collection of poems, with this explanation: "These are littoral poems, shoreline poems—and by extension the whole book—written on that edge where a feminist consciousness floods the structures of patriarchal thought" (unpaginated). She writes that "working on these poems felt aquatic: i was working with subliminal currents in the movements of language, whose direction as 'direction' only became apparent as i went with the drift, no matter how much flotsam seemed at first to be littering the page." Marine metaphors in her poetry speak of breaking down—or perhaps washing away—the grammatical and formal boundaries of language and the restrictiveness of "home":

---

6 Kate Chopin's protagonist in *The Awakening* (1899), for example, "was beginning to realize her position in the universe as a human being [not simply a housewife]"; Edna Pontellier hears "the voice of the sea [which] is seductive; never ceasing, whispering, clamoring, murmuring, inviting the soul to wander for a spell in the abysses of solitude; to lose itself in mazes of inward contemplation" (1,005). Yet even in her suicide by drowning, Edna's final thoughts are of a garden with bees and flowers: "There was the hum of bees, and the musky odor of pinks filled the air" (1,102). Earthy imagery seems necessary here, even in narrating a woman's death by *drowning*.

vi

imagine her in her element. not to be taken in
its restrictive sense as home (is her, closed in).

in her element in other words. blurring the
boundary. it's not that she wants to blur difference, to pretend that out is in, already past
the gate she's past his point of view as central
(hook/lure) to a real she eludes,

free, she multiplies herself in any woman paces
the inside of her mind her skin half in half out
of the common air she drifts along. casting a
thought receives it back this we of an eye com-
plicit in a smile she gathers fish-quick, taking
the measure of their plural depth she who with
every step and never once (-over). desires in
the infinitive to utter (outer) her way through:
litter. wreckage. salvage of pure intent

Contemporary Canadian novelists Hindmarch, Margaret Atwood (*Surfacing*,
1972), and Audrey Thomas (*Intertidal Life*, 1984) all offer deconstructive narratives that pull the solid ground out from beneath the feet of readers. In Thomas'
novel, for instance, the last we know of the heroine, Alice, is her experience
of being "submerged" by an anaesthetic before undergoing surgery—we never
learn the outcome of the operation: "She just didn't care. Floating. Floating. But
not facedown, not the dead man's float. Or not yet, ha ha. Floating down the
hall, horizontal woman" (280). As Alice passes out, the doctor observes: "She's
under now. Let's go" (281).

In "Staking Claims for No Territory: The Sea as Woman's Space" (1994),
Anca Vlasopolos traces a history of such "metaphoric openings to the sea" (73)
in the nineteenth- and early twentieth-century literary works of Jane Austen,
Virginia Woolf, and Kate Chopin. She argues that in their stories the sea represents "the promise of unfettered possibilities outside patriarchy" and becomes
a "nonterritory" of "unexplored depths" where heroines can "[let] go of social
moorings." Her conclusion, that "All three novelists resolutely turn away from
traditional closures, requiring us not merely to read 'beyond the ending' but
to recognize the dead end for women of customary generic conclusions" (86),
could as easily speak for Thomas, Atwood, and Marlatt. These experimental
writers share an interest in the political and metaphorical uses of what they
believe is a limitless and unpolluted region (the sea). They have little interest
in, or knowledge of, the real limits placed upon women who share marine
environments with men (see chapter two). Instead, through their metaphors,
they voice a rejection of and alternative to the traditional metaphors used in

male-authored literature. Symbolized as both "our great sweet mother (*la mer/la mère*)" and "the grey sunken cunt of the world," the sea—like woman—has been constructed as simultaneous opposites, standing for "both the idea of nature as complex inexhaustible life and the threat of individual extinction through engulfment" (van Boheemen 1987, 182).[7] These extreme symbols are not based upon women's experiences at sea. Linked fundamentally to the idea of the home, Western women have only relatively recently enjoyed the freedom to travel "the watery part of the world"; once there, they are likely to encounter the same attitudes and play the same roles they play on land. It is therefore no surprise that of the experimental writers I have discussed here, Gladys Hindmarch (who worked at sea) is alone in depicting in her text the difficult and gender-stereotyped work that women perform at sea. Quantitatively, women's literature remains poised at the edge of the water and has not come much closer, even in this century, to exploring women's real experiences in marine environments. Vlasopolos admits "We remain in the dark" (78) when we look to literature about the lives of women who accompanied men to sea.

Women travel writers viewing the mixed landscape/seascape of the Northwest Coast have chosen to write about the land. It is the more familiar ground: they know better how to describe it, how to differentiate its features. These travelers tend to write about seasickness rather than explore the angle of foam blown off a whitecap or the shade of green in the trough of a wave. This is not true of all women, of course. But for the woman who has learned to identify her place as on land, the sea appears monotonous, foreign, vague, and beyond her powers of description.

Indescribable Landscapes

"'Viewing' landscape," writes Audrey Kobayashi (1989), "is a selective process"; for although "landscape" suggests total environment, "all concepts of landscape are ideologically laden and rooted in specific historical circumstances" (168). The modern concept of landscape refers to a way of seeing the world, "a way of situating oneself simultaneously inside and outside the frame, of arranging a composition before oneself as a viewer and surrendering oneself to the pleasures of the gaze" (Gregory 1992, 292). A concept transplanted from Holland to England in the sixteenth century, landscape has come to mean "a prospect seen from a specific standpoint" (Tuan 1974, 133). As Derek Gregory (1992) reminds us, it has also come to carry "implications of power, domination, and representation" (292). The very creation of landscape is a "process by which human beings produce and reproduce their lives" (Kobayashi 177).

---

7 Unlike the land, the sea is variously associated with both feminine and masculine attributes. For instance, Herman Melville describes "the masculine sea," a "robust and man-like sea [which] heaved with long, strong, lingering swells, as Samson's chest in his sleep" (*Moby-Dick* 649). At the conclusion of James Joyce's *Finnegans Wake*, the river ALP flows into the ocean, the "cold mad feary father" at the moment of death (van Boheemen 182). In the Northwest, Theodore Winthrop (1862) describes the Columbia River as "born to full manhood" (5).

Our sense of place is also a narrative construction (see Ryden 1993, 77); "landscape too is a form of language," writes Kobayashi (164). In a consideration of the journals of Arctic explorers, Barry Lopez (1986) writes about how observations and desires for the landscape become entangled through language:

> Try as we might, we ultimately can make very little sense at all of nature without resorting to such devices [as metaphor]. Whether they are ... bald assertions of human presence ... or the intangible, metaphorical tools of the mind—contrast, remembrance, analogy—we bring our own worlds to bear in foreign landscapes in order to clarify them for ourselves. It is hard to imagine that we could do otherwise. (221)

Despite the notion that tourists experience nature and landscape more simplistically than do explorers or Natives (see Tuan, 63 and 95), the narratives of women traveling the Northwest Coast by boat suggest a great deal about these women's relationships with the regional environment. The manner in which landscapes are both expressed and omitted in these travelogues allows us to locate different standpoints afloat, evoking pieces of "the worlds" women brought to bear in this particular environment.

In the accounts of relatively early female travelers to the region, the emphasis is on human—rather than natural—landscapes. Frances Barkley, for example, who traveled the Northwest Coast in 1787 and 1792 aboard her husband's trading ship, the *Imperial Eagle*, wrote pages about local Natives but virtually nothing about the biophysical world she experienced (Hill 1978). [8] Most of Barkley's journal was lost; however, in 1901 a Captain Walbran published an account "taken chiefly from the original diary" of Barkley. It is worth noting that the limited reference to her sense of landscape focuses on a connectedness to homeland (Britain) and people she knows, not on physical space or place. Walbran records: "Mrs. Barkley notes that in King George's Sound, as she always called Nootka, the climate was the same as in Scotland" (Hill 1978, 35). She concerns herself with recording the names of people for whom the landscape is renamed, rather than descriptions of any topography beyond a "snug" harbor, and she leaves sketching or map making to her husband:

> There was Frances Island, after myself; Hornby peak, also after myself; Cape Beale after our purser; Williams point and a variety of other names, all of which were familiar to us. We anchored in a snug harbour in the island, of which my husband made a plan as far as his knowledge of it would permit. The anchorage was near a large village, and therefore we named it Village Island. (Hill 1978, 37)

When Lady Franklin and her niece, Sophia Cracroft, [9] made their second visit to the coast in 1870, descriptions of natural settings are exceedingly rare in the

---

8 See Frances Barkley, "Reminiscences 1836 Transcript." British Columbia Archives and Records Service, Victoria. A/A/30/B24A.

published journal. Occasional references to the natural environment describe it vaguely as "lovely," while the human environment is offered in specific detail:

> MAY 12. *We anchored in the Harbour at 4 A.M. and on going upon deck, the scene was certainly very lovely. We were near the shore, and the buildings were very distinct—some evidently left by the Russians, colored yellow, with red roofs, with the Dome & Spire (painted green as usual) of the Russian Church, the Indian village being entirely separate. (Cracroft 1)*

The "lovely" aspect of the scene above is enhanced by "noble mountains" show-ing "far away"—their very (safe) distance suggesting their quality as a back-drop to the scene.[10] Further down the page, the journal mentions "a cluster of rocky islets, guarding the harbour to seaward, and from their number *as well as in other ways*, reminding us of the 1000 islands of the St. Lawrence" (1, my emphasis). Here the "rocky islets" are significant to the writer because they appear to guard the inhabited harbor of Sitka, and because they remind her of the more familiar landscape of the St. Lawrence River. Most significantly, Cracroft is without words to describe the islets themselves; they remind her and Lady Franklin of another landscape "in other ways," possibly beyond her powers of description. Wayne Franklin (1979), in his look at the rhetoric of early explorers[11] in the Americas, concludes that early European travelers "were agreed about the inexpressible quality" of the New World (19).

On their earlier visit to the region in 1861, Cracroft and Franklin traveled aboard the Hudson's Bay Company's *Otter* to the mouth of the Fraser River. In another rare description of the natural environment, Cracroft writes: "We had a beautiful view of the mountains as we crossed the Georgian Gulf & entered the Fraser river between low banks covered with tawny reeds, which looked like tracts of cornland ready for harvest" (D.B. Smith 1974, 38). Here she spends more time with a description of the natural environment, appreciating the pas-toral "low banks" and "tawny reeds," virtually transforming a seascape into a *land*scape with imagined "tracts of cornland ready for harvest." Recognizing features of this environment that quite conceivably remind her of her British homeland, Cracroft appears to take more interest in the scene and is able to articulate this particular landscape in greater detail. Relying heavily on meta-phor, she brings her own world into the Fraser River, an act that serves to enhance the colonial aspect of the region (by superimposing the homeland onto the environment) and to suggest her disinterest in or discomfort with seascapes. As Tuan discusses in *Topophilia* (1974), humans of various cultures, periods, and even genders have "canons" of beauty in landscape; clearly for nineteenth-century women travelers, a human element was highly desirable in forming

---

9 These travelers have been introduced in previous chapters as indicated by the index.

10 In an overview of Victorian discovery rhetoric, mary Louise Pratt (1992) notes that landscaptes are typically ordered "in terms of background, foreground, symmetries" (204)—much as Cracroft has done here.

attractive landscapes. That was certainly the case for E. Katharine Bates, who cruised to Alaska in 1889; she writes: "Sitka is by far the most beautifully situated of all the Alaska towns, as it is also the cleanest and most civilized looking" (249).

Women boat travelers of the nineteenth and early twentieth centuries struggled to describe the natural landscapes of the Northwest Coast—even if they had been raised in North America. Following Barkley and Cracroft, many steamship tourists claimed to be incapable of articulating landscapes; those who tried leaned heavily on metaphor and simile—comparing the scenery to more familiar places—or fell into a morass of vague and superlative clichés. The farther north one traveled, the more difficult the task of translating landscape into words; as the mountains grew higher, the glaciers nearer, and the tides steeper, the landscape seemed more foreign and the "Northland" clichés became closer at hand. In 1885, Eliza Scidmore, the American writer for *National Geographic* whose work I examined in chapter three, exclaimed: "Words and dry figures can give one little idea of the grandeur of this glacial torrent flowing steadily and solidly into the sea, and the beauty of the fantastic ice front, shimmering with all the prismatic hues, is beyond imagery or description" (135). Many other women travelers—usually not professional writers such as Scidmore—commented on their inability to capture the landscape with language. Traveling to the Bering Sea, Isabel Shepard writes in 1889 that "It was beyond description beautiful; none but the pen of a Ruskin could do it justice" (198). That same year, Matilda Barns Lukens took a train north to Tacoma, where she and her husband boarded the *Corona* for an Alaskan cruise; in reference to Mount Rainier she notes: "Language is inadequate to give an idea of its grandeur" (2). Farther north she writes: "Above the timber line there is a space of the most brilliant green, which, as the sun shines on it, seems to have a sheen like velvet; above this is the dazzling snow. Words are inadequate to describe the effects of these contrasts" (31). Upon sighting her first glacier, she records that "the grandeur exceeded anything I had ever seen" and that "a clearness indescribable pervaded the atmosphere" (34). Traveling to Alaska in 1892, Mary Holbrook describes the landscape as "'Alps on Alps,' the *whole horizon* majestic and beautiful beyond my power to describe!" (3, her emphasis).[12] Emma Boyd adds a similar protest in her 1909 travelogue but attempts a detailed description nonetheless:

No description of mine could adequately convey the beauty of it, when the sun had set and the sea and sky seemed like a vision of light and colour. Pale gold, ruddy gold, lavender, pink, and soft shades, as of a bird's egg, melted into each other in radiant harmony; while a silver thread of the day-old moon added the last touch of perfection to the picture. (97-98)

---

12 Mary H. Holbrook. "Jottings By the Way." 1892. British Columbia Archives and Records Service, Victoria. NWp/971M/H724j [unpublished brochure, offered as a souvenir to friends].

During several cruises in the 1930s, Rebie Harrington was left generally speechless by the views from her ship; departing Sitka, she writes that the scenery must be seen to be appreciated: "One may describe it; one may photograph it; but neither words nor lens could possibly do justice to these most beautiful scenes" (71).

The "indescribableness" of these landscapes results, in part, from some of the writers' inexperience with writing and also from a desire for emphasis—the landscape is simply "too beautiful for words." But the ineffability of this particular geography was also a result of the lack of popular coastal travel writing; no one had yet definitively prescribed how the landscape *should* be viewed and described. Although she researched Alaska history and was quite familiar with the journals of coastal explorers, Scidmore writes: "There was something, too, in the consciousness that so few had ever gazed upon the scene before us, and there were neither guides nor guide books to tell us which way to go, and what emotions to feel" (139).

Women did know how to feel about other, more familiar places—even if they learned of them through novels or encyclopedias. One descriptive technique, then, was to compare scenery—especially Alaskan scenery—to more familiar terrain, even if the point would be only to conclude that Alaska was "like no place else on Earth." The comparison, it seems, at least allowed a starting point for description. Early in her narrative, Scidmore compares the scenery to the Sierras, to Pike's Peak, to a Florida swamp; she shows how much bigger the scenery is than that of Massachusetts, New Jersey, or even Texas (3). Lukens compares a sunset at Active Pass to a comparable scene in Venice (19), Mount Edgecombe to Vesuvius (41), and Johnstone Strait to the scenery "on the Hudson in the neighborhood of West Point" (20). Boyd makes the frequently made comparison: "It was just like a Norwegian Fiord" (97).

Writing in *A Woman's Trip to Alaska* (1890), Septima Collis—an author whose work I examine in greater detail in chapter three and who is pictured in figure 11—gazes at the landscape through half-closed eyes and writes as if it triggers memories or fantasies of well-known and very well-traveled European and American terrain. Using a heavy hand with similes, she writes:

> I see miles and miles of mountain and table-land covered with snow, the depth of which can be appreciated with the naked eye; there they stand like the palace abodes of some giant race with their facades of purest marble, their turrets, their windows, and their towers; my imagination takes me to Greece, and I stand below the steps of the Acropolis; I am once more in Rome, entranced by the silent magnificence of the Coliseum, and as we pass around the point of another island and I get a glimpse of what looks to me like an avalanche of snow curving over a shelving rock into the abyss below, I think of home and our own Niagara. (72-73)

Fantasy landscapes, fairylands, and wonderlands are not uncommon descriptors. Scidmore offers this vision of the sea at night:

If the beautiful Gulf of Georgia is wonderland and dreamland by day, it is often fairyland by night, and there was an appropriate finale to the last cruise, when the captain came down the deck at midnight and rapped up the passengers. "Wake up! The whole sea is on fire" said the commander. We roused and flung open stateroom doors and windows to see the water shining like a sheet of liquid silver for miles on every side. The water around us was thickly starred with phosphorescence, and at a short distance, the million points of light mingled in a solid stretch of miles of pale, unearthly flame. (296)

Lukens agrees that the coastal traveler was "very far away from the every-day world" (37), and the Alaska Steamship Company would capitalize on the fantastic image in promotional material, claiming: "Within three days' travel from Seattle the pleasure seeker steps ashore in a country which is a fairyland of agreeable surprises and where the true stories of the golden wealth [sic] read like the fanciful and Oriental tales of the Arabian Nights."[13]

"Sublime" is a word commonly connected with the landscape by late nineteenth- and early twentieth-century women boat travelers. It is a word with a history on this coast, having been employed by George Vancouver during his 1792 charting expedition.[14] Vancouver (1984)—impressed by the pastoral aspect of Whidbey Island—used the term to describe the more dramatic landscape farther up the coast. His use of the "sublime" is in keeping with Edmund Burke's definitions, which are based upon John Dennis' "delightful Horrour" and "terrible joy" while viewing mountain scenery in 1688, and James Thompson's connection between sublimity and terror (Boulton 1987, xviii). Vancouver's use of the term connotes simultaneous fear and pleasure felt in the presence of awesome power, while the more recent use of the term connotes exhilaration and exaltation felt in the presence of a God who is demonstrating his goodness and strength through landscape. Abby Johnson Woodman (1889), one of the relatively early women boat tourists on the coast, uses the term in the more traditional sense. Describing a storm that hits the ship just north of Dixon's Entrance, she writes:

The wind was right against us in our course, and actually howled about the ship and whistled in her rigging. The storm continued to increase for more than an hour; the wind held steady, and the ship rose and pitched with every swell, cutting the deep troughs between with unfaltering progress.

The scene was truly a sublime one. I watched the force of the storm upon the ocean until past ten o'clock. (194-95)

---

13 Alaska Steamship Company (Seattle). "A Trip to Wonderful Alaska." MDCCCCVI [sic]. Facsimile 1965, The Shorey Book Store, Seattle, SJS#63. Univ. of British Columbia Special Collections, Vancouver. SPAM 13281.

14 For a discussion of eighteenth-century coastal explorers' attitudes toward landscape, see Tippett and Cole (1977) and Short and Neering (1992).

As more women discovered and described the Northwest Coast, "that sublime land" (Higginson 1906, 338) grew to be a well-worn phrase, in company with "grand" and "majestic" but carrying the additional weight of evangelical Christian ideology. As Christian women (a number of them missionaries) gazed upon the indescribable landscape, it became "God's great masterpiece" (Harrington 1937, 23) and "God's out-of-doors" (French 1923, 7), a paradise and a spectacle. Viewed from the raised deck of a steamship, the "matchless panorama" appeared "like the dawn of creation in some new paradise" (Scidmore 1885, 21). Matilda Lukens (1889) describes how, standing on deck viewing a glacier, she feels as if she is "standing in the audience chamber of the Creator, and looking upon a new creation" (37). This sense of distance and visualism is not limited to overtly religious narratives such as Lukens'. In her unpublished "Diary of a Voyage Around Vancouver Island 1879,"[15] Mary Wilson describes the sense of pleasure and spectatorship she feels from deck while watching an "immense brush fire" burn on shore. The captain apparently gave orders to the crew members to anchor so that passengers could enjoy the view. Wilson writes: "So we had a good view of it and it was certainly a splendid sight to see the fire in all its wild grandeur leaping and running as it willed no fire hose here to throw black jets or fire-men yelling and swearing but all was quiet as the grave" (unpaginated).

Viewing nature from a built platform, perhaps forty feet above the water and acres—even miles—from shore, steamship passengers tend to share a particular pose or standpoint in their depiction of landscape. Mary Louise Pratt (1992) names such depictions "the monarch-of-all-I-survey scene[s]." She argues that in British texts of this style, commonly used referents (such as "pearly," "snowy," "sedgy," and "emerald") work to "tie the landscape explicitly to the explorer's *home* culture, sprinkling it with some little bits of England" (204, my emphasis). The terms these steamship tourists frequently reach for—"splendid," "grand," "beautiful," "majestic," "sublime"—suggest both their unfamiliarity with seascapes and their desire to apply domestic—that is, nationalistic—hyperbole to a relatively "unwritten" landscape. Americans, particularly, were traveling to Alaska to inspect the new colony, and that goal shaped the landscapes they recreated on the page. Even if they could not find words for the place, they saw "home" in it and claimed it as theirs: "I never saw anything that approaches this scene," writes Lukens, "how proud I feel that it belongs to us, that I have an individual share in it" (37).

Women who ventured into launches and rowboats, which brought them closer to the natural world, would offer more concrete and specific descriptions of landscapes. Scidmore (1885), for example, describes "rowing close in where the menzie and merton spruce formed a dense golden-green wall" (268). As women came closer to shore and planted their feet on dry land, their depictions of nature grew more explicit and sure. Not only did women become participants

---

15 Wilson, Mary. "Diary of a Voyage Around Vancouver Island 1879." Olive Wilson Heritage Collection, Box 1. British Columbia Archives and Records Service, Victoria. Add.MSS. 1245.

in the landscape but they began to select familiar and specific terms—repeating, for example, the language of the garden.

As forms of water transportation changed and family cruising became more popular (see chapter one), women had increased access to shore. Local women, more familiar with local terminology, began to experience and narrate the region through pleasure boating. As the next section shows, during the steamship era women who visited the coast saw the natural environment as exotic and collectable—often objectifying nature with their "curio mentality." This initial impulse—to domesticate nature—was created, in part, by the ideology of the home.

Collectable Nature

Accounts from 1870 to the 1930s demonstrate a keen interest in curios, trophies, souvenirs, and artifacts along the Northwest Coast. The purchase and collection of Native artifacts (see figure 16) was an especially common form of curio hunting; collecting indigenous flora and fauna was an extension of that same mentality. In *Captured Heritage: The Scramble for Northwest Coast Artifacts* (1985), Douglas Cole explains that "Indians and their curios rivalled scenery as the major attraction of the [steamship] tour. A chief and seemingly infectious activity of the summer visitors was curio collecting" (96-97). The desire to bring a small, authentic, and controllable piece of primitive wilderness back home was very strong among White travelers. A three-dimensional and sometimes living artifact might serve to translate that "indescribable" landscape into something travelers could manipulate, remember, and perhaps even resell. Because aboriginals were perceived as part of the natural landscape, their artifacts and souvenirs served as evidence that tourists had "penetrated" relatively unexplored regions. Curio collecting was a clear objectification of the natural environment and of First Nations cultures.

When Lady Franklin and Sophia Cracroft traveled to Sitka in 1870, they describe a visit to the nearby Native village as "fruitless" when they fail to acquire curios. At this point in history, tourists were rare that far up the coast, and Native people did not seek boat passengers for commerce. Cracroft describes how a Native man declines to sell the women a carved wooden figure:

Finding that we examined the handles of 2 knives they shewed us wh. were carved in wood, a man pulled down fm. an upper shelf, a large figure exceedingly well carved in wood, of a beast lying down, with an upturned human face. We asked if they wd. sell it, & the price, but they wd. not sell it. (Cracroft 68)

Discouraged by this man who is willing to show them, but not sell to them, the carved prow of a canoe, the women continue looking for curios but find that many of the villagers are away: "There were so many away, who had locked up their houses that few things were offered to us for purchase, & the walk was fatiguing as well as fruitless" (68).

In less than fifteen years, upcoast tourists were buying Native artifacts as a matter of course. Eliza Scidmore describes a pleasant day of curio shopping in *Alaska* (1885): "For another perfect summer afternoon the *Ancon* [see figure 10] lay at the wharf in Kasa-an Bay, and in the mellow, Indian summer sunshine, we roamed the beach, buying the last remaining baskets, bracelets, pipes, and spoons of the Indians" (267). By 1889, Matilda Barns Lukens describes the eagerness of Sitka Natives to sell curios to Pacific Coast Steamship Company passengers: "We went into numerous cabins in the search for curios, and were impressed with the eagerness of the natives to make money" (53).

Figure 16. Alaska women selling baskets and other curios to tourists, about 1900. Photo courtesy of the Oregon Historical Society.

At the beginning of the twentieth century, White women were bragging about their collections of Native curios. In June 1906, Washington State resident and popular author Ella Higginson writes in *Washington Magazine* that if one cruises to Alaska, "you will bring home with you ... Atka baskets, ivories, Kamelinkers, bidarkas, virgin-charms and dozens of other curios that will make your friends die of envy" (336). Higginson confides how she and a friend booked "an extra berth for our Indian baskets" (338) on a Northwestern Steamship Company cruise. Writing for the same magazine the following September, she describes Native women boarding the steamer to sell curios: "The instant the gang-plank is out the squaws swarm silently aboard and squat along the decks, displaying their baskets, bracelets, rings, carved horn spoons, totem poles, inlaid lamps, moccasins and other curios" (60). The Native women whom she describes as "lordly and lazy creatures" (60) undergo a rapid transformation in the concluding installment of her account. As the makers of the baskets she treasures, Native women suddenly become "women with the souls of poets and artists and the patience of angels, weaving their dreams into ravishing beauty and sending them out into the world, where they should be held sacred" (112).

An anonymous tourist diary,[16] written in a booklet issued by the Pacific Coast Steamship Company for a 1909 sailing from Puget Sound to Skagway, suggests the number of opportunities for artifact-collecting in Southeastern Alaska at the time. In an "account" listed at the back of the small diary, this tourist meticulously records:

June		
17	Steamer chairs	6.00
18	lecture by Mr. Duncan, "Meltakatta"	.50
	Basket Ketchican	.75
	Postcards	.90
19	Bracelets	2.25
20	ride to Indian beach Sitka	1.50
	Indian pockets	1.50
	Church	.50
	Contribution church	.25
21	Baskets	5.--
22	ticket to White Pass	5.--
	paper cutter	.50
	Postals	.75
	Baskets	4.25
23	Baskets	7.--
	Postal cards	.75
	" "	.50

The diary suggests this traveler might have spent even more on Native baskets had they been available; on 20 June in Sitka the diary shows that "some of the Indians refuse to sell baskets Sunday." Steamship companies began to capitalize on tourists' desire for artifacts as demand rose and the supply of accessible artifacts declined. A 1929 booklet issued by the Canadian National Steamship Company[17] as "a fitting memento of a happy summer's cruise" (4) lists the ship's services, among them a newsstand that sells "curios."

Most curio-buying transactions took place, however, on or near the docks. Rebie Harrington (1937) describes the reception steamers received coming into Juneau in the 1930s:

On the dock, as each boat with passengers ties up, one observes the quiet Indian squaws seated upon the platform, with moccasins, bags, and odd articles of

---

16 Tourist Diary. Pacific Coast Steamship Company issue, 1909. British Columbia Archives and Records Service, Victoria. Add.MSS. 2014.

17 *The Midnight Sun: Descriptive Notes and Helpful Suggestions on the Journey to Alaska.* Canadian National Steamship Company promotional brochure, 1929. Univ. of British Columbia Special Collections, pam. #6001.

their own manufacture spread out before them for sale. These native women
are also seen on the main street, seated upon boxes or in doorways, mutely
offering specimens of their handiwork to the passer-by. No matter what hour these
passenger boats arrive, even at midnight, they are in evidence. (92)

Harrington explains the savvy necessary for amassing a fine and proper "collection of Alaska curios": the older the curio, the better. Describing how ivory combs grow brown with age, she writes: "A comb that I acquired is very brown. It is my choicest Alaskan possession" (104). Why buy ivory combs that she will never run through her own hair? She explains: "When one grows older and friends grow less, how grand to spend the last of life's moments among pleasant memories, and how much easier to recall to one's mind radiant reminiscences if something tangible is close at hand" (123).

The near-fanatical search for curios affected the way women perceived and described the natural environment. Describing a small island, Scidmore writes: "Its ragged shores hold hundreds of aquariums at low tide, and in the way of *marine curios* there are, besides the skeletons of whales, myriads of star fish and jelly fish and barnacles strewing the beach" (246, my emphasis). Here, the landscape becomes a gathering of collectable items. Wildlife are curios as well; when two small bear cubs are brought on board the *Idaho*, female passengers feed them "cakes and lumps of sugar from the cabin table." Scidmore writes that the cubs were afraid of the male passengers, who teased them, but "For the ladies, who fed them on sugar and salmon berries, both bears showed a great fondness, and the two clumsy pets would trot around the deck after them as tamely as kittens, and stand up and beg for sugar plainly" (293). "Foxes, strange birds, Esquimaux dogs, and other pets," she adds, "have been passengers on the return trips of the steamer" (294). Male tourists appear more likely to capture these animals; officers of the ship present the creatures that survive "to different city gardens and parks"; women, it would seem, undertake the work of domesticating the "pets" on board—or, to borrow a phrase from Vera Norwood—enfolding them into the home. These animals become members of the household afloat, constructed as fellow passengers. When a pair of fawns are "caught as they were swimming the channel near fort Wrangell one morning," they are "quartered [18] on the lower deck" (294). But not all creatures are petted and pampered as they are transformed into curios on this cruise. When the captain shoots a bald eagle, he throws its carcass down onto the deck: "The out-spread wings measured the traditional six feet from tip to tip, and the beak, the claws, and the stiff feathers were rapidly seized upon as trophies and souvenirs of the day" (152). Even the sea itself becomes a curio. On an evening when the sea is filled with shining phosphorescence, "A bucket was lowered and filled with the water, and the marvel of the shining sea was repeated in miniature on deck" (296). That is really the

---

18 It is clear in the context of this passage that the animals were certainly not cut up into quarters but rather were given berth as passengers. Following their capture, "they were visited daily and fed on ... dainties" (294).

definition of a curio, after all—a miniature version of the trip, a thing that stands for the experience.

This "curio mentality" toward fauna is common in women's steamship travel accounts of the region. In 1901 Mrs. James Morris, traveling on the *Queen*, paid two bits for a young seagull in a basket at Muir Glacier: "I hurried my gull to the steward and gained admission for him to the cook's department" (92). She records her intention to give the bird as a gift to "a little invalid boy whom I thought might be pleased with a pet" (92). E. Katharine Bates (1889) records the purchase of another curio as a child's gift near Juneau:

> As we returned to the ship ... we found a boy on the wharf holding a dear little baby bear of four months old by a chain. A gentleman and his wife from the Eastern States had promised their little boy, a child of four years old, to look out for a "real bear" when they started upon this expedition.
>
> The opportunity was too good to be lost. The bear was bought for a few dollars and speedily transferred to the upper deck, where he became a great favourite.
>
> It was a very tame little bear. (242)

Gladys O'Kelly's unpublished account of 1921[19] tells of another small bear being carried along aboard the *Unalga*. This animal

> ... roamed the ship at will, and at night ... relieved the passengers without cabins of their blankets, piling them in a heap and lying on them with a satisfied grunt. Occasionally he raided the sleeping quarters of the sailors, making a collection of their trousers which he used for a couch. He was a great pet. (65)

Not all of the pet stories are so quaint. When Agnes Herbert—introduced to the reader in more detail in chapter three—travels to Alaska to trophy hunt in 1909, she kills a mother bear then takes the cub on board the *Lily* for three weeks until it dies of what she calls "kindness"—that is, malnourishment (119). While alive, the bear is described by Herbert as "just as a St. Bernard puppy" (121).

The curio mentality reaches into the flora of the coast as well. In her unpublished "Jottings by the Way," Mary Holbrook [20] describes collecting natural souvenirs near Portland Canal, in the area of the Alaska border: "we returned to the ship, after breaking off some blue-berry boughs, and getting some specimens of moss and lichens that were hanging in great abundance from the trees, as trophies to remember Alaska by" (16).

Perhaps because women boat travelers sometimes conceived of their role on board as *playing* house, Norwood's (1993) thesis that flora and fauna "carry the emotional weight" of family members and "are due the same consideration as

---

19 Gladys O'Kelly. "A Woman's Log of an Arctic Voyage." 1921. British Columbia Archives and Records Service, Victoria. Add.MSS. 2636.

20 Mary H. Holbrook, "Jottings by the Way." Self-published, 1892. British Columbia Archives and Records Service, Victoria. NWp/971M/H724j.

human members of the household" (52) has its limits when translated from the nature-writing genre into travel discourse. Whereas a female nature writer such as Mary Austin (1903) perceives wild creatures of the American Southwest as "the furred and feathered folk" (17) and "my friend the coyote" (50), and writes of their instincts and animal natures with profound care and respect, these travelers describe bringing bears and deer and birds into the ship's household as amusing toys and appear to have little concern for the animals' fate after the "play" is done. They key to understanding how these tourists could see nature as a trophy or curio may lie in Mary Austin's philosophy of region: "To understand the fashion of any life," she writes—and I believe we may include animals' lives within her frame of reference—"one must know the land it is lived in and the procession of the year" (103). As transitory visitors "playing house"—a temporary child's game—these steamship travelers understood neither the region nor its cyclical changes. They were more interested in animals as curiosities and toys than as lives that would continue in their own homes after the ship had passed.

The curio mentality of women steamship passengers did not seem to significantly damage Northwest Coast environments—a blueberry bough taken here, or a pair of fawns there, would have a limited effect on their natural habitats. [21] However, the widespread impulse to collect living members of the natural environment as curios, as mementos of a new and unusual travel experience, suggests a commonly shared perspective among women steamship passengers. The natural world could be viewed as a distant panorama, a backdrop for human landscapes. Up close, "nature" was valued as a small package, a controllable and understandable pet or curiosity that (she believed) could be domesticated and enfolded into the ship's household.

"An Atavistic Female Instinct"

"The boat," writes T. C. Lethbridge (1952), "is man's greatest triumph over nature" (8). The pleasure and exhilaration of boat travel, adds Michael Stadler (1987), is the "feeling of increased risk [that] arises at sea from the direct confrontation with the forces of nature" (118). Philip Davenport (1953) is more poetic in his articulation of the invitation and challenge of the sea:

> For as long as I can remember I have been fascinated by the sea. I am awed by its infinite power as gale-driven, monstrous waves thunder and crash into foam against the cliffs or contemptuously toss great ships as effortlessly as the smallest chip of clinkers from their fires. I feel the joy and laughter in the blue and dancing ocean when a fresh breeze is brushing caps of white on the wave crests. Its attraction is both a challenge and a promise. (16)

---

21 The "scramble" by tourists, private collectors, and museums to accumulate native curios *did* affect Native culture. Native people lost many of the tools of their heritage (such as ceremonial masks). Cole (1985) writes: "so great was the demand for artifacts, it was reported in 1889, 'that the natives had commenced to despoil the graves of their own relatives'" (101).

Women boat travelers rarely describe this sense of personal confrontation with nature or the sea, largely because women were usually passengers on ships—quite disconnected from operating the vessel or actively "battling" the environment.[22] But Annette Kolodny's *The Land Before Her* (1984) and Maureen Devine's *Woman and Nature: Literary Reconceptualizations* (1992) suggest another reason for woman's "nonconfrontational" relationship with the sea. Because woman has been historically associated with nature (and, more specifically, with "wild" nature), they argue, woman does not conceive of herself as battling nature and emerging reborn from it.[23] The sense of the unexplored landscape as adversary or *bête noire* is a common construct in exploration literature (see Lopez 1986); at sea, the opponent can be the sea itself (as expressed by Davenport and Stadler) or it can be embodied by particular inhabitants of the sea. Melville's *Moby-Dick* is a symbol of the force of nature to be engaged in battle; the "man-eating" shark is a more common example to be found in sea literature.

When sailors could capture a shark, they would, as a matter of course and tradition, regularly torture the creature as a demonstration of their power over nature and the sea; Betty Jacobsen—the young woman shown uneasily sharing space with a male crew in chapter two—describes the tradition and her response to it in *A Girl Before the Mast* (1934):

> *I had often heard of how sailors hated sharks, but I never realized how much until I saw these usually calm young boys turn into vicious torturers. They ram a capstan bar down his throat into his stomach, and his teeth set hard into it but can do no harm. They hurl knives into him to watch his body quiver and jump; they strike him with belaying pins, capstan bars, marlinspikes, anything and everything that comes to hand. (181)*

"What chance has a poor shark," she asks, against the young men who "rip his backbone out while he still lives, chop off his tail with an axe, carve off his fins, and tear hard leather from his back" (181). Feeling more than a little persecuted by her male peers, who superstitiously threaten her for being female (and for bringing bad luck aboard), she feels compassion for the creature and is baffled by the sailors' treatment of him: "What harm had this poor shark done, that he should be so hurt and maimed and cut, and murdered a hundred times over on

---

22 Women who travel as captains and navigators do narrate confronting nature at sea. Stephanie Quainton Steel (1991), an active British Columbia kayaker, writes of her "confrontation with the sea's fierceness" (23). However, this confrontation is not the main theme of her book; instead, Steel's book is about her "floating studio," her "kayak as a method" to gain access to "the world of water, beckoning [her] into the exquisite heart of a painting" (15). Her kayak, *Raven Moon*, becomes a vehicle for drawing closer to nature: "I can take you to where painting would be meaningful—truthful, offered the kayak" (15). Steel does not, then, emerge victorious from a self-defining "battle" with the sea.

23 In this discussion, Kolodny is interested in women's participation in the myths that shape the essential or central "American" experience. Her work explores how women had different views of pioneer mythology—for example, the Garden of Eden myth.

a sailing-ship's deck in the tropic sun? Perhaps I am soft; perhaps men are more primitive than I knew" (182).

This "man versus nature" battle, enacted with a shark or described in *Moby-Dick*, is the driving force, the source of energy and interest in the genre of canonical sea literature. Bert Bender (1988) claims that "All writers in the tradition of American sea fiction after Melville have been guided by biological thought," that "no writer thereafter could depict the ocean reality without focusing on the mechanism of evolution by natural selection" (x). The "evolutionary thrust" (xi) of Darwinian thought figures prominently in Bender's analysis; he writes, for instance, of Darwin's "law of battle" in the many sea stories, which typically narrate "a young seaman's struggle to survive and become a man" (102). Women's Northwest Coast travel accounts show little interest in such confrontations. If there is an energy that connects these travelers' narratives, it is in the tradition of the American nature essay, based on the experience of travel. Thomas Lyon (1989) writes that this genre's "charge of interest comes from the excitement of crossing the frontier between civilization and wilderness" (88). Just where that line between civilization and wilderness lies varies over time. For nineteenth-century steamship tourists, the line had already been crossed before reaching Puget Sound; as a result, mountains in the southerly Cascade Range are viewed as grand and wild. As women from San Francisco, Portland, and Seattle begin cruising, the waters of Washington State become familiar and the British Columbia coast are the new wilderness. In 1910, Joseph and Annie Pyle describe their departure aboard a ninety-two-foot yacht (see figures 4 and 5) as follows: "The beginning of the *Lotus's* voyage was almost pastoral. A few hours' run from Seattle brought us to Whidbey Island—long, low, fruitful, idyllic as a bit of land cut out from surroundings occupied for centuries" (13,297). Passing "Nanaimo, the last outpost of cities," the Pyles notice how "the scenery begins to doff its garb of quiet loveliness and to assume a certain severity of grandeur" (13,298). The landscape is described as "dark," "sheer," "black," "morose," "gigantic," and "mighty" and is defined as a wilderness: "And so the days slip into weeks, and you feel that you have been in the wilderness for a lifetime" (13,297). As settlement moved upcoast, the "wilderness line" moved with it. Today the boat traveler can find "nature" all along the Inside Passage and will note the changing geography from south to north; however, many travelers believe they must go north into Alaska—beyond the large cities of Southeast Alaska and on to the glaciers—to find "wilderness."

Women boat travelers use the theme of crossing into wilderness [24] to generate a degree of tension in their narratives; but once in a wilderness setting, women's accounts emphasize features of the wilderness that are familiar and reminiscent of home. Moments of epiphany or passion occur on dry land, frequently in a garden-like setting. On these occasions, women emphasize the comfort and joy they take in the beauty of landscapes that allow a corner of domesticity to thrive

---

24 Proof of this crossing was the collection of curios.

in a northern wilderness. In 1889, Isabel Shepard took special pleasure when she "found a soft, dry seat on the rich, thick carpet of moss and dried grass":

I asked myself, could this be the same spot which, till within so short a time
had been so cold, gloomy and wintry, so dreary and uninviting...? Wildflowers
bloomed at my feet and all around me in profusion. The sun's warm beams
diffused a gentle heat, which made all nature seem to expand and grow—each little
flower lifting its face to greet the unwonted blessing. (111)

Ella Higginson (1906) insists that a walk among flowers was the most delightful part of her cruise to Alaska. After listing the varieties of flowers, their size, and their distribution over whole slopes, she describes gathering and carrying armfuls of them. The presence of flowers juxtaposed with "wild" nature in the area of Dutch Harbor makes the scene "perfect" and the air "the sweetest I have ever breathed, mixed with sun light, flowers, sea and snow" (112). In Toba Inlet, Florence Kell (1911) finds the combination of flowers and wilderness extremely desirable as well; the "delicate perfume of wild flowers mingled with the cold breath of an icy gale breathed a sweetly welcome" (10).

Flowers invited women to use their powers of description to translate the "indescribable" landscape into concrete images. Women travelers often knew the nomenclature and growing conditions of plants and could find the words to write specifically about this aspect of nature. And clearly, they found the subject worthy of attention; Gladys O'Kelly writes in her unpublished account:

The island was a carpet of glorious flowers. A garden could not have grown
more densely than here. The predominating color was blue, forget-me-nots on long
slender stems stretched away as far as the eye could see, lovely little daisies,
mauve and yellow, reared themselves above the grasses, Marguerites and Painter's
Brush shaded from cream to deep wine, lent a riot of color to the gently rolling
surfaces. There are over sixty five varieties of flowers each of which grows in
abundance. The Alpine poppy, too, with its delicate little yellow flower thrives
in this chilly clime and all these plants mature with their little toes on the icy
ground beneath. (27)

O'Kelly juxtaposes the smallness of the "lovely," "slender," and "delicate" flowers against the vast landscape and "chilly" climate; she uses the adjective "little" three times here to emphasize the delicacy (and perhaps even the "femininity") of the flora. Her description continues with a discussion of the heat and light necessary for these species and the cultivation of cabbages and hardy vegetables—illustrating both the botanical interest and general knowledge of cultivation she has brought with her from home.

Surrounded by water and unfamiliar terrain, women traveling or temporarily stationed along the Northwest Coast describe flowers as "more precious here than anywhere I have ever been" (Beaman 1987, 231). They also use garden imagery to describe the less-familiar sea life. In her unpublished booklet, "Memoirs of the Pribilof Islands: Nineteen Years on St. George and St. Paul Islands Alaska (1894-1913),"[25] Helen Judge McAllister carefully describes a sea anemone as closing "like a passion flower" (14). Florence Kell describes a beach at low tide in the fashion of a garden:

> I was up early the next day and out for a last row through this garden of marine life. The tide was low and the mirror of water reflected colors of rarest harmony and pictures of endless variety. On the crusted ledges hung great colonies of barnacles, and vivid pink and royal purple starfish clung to the glowering crags. Overhanging the water's edge grew festoons of bright yellow seaweed, and resting on the surrounding rocks were countless water birds. (12)

As pleasure boating with small craft grew prevalent in the twentieth century (see chapter one), women became "first mates" or co-pilots rather than passengers. Although the male head of the household is traditionally the "captain" in charge of navigation and the operation of the boat (see chapter two), boating partners can discuss routes, weather conditions, safety, and boat-handling techniques. Women are sometimes asked to "relieve" the captain while he checks the chart or takes a break; they generally help with docking and anchoring. As women became more active participants on the water, descriptions and "readings" of the seascape entered their narratives. Rapids, for instance, are of particular interest because they must be navigated with intelligence and finesse. For Kathrene Pinkerton (1940), "mate" of a family crew that cruised to Alaska over several years in the 1920s, the powerful "Yucluetaws Rapids" warrant careful attention and detailed description:

> Little Dent Island lies in midchannel and forces the tide into its narrowest and swiftest place. The flood began with a low mutter, and the current swept along, fast and smooth and straight. Eddies formed along the shore with a line of small whirlpools to mark the preliminary skirmish with the torrent. (83)

As she watches, her emphasis is on the emotion, sensuality, and drama of the topography; her consideration of how their boat would pass through this stretch of water comes as an afterthought:

> Rivers and cataracts have settled and regular movement. Here the tide snarled and surged and doubled its might in savage thrusts as it crowded through the narrow channel. And when the great tidal push increased in power, the roar intensified. The whole surface of the channel would lift suddenly. Then I understood why the Yucluetaws had been known to put a large steamship on its beam ends and hold it there, helpless in the rapid's grasp.

---

25 Helen Judge McAllister Papers (V.F. 476). Univ. of Washington Manuscripts and Archives, Seattle.

We sat tense and thrilled as the spring flood built to a climactic burst of power. I was conscious of a tremendous inner excitement while I watched. Occasionally someone would call attention to a newly forming whirlpool or a mounting boil. I didn't speak. I was exalted. Only a few great symphonies have moved me more. In the end, I was very weak and very tired.

And I began to wonder how the little Yakima *would fare when we went through the next morning. (83-84)*

Muriel "Capi" Blanchet (figure 15), a widow and captain of her small boat, *Caprice*, sees rapids through the perspective of the navigator and commander of the vessel. As examined in more detail in chapter three, with *The Curve of Time* (1961) she recalls the experiences of boating the British Columbia coast with her children in the 1930s. Describing the narrows at the entrance to Princess Louisa Inlet, she writes:

The entrance is a little tricky to get through at low tide unless you know it, but there is plenty of water. From water level, the points on one side and the coves on the other fold into each other, hiding the narrow passage. It is not until you are rushed through the gap on a rising tide that the full surprise of the existence and beauty of this little hidden inlet suddenly bursts on you. It is always an effort to control the boat as you hold her on the high ridge of the straight run of water down the middle. Then, as you race past the last points, the ridge shatters into a turmoil of a dozen different currents and confusions. Your boat dashes towards the rocky cliff beyond the shallow cove on your right; and the cliff, equally delighted, or so it seems, rushes towards your boat. You wrestle with the wheel of your straining boat, and finally manage to drag the two apart. (21-22)

Very few women along the Northwest Coast share Blanchet's exuberance for, and experience with, navigation. Experience in the seascape allows women to understand it, to find words for it, and even to equate themselves with it; for example, Frances Brown, daughter of the lightkeeper at Porlier Pass early in the twentieth century, describes the pass in Saeko Usukawa's (1984) collection of oral histories: "It's a short pass, but it's a strong pass. I think we run about nine knots at the strongest tide, somewhere between six and nine, which is quite strong. We like to boast that we're the strongest of the two tiderips on the island" (252). Women unfamiliar with the seascape are more likely to construct it as foreign and malevolent. Kaisa Riksman recalls her fearful arrival at Sointula on Malcolm Island in 1902: "all the bay was covered with these big kelps—these great big snakes in the water with these great big heads on them" (Usukawa 62-63). Caroline Leighton (1995), traveling from Puget Sound to San Francisco in the spring of 1875, describes how fearful she was in her ignorance of sailing. When the captain takes the time to explain the workings of the boat to her and shows her the perspective he most enjoys on the water, her fear is dispelled:

One day [the voyage] was more than I could enjoy. The wind roared so loud, and the sound of the waves was so heavy, that I retreated to my berth, and lay down; but I could not keep my mind off the thought of how deep the water was under us. After a while I went on deck and sat there again, and the vessel began to plunge so that it seemed as if it were trying to stand upon one end. I felt so frightened that I thought I would speak to the captain.... I spoke to him, and he did not give me much of an answer; but, a little while after, he came to me, and said, "Are you able to go to the forward part of the ship with me? I should like to have you, if you can." So he helped me along to the bow, where it seemed almost too frightful to go, and said, "Kneel down;" and knelt down by me, and said, "Look under the ship." It was one of the most beautiful sights I ever saw,—such a height of foam, and rainbows over it. The dark water beside it seemed full of little, sharp, shining needles. I suppose it was moving so quickly that made the elongated drops appear so. Then he took me to the other side, that was in shadow; and there the water whirled into the most beautiful shapes, standing out distinct from each other, from the swiftness of the motion, that held them poised, like exquisite combinations of snowflakes, only more airy.

Presently he said, "Men don't often speak of these things to each other, but I feel the beauty of it. Nights when the vessel is moving so fast, I come and watch here for hours and hours, and dream over it." When I thought about it afterward, I wondered how he could know the way to answer my fear was to show me what was so beautiful. I was not afraid any more, whatever the vessel did. (117-18)

The ease Leighton gains when the captain shares his experience and perspective with her allows her the relaxed, contemplative moments she needs to take in the beauty created by the ship passing through the sea and to recreate it for her readers.

Because women have "naturally" been associated with the land, and have been "taboo" in the marine environment (see chapter two), women's cruising accounts commonly link femininity with a desire for shore, flora, and soil. Kathrene Pinkerton is explicit on this subject with *Three's a Crew* (1940). While cruising, the Pinkertons visit with loggers' wives; these women live in wooden shacks that rise and fall with the tides, moored to the steep, rocky slopes of the inlets. She writes:

Women in the float houses of that hybrid country of land and sea fascinated me. All revealed a yearning for contact with earth. Window boxes, pots of growing things around the float, did not satisfy. Women and hens—they must put their feet on land. Kinship with the earth is femaleness and as insistent as the male instinct for boats. (156)

This "kinship" is alive and well for Pinkerton and her daughter, Bobs; she discusses her husband's marvel at her need to "feel the earth":

He marveled at Bobs' and my elaborate preparations for an afternoon on land and would hand down to the dinghy all our impedimenta—towels, books, sewing, paints, notebooks and pencils—with the remark that girls made a lot of trouble for themselves. If he joined us later for exploring, it was from a desire to see the county and not because his feet, like mine, demanded the feel of earth. Every so often I had to smell the perfume of crushed sweet fern and to walk in open places. (156)

What she calls "an atavistic female instinct" (223), a desire to move ashore, hits her especially hard with the coming of autumn: "I had an odd dislocated feeling. Perhaps it was a fall nostalgia for the land," she writes. While "Betty had gone south to her home and garden," the Pinkertons attempted to live aboard all winter. By consciously defining the boat as a home afloat, she overcomes this desire to move on shore:

I was at home in what was practically an apartment. I was surrounded by my own things. I was fully occupied and very comfortable. And we had not swung at anchor for more than a day before the strangeness of a fall home at sea left me completely.
"It must have been an atavistic female instinct," I said. "That first autumn chill makes a woman think of leaving water for the land, even when there's no rhyme nor reason to it." (223)

Because she resists defining a boat as a home, Beth Eberhart (1961) is never at home afloat: "'I just don't like it, being on the boat. It's so small and cramped. And I don't like the water'" (151).[26] Fishing and traveling on her husband's fishing boat in Southeastern Alaska interferes with Eberhart's comfort. "'You can't keep clean on a boat,'" she says, and there's "'nothing to look at but water and sky and more boats'" (152, 25).

As analyzed in depth in chapter two, Eberhart's narrative is constructed as a "battle of the sexes," of sorts—a battle she wins when her husband eventually sells his fishing boat and the couple move to a house on solid land in the Seattle area. Like other female boat travelers, she takes special pleasure in "stroll[ing] along, enjoying the feel of being on land. Good solid earth, soft underfoot" (226). Stopping over in Wrangell, she describes an uncommon moment of pleasure: "Oh, it was wonderful to have my feet on the ground once more, and such luxuriant growth. What if [the dandelions] were only weeds? ... I had a longing for a garden, to dig in the soil once more, to plant seeds and watch them grow!" (130). This longing or need for the earth is narrated as an elemental difference between women and men in Eberhart's *A Crew of Two.* Whereas women need a garden to tend and a comfortable home, men need fish to catch and a sea-battle to fight. Regarding fishing with her husband, she writes:

---

26 See my more thorough discussion of Eberhart's and Margaret Sharcott's experiences on the water in chapter two.

So this was it! The reason small boys sit beside some quiet stream, dabbling for hours with a piece of string and a bent pin; the urge that drives those same boys, grown to manhood, into untold hardships with battling waves and freezing gear. The irresistible attraction of fishing, whether for minnows or whales. Yes, this was it, and they could have it, I thought, as I leaned to pick up a fish from the deck and got a slimy slap across the face. (267)

Traveling with her husband aboard their fishing boat, Margaret Sharcott (1957)—whose account I also analyze in more detail in chapter two—expresses her felt connection with the earth less directly. "[N]ot a good sailor" (95), she perceives "the ever-present terror of the hungry seas" in the seascape (18). Because Sharcott and her husband have distinct gender roles on board—he does all navigating and steering; she does all "housework" below deck—she views the seascape with vague horror and a sense of utter powerlessness. Her narrative is dominated by her feelings of stress and her descriptions of the difficulties of keeping house in a restrictive and pitching galley. But as the boat passes Hornby Island, where she was raised, Sharcott experiences a rare moment of calm and engagement with the natural world. "A longing to write of those first fourteen years stirred in my heart," she confides. "I wanted to write of the pleasure of digging in warm, black loam in the garden, the smell of fresh-cut hay mingling with honeysuckle" (122). Her most detailed description of the natural environment comes as they pass close to shore and through Dodd's Narrows; her longing to write of gardening leads her to brush careful touches of detail into the scene:

We squeezed through the Narrows, swirling tide racing by us. Tree-lined shore reached out to touch tree-lined shore. Rocks, black with moisture, small pale green ferns rooting in their crevices, curved to the grey channel water. Yellow-green moss clung to the rocks and lost itself in the bush above. (139)

Sharcott, raised on a island, remains in many respects a foreigner to the marine environment that surrounds her. Because the ideology of the home ties her explicitly to the galley and the "housework" below deck, she does not learn how to operate her husband's fishing boat nor to read the waterscape he navigates. As a result, from the boat she sees the seascape vaguely and with a sense of powerlessness. Her attention is drawn to the aspect of the natural world that she knows how to articulate: the soil. Even when she describes a feature of the marine environment, her focus is the shore, with its rocks, moss, ferns, and trees. For Sharcott and for many adult women boat travelers, this link to dry land is perceived as "atavistic" and "natural." Woman's "atavistic female instinct" for the shore would seem (to them) to justify any inexperience and discomfort afloat. At the same time, it justifies a world order in which women have been associated with home and with nature—legitimizing their "natural" place in the galley and on dry land. As adult women, such as Muriel Blanchet, move into less "natural" roles as boat owners and captains, they become better able to read and describe the waterscape.

Daughters of the Coast

Girls, unlike adult women, seem uniquely comfortable in the waterscape along the Northwest Coast. This ease may result from a lack of defined and separate spheres based on gender for pre-adult girls in a frontier environment. For instance, when Burgess Cogill (1990) traveled to Puget Sound aboard her father's trade schooner between 1902 and 1910, her mother had a very defined role and spatial territory aboard the ship (see chapter two). However, for the adolescent Burgess and her sister, "we accepted ourselves as part of the crew" (106). The girls regularly played "house" not just below deck, but on deck among coils of rope and stacks of lumber (figure 17). Believing that the ship was her own, she writes, "Women's lib had a big start in that first decade of my life with Father" (106).

Cogill also enjoyed cruising in a small boat with her father. Although "Mother was never really crazy about these excursions" or her father's wet "maneuvers," the girls "never seemed to mind, not even getting a bit wet" (70). Her comfort with boats led her to appropriate a man's skiff and learn how to row:

I had eyes for nothing else but the little blue boat. Looking into it, I saw neatly placed oars, the boat all clean, shipshape, and blue inside and out. I got in and pushed the boat out from the float and pulled it back a few times, leaving the painter tied as the water lapped gently against the sides. Then I tried the oars. I had an ecstatic few hours in the morning sunshine, rowing (somewhat), listening to the click of the oarlocks, the water dripping quietly from the oars back into the bay. (73)

After her father discovers her efforts to row, he gives her a lesson.

After I learned, I couldn't get enough of rowing in Sam Bagley's blue skiff, though I managed to forget that it belonged to him. Actually I was rowing in my *boat,* my *own small ship, to steer, to navigate, to change course as I wanted, to explore the far corners of the small world of water surrounding Snow & Burgess, while blissful hours slipped by. (71, 73; her emphasis)*

Rowing offers the girl a great deal of freedom; her learned skill and new-found mobility also bring her close to the natural world under the sea:

From then on, time in the sun was spent in my boat, first perfecting my rowing, then guiding the boat wherever I wanted to go. I even learned to feather my oars! Once this was accomplished, great explorations of the small sea and bay tides and marine life were the order of the day. I spent hours watching the clear waters from the drifting boat, hanging over the stern and watching the fish swim by; moving in close to the wharf, seeing red starfish and purple mussels attached to the pilings; barnacles like tiny snow-covered volcanoes clustered on the pilings beneath the water. (74-75)

Figure 17. "Her decks made a fine playground" (Cogill 1990; photo courtesy of the Peabody Museum of Salem).

Alone and competent, she is entirely comfortable on the water: "mostly I was alone in my sheltered sea-world," she writes. "It was a completely safe place for me to be" (75).

Safety, in fact, is a significant issue in the assignment of gender roles. The Women and Geography Study Group (1984) notes that safety appears to be a reason for limiting the space allocated to adolescent girls: "it seems that little girls are allowed far less freedom of movement than little boys, in part because of the apparently higher chance of sexual attack they face. In adolescence, the identification of public space with boys, and private space with girls, seems to become even more marked" (29). In frontier environments, this separation of spheres may have been more difficult to enforce on adolescent girls; Cogill's opportunity to investigate the underwater world and to row herself away from human society at will may have resulted in part from growing up in a frontier environment. In *The Last Best West: Women on the Alberta Frontier 1880-1930* (1984), Eliane Leslau Silverman describes how the frontier landscape offered girls a measure of freedom. Silverman hypothesizes that although first-generation settlers on the prairie could become insane and embittered "prairie women," beaten down physically and emotionally by the new landscape, the daughters of these women, born on the prairie, had a very different response to their environment. "The open land," she writes, "with its possibilities for running wildly and freely, and seemingly eternally, offered girls a glimpse of something like freedom" (16). The combination of frontier society and the prairie landscape, she explains

> ... evoked the knowledge that life could be transitory and tenuous, and not well-rooted in the past. The understanding of hierarchy, of place, and of obedience was a bit harder to instill in frontier children than in children growing up in more settled places. Even as girls were absorbing the knowledge of roles appropriate to their gender, they also heard the whisper of the inappropriate. (16)

That whisper, I think, came not just from the prairie landscape. A number of girls born on the coast near the end of the nineteenth century describe "getting their dresses wet": that is, participating in the marine environment in a way that ignored gender roles "appropriate" for non-frontier society of the time. In her oral history, Etta Leightheart Egeland, who was born in 1896 and raised on San Juan Island, recalls riding logs with her half-sister, Winifred:

> When Winifred Leightheart and I were about nine, ten, or eleven years old, we used to ride on big logs that would come rolling in [to the beach], out in front of my grandfather Leightheart's log cabin a mile west of Sunset Point. Winifred and I would get on them and paddle around. We were hardy little rascals. If I saw my children doing that. (Strickland 1990, 69; her emphasis)

Egeland describes the girls' brazen confidence and the skill with which they read the tides. Even if the landscape of the inland sea is not obviously "open," these girls know the water could carry them anywhere:

> I was wearing a dress while riding on a log. We didn't fall in the water. I don't know what we'd have done. We straddled the logs but getting our dresses wet never bothered us. I imagine we were just like ice when we got out of that water.
>   Winifred Leightheart and I knew the tides. We knew when the tide was going out and when it was coming in. And we didn't go out on an outgoing tide or we would be in some other country by now. (69)

Winifred was especially daring; she helped construct a raft and set out on the tide with a boy: "Winifred and a boy that my grandfather got from the orphan's home in Seattle, Frank Miller, he and Winifred made a raft and started out, going south, and a purse seiner saw them and took them aboard, much against their will, and set the raft adrift into the tide rips. Winifred had a great desire to be adventuresome" (69-70).

Two female cousins raised on a B.C. Gulf Island shared a similar sense of autonomy and freedom on the water. When their fathers came from England in the 1880s, the families were unable to maintain their upper-class British way of life in British Columbia. As a result, Dorothy Payne Richardson explains, "We had far more freedom in many ways" (Orchard and Reimer 1984, 109):

> We had guns, we had boats. We were allowed to use tools. When we went log salvaging, my brother and I rented a big logging-jack from our uncle, and peavies—all kinds of things. And we used to take off for a whole day if we felt like it. Nobody would say: "Where are you going?" or "When are you going to be back?" We'd just go off. It might be by boat, it might be by land—but more often by boat—and if we didn't come back for two meals in a row, somebody would come and look for us, perhaps, but very rarely. We all did it. (109)

Richardson's cousin Dora Payne learned to row by the age of four; the water, Payne explains, was a significant part of their lives from birth:

> We were on the water almost as much, I would say, as we were on land, because we used to play on the beach, we used to fish, we used to row. On all our picnics we went on the water; every time we wanted to get mail we went by water. We just didn't have any fear of the water at all. (109-10)

By the age of ten, Payne and her twelve-year-old brother were salvaging logs in the Georgia Strait during the winter. It was the sort of activity that an upper-class girl would never have the opportunity to engage in outside a frontier context.

Playing and working on the water was apparently not taboo for young girls as it was for adult women (see chapter two). Viola Wood (1983), raised on the Queen Charlotte Islands/Haida Gwaii, recalls how rowing was a common activity and hard work:

> Usually we rowed the ten miles from Watun to Masset, using the tide to our advantage, and sometimes it was dark as we pulled up the inlet for home. Depending on the swiftness of the tide, we more or less went by guess and by God to estimate when we were approaching the Watun, craning our necks over our right shoulders to seek the lamplight in the window that would guide us home. (11)

She describes how she and a girlfriend worked independently at log salvaging:

> I remember Ethel, the eldest Ormbrak girl, and how we worked with the tide to peavy some logs to the water's edge, stapling each one and securing them all with ropes. The plan was to tow them to Art Robertson's mill in Masset and try to sell them for ten dollars. We borrowed an anchor from Ed Finney and set off confidently, edging into midstream where the current would carry us. We made the tow in record time and pulled our precious logs into Delkatla Slough. Then we ran into problems. (11)

The opportunity to "run into problems" on the water, and to learn how to work safely in that environment, enables young women to grow capable and confident afloat. Wood describes how she used a rowboat for pleasure, gaining access to a favorite lagoon:

> Jim May, the maintenance man, loaned me his rowboat to make excursions around the small islands. My favorite spot was an almost landlocked lagoon where I could ship the oars and note an eagle soaring overhead, or watch a deer mincing to the water's edge, curious and unafraid. Perhaps a bluejay would scold my intrusion, and I would laugh back at him. I belonged there too, no matter what he thought. (13)

This sense of belonging in the natural seascape/landscape results from her comfort and expertise on the water, a result of having been born and raised near water, and of the relaxed gender roles for frontier girls.

In "Listening to the Voices of the Coast," Charles Lillard (1992) explores how "the early daughters of the coast" were the first writers to express the "call of the coast," or the "coastal spell" felt by White settlers:

> These women were the ones who frequently found this coastal spell impossible to break, maybe because they were not supposed to know of its existence—"a woman's place is in the home" and all that entails. Barrett Willoughby was the first to break free and write. (157)

Willoughby's romance novel, *Spawn of the North* (1932), centers on a daughter of the coast—a girl who, in adolescence, would have shared much in common with Viola Wood and Burgess Cogill: "A love of keels and salt-water things had been Dian Turlon's all of her twenty-four years; at least, ever since her baby feet had taken their first wavering steps along the deck of the *Star of Alaska*" (6-7).

Willoughby's fiction glamorizes the necessity of boat travel along the coast; Dian Turlon does not salvage logs, she speeds about in her cruiser, running "her supple hands over the [steering] wheel to feel again that sense of restrained power that always came to her from the contact" (1-2). The novel begins:

> The girl, slender, blonde, in a jersey of silver green, seemed a part of the radiant Alaska morning. She stood alone at the wheel in the pilot-house of the small cabined cruiser, Golden Hind, *and with a sureness that lent a lean, daring grace to her movements, swung the speeding craft down the channel between spruce-green islands. (1)

A girl as the book opens, Turlon is about to change into a woman. Rigorously symbolized as the very embodiment of natural Alaska, Turlon has returned to the North from a college in the Lower Forty-eight States, much as a salmon spawned in Alaska returns home: "It was almost as if she were a part of the mighty tide of life that moves northward each spring" (3). Turlon's body, echoing the landscape about her, positively throbs with desire:

Everywhere now in the vast country about her pulsed the stir of procreation. In the forests, in the sea, on the tundras, in every broad river and mountain stream that threaded the wilderness. She felt it, the quick passion of the North, strong, productive; and feeling it, knew a brief, rapturous inebriation, a keen awareness of life and the power for life in herself. (3)

As the "spawn" of Alaska, Turlon is part this landscape, an extension of her homeland. Her connection to the earth is a result of her innate "Northness," not her femaleness:

As she moved on through the darkness, it seemed to her that Dian Turlon of the civilized South had stepped outside her body and was watching Dian of the North, a night-treading creature who was a part of the wilderness.... She enjoyed that. She liked the sibilant lap of small waves on her left, the sense of the damp rocky cliff on her right. She splashed on through tide pools feeling close to the earth; feeling of the earth. (284-85)

With *Spawn of the North*, Willoughby creates a daughter of the coast whose connection to the natural world is based not upon woman-as-nature assumptions but upon birthright. Born to overthrow the stereotype that "women and fish don't mix" (21) and that "women had no place" in the Ketchikan fishery (9), she saves the fishery from piracy.

Eventually, however, this daughter of the coast must come of age within the romantic construct of the novel. Meeting her match in the insolent and rugged "Jim," Dian Turlon's physical and psychic connections with the natural environment appear to make romance inevitable:

She was acutely conscious of him and of herself—two magnetic beings charged with mysterious emotions and strangely akin to the wilderness about them—the trees, the clean scent of elder blossoms, the running water, the cool and liquid sounds made by early silver salmon going up two and two through the crystal darkling waters that led inland to the spawning grounds. (61)

As she matures, this girl wants to give up cruising alone in her speedboat; through Jim, she comes to see the marine environment as a battleground and herself as someone needing protection and shelter from nature:

In this moment when her guard was down against [Jim] she wished she might, in reality, go cruising with him through the night.... In some mysterious way he had put a glamour on the world for her. He was one of those who seem to epitomize man's [sic] proud and splendid way of adventuring; the romance of man's long, successful struggle with Nature: Dominion over more powerful, though less intelligent creatures. Shelter from the elements. Safety on the ruthless, uncertain sea. (105)

Finding safety in her marriage to Jim, Dian Turlon is no longer the adolescent daughter of the coast, standing alone at the wheel of the *Golden Hind*. As the novel concludes, Dian and Jim elope aboard her boat, "setting out standing at the wheel together" (349). Thus, in this little-known romantic drama, Willoughby offers a momentary illustration of shared power afloat—a rare vision, achieved through a shared belief in "man's long, successful struggle with Nature." Belief in the righteousness of that struggle—so crucial to the frontier mentality of the Northwest Coast—is what characterizes Dian as "Northern":

> *All about was a sense of the illimitable, beckoning vastness of Alaska lying beyond; a listening country, lovely, wild, untouched—and waiting. It made Dian conscious of herself and of the tall man by her side: They were both of this country—North-born; a man and a woman of a new, vigorous race, proud and valiant and splendidly strong; potent to mould the beginnings of their wilderness land. (208)*

This theme of a "new race" of strong and vigorous people (often described in narratives that also stereotype Native people as old, fat, weak, and cowardly) is a common construct of Northwest Coast writing, going back as least as far as Theodore Winthrop (1862).[27]

Here at the conclusion of Willoughby's novel, the daughter of the coast accepts her heritage as a shaper and conqueror of the landscape. Leaning back against Jim, who steers her boat with one hand, she has learned to accept the hierarchy of man over nature. It is a glamorous moment on a romanticized frontier, happily ignorant of woman's position in that hierarchy.

---

27 Roderick Haig-Brown (1980), for example, characterizes different generations of Northwest timber workers as the "new" and "old" race of men, based upon their ability to process lumber.

BIBLIOGRAPHY

Aitken, Maria. *A Girdle Round the Earth*. London: Constable Press, 1987.

Allison, Charlene J., Sue-Ellen Jacobs, and Mary A. Porter, eds. *Winds of Change: Women in Northwest Commercial Fishing*. Seattle: Univ. of Washington Press, 1989.

Anderson, Lorraine, ed. *Sisters of the Earth: Women's Prose and Poetry About Nature*. New York: Vintage, 1991.

Ardener, Shirley, ed. *Women and Space: Ground Rules and Social Maps*. London: Croom Helm, 1981.

Armitage, Susan H. "The Challenge of Women's History." Ed. Karen J. Blair. *Women in Pacific Northwest History: An Anthology*. Seattle; London: Univ. of Washington Press, 1988. 233-45.

Atwood, Margaret. *Surfacing*. Toronto: General Publishing, 1972.

Auerbach, Nina. *Woman and the Demon: The Life of a Victorian Myth*. Cambridge: Harvard Univ. Press, 1982.

Austin, Mary. *The Land of Little Rain*. Albuquerque: Univ. of New Mexico Press, 1974 (1903).

Aylmer, Fenton, ed. *A Cruise in the Pacific: From the Log of a Naval Officer*. 2 Vols. London: Hurst and Blackett, 1860.

Bachelard, Gaston. *The Poetics of Space*. Trans. Maria Jolas. Boston: Beacon Press, 1969 (1958).

Balderston, Lydia Ray. *Housewifery: A Manual and Text Book of Practical Housekeeping*. Philadelphia: Lippincott, 1921.

Bancroft, Hubert Howe. *History of the Northwest Coast*. New York: Bancroft Co., 1884.

Barman, Jean. *The West Beyond the West*. Toronto: Univ. of Toronto Press, 1991.

Barrett-Lennard, C. E. *Travels in British Columbia, with the Narrative of a Yacht Voyage Round Vancouver's Island*. London: Hurst and Blackett, 1862.

Barrow, Francis. *Upcoast Summers*. Ed. Beth Hill. Ganges, B.C.: Horsdal and Schubart, 1985.

Bates, E. Katharine. *Kaleidoscope: Shifting Scenes from East to West*. London: Ward and Downey, 1889.

Beaman, Libby. *Libby: The Alaskan Diaries and Letters of Libby Beaman, 1879-1880, as Presented by her Granddaughter Betty John*. Boston: Houghton Mifflin, 1987.

Beecher, Catherine E. *A Treatise on Domestic Economy: For the Use of Young Ladies at Home and at School*. New York: Harper, 1849.

————, and Harriet Beecher Stowe. *The American Woman's Home*. New York: J. B. Ford, 1869.

Bemelmans, Ludwig. "Ship-Owner." In *Tell Them It Was Wonderful*. New York: McGraw-Hill, 1987. 293-304.

Bender, Bert. *Sea Brothers: The Tradition of American Sea Fiction from* Moby-Dick *to the Present*. Philadelphia: Univ. of Pennsylvania Press, 1988.

Bennett, Dery, ed. *The Seaside Reader*. New York: Lyons and Burford, 1992.

Biehl, Janet. *Rethinking Ecofeminist Politics*. Boston: South End Press, 1991.

Binns, Archie. *The Roaring Land*. New York: McBride, 1942.

Birkett, Dea. *Spinsters Abroad: Victorian Lady Explorers*. Oxford; New York: B. Blackwell, 1989.

Birtles, Dora. *North-West by North: A Journal of a Voyage*. London: Virago, 1985 (1935).

Bish, Robert L., et al. *Coastal Resource Use: Decisions on Puget Sound*. Seattle: Univ. of Washington Press, 1975.

Blair, Karen J., ed. *Women in Pacific Northwest History: An Anthology*. Seattle: Univ. of Washington Press, 1988.

Blanchet, M. Wylie. *The Curve of Time*. Sidney, B.C.: Gray's, 1980 (1961).

Boulton, James T. Editor's Introduction to *A Philosophical Enquiry into the Origin of Our Ideas of the Sublime and Beautiful*, by Edmund Burke. Rev. ed. Oxford: Basil Blackwell, 1987. vii-xlviii.

Boyd, Emma S. *Many Coloured Mountains and Some Seas Between*. London: John Long, 1909.

Brown, Gillian. *Domestic Individualism: Imagining Self in Nineteenth-Century America*. Berkeley: Univ. of California Press, 1990.

Brown, H. Douglas. "We Went A-Boating." *Hobbies* 59 (October 1954): 154-55.

Brown, Jennifer. *Strangers in Blood: Fur-Trade Company Families in Indian Country*. Vancouver: Univ. of British Columbia Press, 1980.

Brown, Richard Maxwell. "Rainfall and History: Perspectives on the Pacific Northwest." In *Experiences in a Promised Land*. Ed. G. Thomas Edwards and Carlos Schwantes. Seattle: Univ. of Washington Press, 1986. 13-27.

Brownmiller, Susan. *Femininity*. New York: Linden Press, 1984.

Buerge, David M. Introduction to *West Coast Journeys, 1865-1879: The Travelogue of a Remarkable Woman* by Caroline C. Leighton. Seattle: Sasquatch, 1995. vi-x.

Burke, Katy. *The Handbook for Non-Macho Sailors*. Newport, R.I.: Seven Seas Press, 1985.

Butler, Judith. *Gender Trouble: Feminism and the Subversion of Identity*. New York: Routledge, 1990.

Calhoun, Bruce. "Northwest Dividends for Small-Boat Yachtsmen." In *Northwest Passages: A Collection of Pacific Northwest Cruising Stories*. Ed. Bruce Calhoun. San Francisco: Miller Freeman, 1969. 8-10.

Cantwell, Robert. *The Hidden Northwest*. Philadelphia: J. B. Lippincott, 1972.

Carr, Emily. *Klee Wyck*. Toronto: Irwin, 1941.

Carson, Rachel L. "Winds Blowing Seaward." In *The Seaside Reader*. Ed. Dery Bennett. New York: Lyons and Burford, 1992. 55-62.

Carter, Paul. *The Road to Botany Bay: An Exploration of Landscape and History*. Chicago: Univ. of Chicago Press, 1989 (1988).

Chambers, Anne. *Granuaile: The Life and Times of Grace O'Malley c. 1530-1603*. Dublin: Wolfhound Press, 1979.

Chasan, Daniel Jack. *The Water Link: A History of Puget Sound as a Resource*. Seattle: Univ. of Washington Press, 1981.

Chaudhuri, Nupur, and Margaret Strobel, eds. *Western Women and Imperialism: Complicity and Resistance*. Bloomington; Indianapolis: Indiana Univ. Press, 1992.

Chopin, Kate. *The Awakening*. In *The Norton Anthology of Literature by Women*. Ed. Sandra M. Gilbert and Susan Gubar. New York: Norton, 1985 (1899). 993-1,102.

Clark, Arthur H. *The History of Yachting, 1600-1815*. New York; London: Putnam's, 1904.

Clark, Sally. "Boating is a Family Sport." *Seattle Times* (20 April 1958). Sec. 6.

Clifford, James. "Introduction: Partial Truths." In *Writing Culture: The Poetics and Politics of Ethnography*. Ed. James Clifford and George E. Marcus. Berkeley: Univ. of California Press, 1986. 1-26.

Cogill, Burgess. *When God Was an Atheist Sailor: Memories of a Childhood at Sea, 1902-1910*. New York: Norton, 1990.

Cole, Douglas. *Captured Heritage: The Scramble for Northwest Coast Artifacts*. Seattle; London: Univ. of Washington Press, 1985.

Collis, Septima. *A Woman's Trip to Alaska*. New York: Cassell, 1890.

Cooper, Carol. "Native Women of the Northern Pacific Coast: An Historical Perspective, 1830-1900." *Journal of Canadian Studies* 27/4 (Winter 1992-93): 44-75.

Cooper, Morley. *The Cruising Yacht*. New York: McGraw-Hill, 1945.

Corwin, Joan. "Travel Literature." In *Victorian Britain: An Encyclopedia*. Ed. Sally Mitchell. New York: Garland, 1988. 818-19.

Cracroft, Sophia. *Lady Franklin Visits Sitka, Alaska: The Journal of Sophia Cracroft, Sir John Franklin's Niece*. Ed. R. N. DeArmond. Anchorage: Alaska Historical Society, 1981.

Creese, Gillian, and Veronica Strong-Boag, eds. *British Columbia Reconsidered: Essays on Women*. Vancouver: Press Gang, 1992.

Crosby, Marcia. "Construction of the Imaginary Indian." In *Vancouver Anthology: The Institutional Politics of Art*. Ed. Stan Douglas. Vancouver: Talonbooks, 1991. 267-91.

Cruikshank, Julie, with Angela Sidney, Kitty Smith, and Annie Ned. *Life Lived Like a Story: Life Stories of Three Yukon Elders*. Lincoln: Univ. of Nebraska Press, 1990.

Cunnington, C. Willett. *Feminine Attitudes in the Nineteenth Century.* London: William Heinemann, 1935.

Currie, Noel. *Captain Cook at Nootka Sound and Some Questions of Colonial Discourse.* Ph.D. Thesis, Univ. of British Columbia. Canadian Theses on Microfiche 953306. Ottawa: National Library of Canada, 1994.

Daly, Mary. *Gyn/Ecology: The Metaethics of Radical Feminism.* Boston: Beacon, 1978.

Davenport, Philip. *The Voyage of "Waltzing Matilda."* London: Hutchinson, 1953.

Davies, Karen. *Women and Time: Weaving the Strands of Everyday Life.* Lund, Sweden: Karen Davies, 1989.

Davies, Miranda, and Natania Jansz, eds. *Women Travel: Adventures, Advice and Experience.* London: Rough Guides, 1993 (1990).

Davion, Victoria. "Is Ecofeminism Feminist?" In *Ecological Feminism.* Ed. Karen J. Warren. London; New York: Routledge, 1994. 8-28.

Davison, Ann. *Florida Junket: The Story of a Shoestring Cruise.* London: Peter Davies, 1964.

———. *Last Voyage.* New York: William Sloane, 1952 (1951).

Dawson, Jan C. "Landmarks of Home in the Pacific Northwest." *ISLE: Interdisciplinary Studies in Literature and the Environment* 2:2 (Winter 1996): 1-23.

Dawson, Will. *Ahoy There!* Toronto; Vancouver: J. M. Dent and Sons, 1955.

Day, David. "Eustace Smith: The Last Authority." In *Raincoast Chronicles Six/Ten.* Ed. Howard White. Madeira Park, B.C.: Harbour Publishing, 1983. 272-75.

d'Eaubonne, Françoise. "Feminism or Death." In *New French Feminisms: An Anthology.* Trans. Betty Schmitz. Ed. Elaine Marks and Isabelle de Courtivron. Amherst, Mass.: Univ. of Massachusetts Press, 1980 (1974). 64-67.

De Laguna, Frederica. *The Archaelogy of Cook Inlet, Alaska.* Philadelphia: Univ. of Pennsylvania Press, 1934.

de Montauban, G. *The Cruise of a Woman Hater.* 5th ed. Boston: Ticknor, 1887.

Devine, Maureen. *Woman and Nature: Literary Reconceptualizations.* London: Scarecrow Press, 1992.

Diamond, Irene, and Gloria Feman Orenstein, eds. *Reweaving the World: The Emergence of Ecofeminism.* San Francisco: Sierra Club, 1990.

Distad, N. Merrill. "Travel and Exploration." In *Victorian Britain: An Encyclopedia.* Ed. Sally Mitchell. New York: Garland, 1988. 814-16.

Douglas, Ann. "Heaven Our Home: Consolation Literature in the Northern United States, 1830-1880." In *Death in America.* Ed. David E. Stannard. Philadelphia: Univ. of Pennsylvania Press, 1975. 49-68.

Douglas, Gilean. "The Bible Barge to Kingdom Come." In *Raincoast Chronicles Six/Ten.* Ed. Howard White. Madeira Park, B.C.: Harbour Publishing, 1983. 230-36.

Douglas, Mary. "The Idea of a Home: A Kind of Space." In *Home: A Place in the World.* Ed. Arien Mack. New York: New York Univ. Press, 1993. 261-81.

Drushka, Ken. *Against Wind and Weather: The History of Towboating in British Columbia.* Vancouver: Douglas and McIntyre, 1981.

Eberhart, Beth. *A Crew of Two.* Garden City, N.Y.: Doubleday, 1961.

Emberley, Julia V., ed. *Thresholds of Difference: Feminist Critique, Native Women's Writings, Postcolonial Theory.* Toronto: Univ. of Toronto Press, 1993.

Fabian, Johannes. *Time and the Other: How Anthropology Makes its Object.* New York: Columbia Univ. Press, 1983.

Fee, Margery. "Romantic Nationalism and the Image of Native People in Contemporary English-Canadian Literature." In *The Native in Literature.* Ed. Thomas King, Cheryl Calver, and Helen Hoy. Oakville, Ont.: ECW Press, 1987. 15-33.

Finch, Robert, and John Elder. Introduction to *The Norton Book of Nature Writing.* Robert Finch and John Elder, eds. New York: Norton, 1990. 19-28.

Fisher, Robin. *Contact and Conflict: Indian-European Relations in British Columbia, 1774-1890.* Vancouver: Univ. of British Columbia Press, 1977.

————, and Hugh Johnston, eds. *From Maps to Metaphors: The Pacific World of George Vancouver.* Vancouver: Univ. of British Columbia Press, 1993.

Ford, Susan. "Landscape Revisited: A Feminist Reappraisal." In *New Words, New Worlds: Reconceptualising Social and Cultural Geography.* Ed. Chris Philo. Lampeter, Dyfed, Wales: Dept. Geography, St. David's Univ. College, 1991. 151-55.

Foster, Shirley. *Across New Worlds: Nineteenth-Century Women Travellers and Their Writings.* New York: Harvester Wheatsheaf, 1990.

Fox, Uffa. *According to Uffa: Handling Sailing Boats.* London: Newnes, 1960.

Francis, Daniel. *The Imaginary Indian: The Image of the Indian in Canadian Culture.* Vancouver: Arsenal Pulp Press, 1992.

Frankel, Michael F., ed. *Gently with the Tides: The Best of Living Aboard.* Camden, Maine: International Marine, 1993 (1990).

Franklin, Wayne. "Speaking and Touching: The Problems of Inexpressibility in American Travel Books." In *America: Exploration and Travel.* Ed. Steven E. Kagle. Bowling Green, OH: Bowling Green State Univ. Popular Press, 1979. 18-38.

Frawley, Maria H., ed. *A Wider Range: Travel Writing by Women in Victorian England.* Rutherford, N.J.: Fairleigh Dickinson Univ. Press; London; Cranbury, N.J.: Associated Univ. Press, 1994.

Frederick, Christine. *The New Housekeeping: Efficiency Studies in Home Management.* Garden City, N.Y.: Doubleday, Page, 1914.

French, Mrs. H. P. [Anna]. "A Trip to Alaska." *Woman's Home Missions* XL/2 (February 1923): 6-10.

Fulford, Robert. "The Trouble with Emily." *Canadian Art* 10/4 (Winter 1993): 32-39.

Gilbreth, Lillian, Orpha Mae Thomas, and Eleanor Clymer. *Management in the Home: Happier Living Through Saving Time and Energy.* New York: Dodd, Mead, 1954.

Goodnow, Cecelia. "Nautical Chic." *Seattle Post-Intelligencer* (11 August 1986). Sec. C1, cols. 2-5.

Gordon, Deborah. "Introduction: Feminism and the Critique of Colonial Discourse." *Inscriptions* 3/4 (1988): 1-5.

Gough, Barry M. *Gunboat Frontier: British Maritime Authority and Northwest Coast Indians, 1846-90.* Vancouver: Univ. of British Columbia Press, 1984.

————. *The Northwest Coast: British Navigation, Trade, and Discoveries to 1812.* Vancouver: Univ. of British Columbia Press, 1992.

Graham, R. D., *Rough Passage*; M. Helen Graham, *The Adventure of the Faeroe Islands.* London: Rupert Hart-Davis (The Mariners Library series), 1950 [simultaneous publication].

Graulich, Melody. "Opening Windows toward the Sea: Harmony and Reconciliation in American Women's Sea Literature." In *Iron Men, Wooden Women: Gender and Seafaring in the Atlantic World, 1700-1920.* Ed. Margaret S. Creighton and Lisa Norling. Baltimore: Johns Hopkins Univ. Press, 1996. 204-26.

Gray, Rockwell. "Travel." In *Temperamental Journeys: Essays on the Modern Literature of Travel.* Ed. Michael Kowalewski. Athens: Univ. of Georgia Press, 1992. 33-50.

Green, Martin. *Dreams of Adventure, Deeds of Empire.* New York: Basic Books, 1979.

Gregory, Derek. Epilogue to *Vancouver and its Region.* Ed. Graeme Wynn and Timothy Oke. Vancouver: Univ. of British Columbia Press, 1992. 291-97.

Griffin, Susan. *Woman and Nature: The Roaring Inside Her.* New York: Harper and Row, 1980 (1978).

Guppy, Neil. "Labouring at Sea: Harvesting Uncommon Property." In *Uncommon Property: The Fishing and Fish-Processing Industries in British Columbia.* Ed. Patricia Marchak, Neil Guppy, and John McMullan. Toronto: Methuen, 1987. 173-98.

———. "Labouring on Shore: Transforming Uncommon Property into Marketable Products." In *Uncommon Property: The Fishing and Fish-Processing Industries in British Columbia.* Ed. Patricia Marchak, Neil Guppy, and John McMullan. Toronto: Methuen, 1987. 199-222.

Haig-Brown, Roderick. *Woods and River Tales.* Toronto: McClelland and Stewart, 1980.

Hanson, Susan, and Geraldine Pratt. *Gender, Work, and Space.* London; New York: Routledge, 1995.

Hareven, Tamara K. "The Home and the Family in Historical Perspective." In *Home: A Place in the World.* Ed. Arien Mack. New York: New York Univ. Press, 1993. 227-59.

Harrington, Rebie. *Cinderella Takes a Holiday in the Northland: Journeys in Alaska and Yukon Territory.* New York: Fleming H. Revell Co., 1937.

Hayden, Dolores. *The Grand Domestic Revolution: A History of Feminist Designs for American Homes, Neighborhoods, and Cities.* Cambridge: MIT Press, 1983.

Heaton, Peter, ed. *The Sea Gets Greyer: More Small Boat Wanderers and Their Writings.* London: Adam and Charles Black, 1966.

Herbert, Agnes. *Two Dianas in Alaska.* London: T. Nelson, 1909.

Higginson, Ella. "Alaska—The Dream Voyage." *Washington Magazine* 2/1 (September 1906): Part 1. 12-17, 59-64.

———. "Alaska—The Dream Voyage." *Washington Magazine* 2/2 (October 1906): Part 2. 101-12.

———. "The Voyage of All Voyages." *Washington Magazine* 1/4 (June 1906): 336-39.

Hill, Beth. "If Such a Frightful Apendage [*sic*] Can Be Called Ornamental...." In *Raincoast Chronicles Six/Ten.* Ed. Howard White. Madeira Park, B.C.: Harbour Publishing, 1983. 148-50.

———. *The Remarkable World of Frances Barkley: 1769-1845.* Sidney, B.C.: Gray's, 1978.

Hill, Gwyn Gray. "Searching for Cape St. Elias: An Alaskan Odyssey." In *Raincoast Chronicles Six/Ten*. Ed. Howard White. Madeira Park, B.C.: Harbour Publishing, 1983. 238-45.

Hindmarch, Gladys. *The Watery Part of the World*. Vancouver: Douglas and McIntyre, 1988.

Hollander, John. "It All Depends." In *Home: A Place in the World*. Ed. Arien Mack. New York: New York Univ. Press, 1993. 27-45.

Horsley, Robert, and Eric Carlson. "The Bourgeoisification of Boating." *The Weekly: Seattle's Newsmagazine* 1/44 (26 January 1977): 9-11.

Hume, Stephen. "The Spirit Weeps." In *The Norton Reader*. Ed. Arthur M. Eastman. Shorter 8th ed. 552-62. (*Edmonton Journal*, February 1988).

Iglauer, Edith. *Fishing with John*. Madeira Park, B.C.: Harbour Publishing, 1988.

Jacknis, Ira. "George Hunt, Collector of Indian Specimens." In *Chiefly Feasts: The Enduring Kwakiutl Potlatch*. Ed. Aldona Jonaitis. Seattle; London: Univ. of Washington Press, 1991.

Jacobsen, Betty. *A Girl Before the Mast*. New York: Charles Scribner and Sons, 1934.

Jameson, Elizabeth. "Women as Workers, Women as Civilizers: True Womanhood in the American West." In *The Woman's West*. Ed. Susan Armitage and Elizabeth Jameson. Norman; London: Univ. of Oklahoma Press, 1987. 145-164.

Jedamski, Doris. *Images, Self-Images and the Perception of the Other: Women Travellers in the Malay Archipelago*. Hull Centre for South-East Asian Studies: Univ. of Hull, 1995.

Jensen, Vickie. *Saltwater Women at Work*. Vancouver: Douglas and McIntyre, 1995.

Jerome, Jerome K. *Three Men in a Boat*. Harmondsworth: Penguin, 1976 (1889).

Johnston, Gordon. "An Intolerable Burden of Meaning: Native Peoples in White Fiction." In *The Native in Literature*. Ed. Thomas King, Cheryl Calver, and Helen Hoy. Oakville, Ont.: ECW Press, 1987. 50-66.

Kaplan, Cora. *Sea Changes: Essays on Culture and Feminism*. London: Verso, 1986.

Karlsson, Elis. *Cruising off Mozambique*. London: Oxford Univ. Press, 1969.

Kazin, Alfred. *A Writer's America: Landscape in Literature*. New York: Knopf, 1988.

Kearns, Lionel. *Convergences*. Toronto: Coach House Press, 1984.

Kell, Florence. "Motor Boating in Northwestern Waters." *Kansas Magazine* (March-April 1911): 9-13.

Kimbrough, Emily. *And a Right Good Crew*. New York: Harper and Brothers, 1958.

Kirstein, Jane, and Mary Leonard. *Family Under Sail: A Handbook for First Mates*. Toronto: Collier-MacMillan, 1970.

Kirton, J. W. *Happy Homes, and How to Make Them; Or, Counsels on Love, Courtship and Marriage*. London: Frederick Warne and Co., 1870. Micropublished in "History of Women." New Haven: Research Publications, Inc., 1975. #2788.

Klein, Laura F. "Contending With Colonization: Tlingit Men and Women in Change." In *Women and Colonization: Anthropological Perspectives*. Ed. Mona Etienne and Eleanor Leacock. New York: Praeger, 1980. 88-108.

Knight, Rolf. *Indians at Work: An Informal History of Native Indian Labour in British Columbia 1858-1930*. Vancouver: New Star Books, 1978.

Knox, Adeline (Trafton). *An American Girl Abroad*. Boston: Lee and Shepard; New York: Lee, Shepard, and Dillingham, 1872. Micropublished in "History of Women." New Haven: Research Publications, Inc., 1976. #2789.

Kobayashi, Audrey. "A Critique of Dialectical Landscape." In *Remaking Human Geography*. Ed. Audrey Kobayashi and Suzanne Mackenzie. Boston; London: Unwin Hyman, 1989. 164-83.

Kolodny, Annette. *The Land Before Her: Fantasy and Experience of the American Frontiers, 1630-1860*. Chapel Hill: Univ. of North Carolina Press, 1984.

———. *The Lay of the Land: Metaphor as Experience and History in American Life and Letters*. Chapel Hill: Univ. of North Carolina Press, 1975.

Koppel, Tom. "Indian Shell Middens: Piling Up the Evidence." *Oceans* (May 1985): 18-22.

Kröller, Eva-Marie. "First Impressions: Rhetorical Strategies in Travel Writing by Victorian Women." *Ariel* 21/4 (October 1990): 87-99.

Lakoff, Robin. *Language and Woman's Place*. New York: Harper Colophon, 1975.

Laskin, David. *Rains All the Time: A Connoisseur's History of Weather in the Pacific Northwest*. Seattle: Sasquatch Books, 1997.

Lawrence, Iain. *Sea Stories of the Inside Passage: In the Wake of the Nid*. Bishop, Calif.: Fine Edge Productions, 1997.

Lawrence, Karen R., ed. *Penelope Voyages: Women and Travel in the British Literary Tradition*. Ithaca: Cornell Univ. Press, 1994.

Lawrence, Ruth. "Boat Interior Decorating." In *The Woman's Guide to Boating & Cooking*. Ed. Lael Morgan. Rev. ed. Garden City, N.Y.: Doubleday, 1974 (1968). 34-42.

Leighton, Caroline C. *Life at Puget Sound with Sketches of Travel in Washington Territory, British Columbia, Oregon, and California 1865-1881*. Boston: Lee and Shepard, 1884.

———. *West Coast Journeys, 1865-1879: The Travelogue of a Remarkable Woman*. Ed. David M. Buerge. Seattle: Sasquatch, 1995.

Lethbridge, T. C. *Boats and Boatmen*. London: Thames and Hudson, 1952.

Lillard, Charles. "Afterword: Listening to the Voices of the Coast." In *The Call of the Coast*. Ed. Charles Lillard. Victoria: Horsdal and Schubart, 1992. 157-164.

———. "Foreword: What the Pinks Saw." In *Three's a Crew*, by Kathrene Pinkerton. Ganges, B.C.: Horsdal and Schubart, 1991. 7-12.

Line, Lila. *Waterwomen*. Queenstown, Md.: Queen Anne Press, 1982.

Livingston, Margie. *The Yachtsman's Mate's Guide*. New York: Ziff-Davis, 1980.

Lopez, Barry. *Arctic Dreams: Imagination and Desire in a Northern Landscape*. Toronto: Bantam, 1987 (1986).

Lukens, Matilda Barns. *The Inland [sic] Passage: A Journal of a Trip to Alaska*. Canadian Institute for Historical Micro-reproductions 15530 (1889).

Lyon, Thomas J. "Nature Writing as a Subversive Activity." *North Dakota Quarterly* 59/2 (Spring 1991): 6-16.

———, ed. *This Incomperable [sic] Lande*. Boston: Houghton Mifflin, 1989.

MacCannell, Dean, and Juliet Flower MacCannell. "The Beauty System." In *The Ideology of Conduct: Essays on Literature and the History of Sexuality.* Ed. Nancy Armstrong and Leonard Tennenhouse. New York: Methuen, 1987. 206-38.

MacCormack, Carol P. "Nature, Culture and Gender: A Critique." In *Nature, Culture and Gender.* Ed. Carol P. MacCormack and Marilyn Strathern. Cambridge; London: Cambridge Univ. Press, 1980. 1-24.

Maillart, Ella K. *Gypsy Afloat.* London: William Heinemann, 1942.

Mallinson, Florence Lee. *My Travels and Adventures in Alaska.* Seattle: Seattle-Alaska Co., 1914.

Marine Retirees Association. *A History of Shipbuilding in British Columbia.* Vancouver: Marine Retirees Association, 1977.

Marlatt, Daphne. *Salvage.* Red Deer, Alberta: Red Deer College Press, 1991.

———. "Subverting the Heroic: Recent Feminist Writing on the West Coast." In *British Columbia Reconsidered.* Ed. Gillian Creese and Veronica Strong-Boag. Vancouver: Press Gang, 1992. 296-306

Martin, Biddy, and Chandra Talpade Mohanty. "Feminist Politics: What's Home Got to Do with It?" In *Feminist Studies/Critical Studies.* Ed. Teresa de Lauretis. Bloomington: Indiana Univ. Press, 1986. 191-212.

Massey, Doreen. "Flexible Sexism." In *Space, Place, and Gender.* Minneapolis: Univ. of Minnesota Press, 1994 (1991). 212-48.

———. "Politics and Space/Time." In *Space, Place, and Gender.* Minneapolis: Univ. of Minnesota Press, 1994 (1992). 249-72.

———. "Space, Place and Gender: Introduction." In *Space, Place, and Gender.* Minneapolis: Univ. of Minnesota Press, 1994. 177-84.

———, and Linda McDowell. "A Woman's Place?" In *Space, Place, and Gender.* Minneapolis: Univ. of Minnesota Press, 1994 (1984). 191-211.

McCarthy, Aine. *Get Up & Go: A Travel Survival Kit for Women.* Dublin: Attic Press, 1992.

McCormick, J. A. "Cruise of the Calcite." In *Northwest Passages: A Collection of Pacific Northwest Cruising Stories.* Vol. 1. Ed. Bruce Calhoun. San Francisco: Miller Freeman, 1969. 185-90.

Meeker, Ezra. "A Cruise on Puget Sound." In *The Call of the Coast.* Ed. Charles Lillard. Victoria: Horsdal and Schubart, 1992 (1905). 2-18.

———. *Ventures and Adventures of Ezra Meeker or Sixty Years of Frontier Life.* Seattle: Rainier Printing Co., 1909 (1908).

Meggs, Geoff, and Duncan Stacey. *Cork Lines and Canning Lines: The Glory Years of Fishing on the West Coast.* Vancouver: Douglas and McIntyre, 1992.

Melville, Herman. *Moby-Dick.* New York: Penguin, 1982 (1851).

Merchant, Carolyn. *The Death of Nature: Women, Ecology, and the Scientific Revolution.* San Francisco: Harper and Row, 1980.

Mills, Patricia Jagentowicz. *Woman, Nature, and Psyche.* New Haven; London: Yale Univ. Press, 1987.

Mills, Sara. *Discourses of Difference: An Analysis of Women's Travel Writing and Colonialism.* London: Routledge, 1991.

Modzelewski, Michael. *Inside Passage: Living with Killer Whales, Bald Eagles, and Kwakiutl Indians.* New York: HarperCollins, 1992 (1991).

Moi, Toril. *Sexual/Textual Politics: Feminist Literary Theory.* London; New York: Routledge, 1985.

Monk, Janice. "Approaches to the Study of Women and the Landscape." *Environmental Review* 8/1 (Spring 1984): 23-33.

Morgan, Lael. *The Woman's Guide to Boating & Cooking.* Rev. ed. Garden City, N.Y.: Doubleday, 1974 (1968).

Morison, Samuel Eliot. *Spring Tides.* Boston: Houghton Mifflin, 1965.

Morris, (Mrs.) James Edwin. *A Pacific Coast Vacation.* London; New York; Montreal: The Abbey Press, 1901.

Morris, Mary. ed. *Maiden Voyages: Writings of Women Travellers.* New York: Vintage, 1993.

———. "Women and Journeys: Inner and Outer." In *Temperamental Journeys: Essays on the Modern Literature of Travel.* Ed. Michael Kowalewski. Athens: Univ. of Georgia Press, 1992. 25-32.

Mourelle de la Rúa, Francisco Antonio. *Voyage of the Sonora from the 1775 Journal of Don Francisco Antonio Mourelle as Translated by Daines Barrington.* Fairfield, Wash.: Ye Galleon Press, 1988 (1780).

Mullen, Richard. *Birds of Passage: Five Englishwomen in Search of America.* New York: St. Martin's Press, 1994.

Murphy, Patrick D., ed. *Literature, Nature, and Other: Ecofeminist Critiques.* Albany: State Univ. of New York Press, 1995.

Nelson, Richard. *The Island Within.* New York: Vintage, 1991 (1989).

Nicolls, Nan, ed. *North of Anian: The Collected Journals of Gabrielle III Cruises in British Columbia Coastal Waters 1978-1989.* Vancouver: Dick Sandwell, 1990 [private, 250 numbered copies].

Nordquist, Joan. *Ecofeminist Theory: A Bibliography.* Santa Cruz: Reference and Research Services, 1994.

Norwood, Vera. *Made From This Earth: American Women and Nature.* Chapel Hill: Univ. of North Carolina Press, 1993.

———. "Women's Place: Continuity and Change in Response to Western Landscapes." In *Western Women: Their Land, Their Lives.* Ed. Lillian Schlissel, Vicki L. Ruiz, and Janice Monk. Albuquerque: Univ. of New Mexico Press, 1988. 155-81.

Nunn, Betty. "Alaska . . . Not Just a Place to Reach." In *Northwest Passages: A Collection of Pacific Northwest Cruising Stories.* Ed. Bruce Calhoun. San Francisco: Miller Freeman, 1969. 222-26.

Oakes, Guy. "The Problem of Women in Simmel's Theory of Culture." In *Georg Simmel: On Women, Sexuality, and Love,* by Georg Simmel. Trans. Guy Oakes. New Haven: Yale Univ. Press, 1984. 3-62.

Ogden, Charles D. "Puget Sound and Vancouver Waters." In *Yachting in North America.* Ed. Eugene V. Connett. New York: D. Van Nostrand, 1948. 679-712.

"One of Six Seattle Families Owns Pleasure Craft." *Seattle Times* (24 November, 1961). 10C.

Orchard, Imbert, and Derek Reimer, collectors. "Free and Fearless: Children of the Backwoods." In *Sound Heritage: Voices from British Columbia*. Ed. Saeko Usukawa. Vancouver; Toronto: Douglas and McIntyre, 1984. 104-10.

Ormsby, Margaret A. *British Columbia: A History*. Vancouver: Macmillan, 1958.

Pagh, Nancy. "Offshore Women: A Personal Log." In *Private Voices, Public Lives: Women Speak on the Literary Life*. Ed. Nancy Owen Nelson. Denton, Tex.: Univ. of North Texas Press, 1995. 125-40.

Pattison, Mary. *Principles of Domestic Engineering: Or the What, Why and How of a House*. New York: Trow Press, 1915.

Perkins, Joan. *Victorian Women*. London: John Murray, 1993.

Peterson, Brenda. *Living by Water: Essays on Life, Land & Spirit*. Anchorage; Seattle: Alaska Northwest Books, 1990.

Phillips-Birt, Douglas. *The History of Yachting*. London: Hamish Hamilton; New York: Stein and Day, 1974.

Pinkerton, Kathrene. *Three's a Crew*. Ganges, B.C.: Horsdal and Schubart, 1991 (1940).

Plumwood, Val. *Feminism and the Mastery of Nature*. London; New York: Routledge, 1993.

Pollock, Griselda. *Vision and Difference: Femininity, Feminism, and Histories of Art*. London; New York: Routledge, 1988.

Porteous, J. Douglas. *Landscapes of the Mind: Worlds of Sense and Metaphor*. Toronto: Univ. of Toronto Press, 1990.

Pratt, Daniel L. "Motor Boating on Puget Sound." *Pacific Monthly* 18/1 (July 1907): 113-21.

Pratt, Mary Louise. *Imperial Eyes: Travel Writing and Transculturation*. London; New York: Routledge, 1992.

Pritchard, Allan. "West of the Great Divide: A View of the Literature of British Columbia." *Canadian Literature* 94 (Autumn 1982): 96-112.

———. "West of the Great Divide: Man and Nature in the Literature of British Columbia." *Canadian Literature* 102 (Autumn 1984): 336-533.

Putnam, Tim. "Beyond the Modern Home: Shifting the Parameters of Residence." In *Mapping the Futures: Local Cultures, Global Change*. Ed. Jon Bird et al. London: Routledge, 1993. 150-65.

Pyle, Joseph Gilpin, and Annie Sanborn Pyle. "Six Hundred Miles in a Houseboat: A Leisurely Cruise Along the Coast of British Columbia in the First Modern Houseboat in Pacific Waters." *The World's Work* (10 August 1910). 13,295-13,302.

Rigby, Elizabeth [Lady Eastlake]. "Lady Travellers." *Quarterly Review* LXXVI/CLI (1845): 98-137.

Robinson, Jane. *Wayward Women: A Guide to Women Travellers*. Oxford: Oxford Univ. Press, 1990.

Rock, Cynthia, Susan Torre, and Gwendolyn Wright. "The Appropriation of the House: Changes in House Design and Concepts of Domesticity." In *New Space for Women*. Ed. Gerda R. Wekerle, Rebecca Peterson, and David Morley. Boulder, Colo.: Westview Press, 1980. 83-100.

Rogers, Woodes. *A Cruising Voyage Round the World First to the South Seas Thence to the East Indies and Homeward by the Cape of Good Hope*. Facsim. of 1712 ed. New York: Da Capo Press; Amsterdam: N. Israel, 1969.

Rushton, Gerald A. *Whistle up the Inlet: The Union Steamship Story*. Vancouver: J. J. Douglas, 1974.

Ruskin, Olga. "By Boat to Desolation Sound." *Western Living* 7/6 (June 1977): 18-20, 22.

Rybczynski, Witold. *Home: A Short History of an Idea*. New York: Viking, 1986.

Ryden, Kent C. *Mapping the Invisible Landscape: Folklore, Writing, and the Sense of Place*. Iowa City: Univ. of Iowa Press, 1993.

Saegert, Susan, and Gary Winkel. "The Home: A Critical Problem for Changing Sex Roles." In *New Space for Women*. Ed. Gerda R. Wekerle, Rebecca Peterson, and David Morley. Boulder, Colo.: Westview Press, 1980.

Said, Edward. *Orientalism*. New York: Pantheon, 1978.

Samson, Pat, and John Samson. *The New Way of Life*. Richmond, B.C.: Samson Marine Design Enterprises Ltd., 1970.

Sandwell, Agnete. "The Care and Feeding of Yachtsmen in B.C. Waters." In *North of Anian: The Collected Journals of Gabrielle III Cruises in British Columbia Coastal Waters 1978-1989*. Ed. Nan Nicolls. Vancouver: Dick Sandwell, 1990 [private, 250 numbered copies]. 310-15.

Sass, George. "Living Aboard a Grand Banks." In *Gently with the Tides: The Best of Living Aboard*. Ed. Michael F. Frankel. Camden, Maine: International Marine, 1993 (1990). 60-63.

Schriber, Mary Susan, ed. *Telling Travels: Selected Writings by Nineteenth-Century American Women Abroad*. DeKalb: Northern Illinois Press, 1995.

Schwantes, Carlos. *The Pacific Northwest: An Interpretive History*. Lincoln: Univ. of Nebraska Press, 1989.

Schriber, Mary Susan, ed. *Telling Travels: Selected Writings by Nineteenth-Century American Women Abroad*. Dekalb: Northern Illinois Press, 1995.

Scidmore, E. Ruhamah. *Alaska, Its Southern Coast and the Sitkan Archipelago*. Boston: D. Lothrop and Co., 1885.

Sharcott, Margaret. *Troller's Holiday*. Toronto: British Book Service, 1957.

Sheets, Robin. "Womanhood." In *Victorian Britain: An Encyclopedia*. Ed. Sally Mitchell. New York: Garland, 1988. 863-64.

Sheldon, Sidney R. "Eighteen Feet to Alaska." In *The Call of the Coast*. Ed. Charles Lillard. Victoria: Horsdahl and Schubart, 1992 (1959). 37-45.

Shepard, Isabel S. *The Cruise of the U.S. Steamer "Rush" in Behring* [sic] *Sea Summer of 1889*. San Francisco: Bancroft, 1889.

Short, Steve, and Rosemary Neering. *In the Path of the Explorers*. Vancouver; Toronto: Whitecap Books, 1992.

Silverman, Eliane Leslau. *The Last Best West: Women on the Alberta Frontier 1880-1930*. Montreal: Eden Press, 1984.

Simmel, Georg. *Georg Simmel: On Women, Sexuality, and Love*. Ed. and trans. Guy Oakes. New Haven: Yale Univ. Press, 1984 (1911).

Skogan, Joan. *Voyages: At Sea with Strangers*. Toronto: HarperCollins, 1992.

Smith, Dorothy Blakey, ed. *Lady Franklin Visits the Pacific Northwest*. Victoria: Provincial Archives of British Columbia, 1974.

Smith, Roland, and Janice Smith. "Male/Female Relations." In *Gently with the Tides: The Best of Living Aboard*. Ed. Michael L. Frankel. Camden, Maine: International Marine, 1993 (1990). 86-87.

Spain, Daphne. *Gendered Spaces*. Chapel Hill: Univ. of North Carolina Press, 1992.

Speed, Maude. *A Yachtswoman's Cruises and Some Steamer Voyages*. London: Longmans, Green and Co., 1911.

Stadler, Michael. *The Psychology of Sailing: The Sea's Effects on Mind and Body*. Trans. Sally A. R. Bates. Camden, Maine: International Marine, 1987.

Steel, Stephanie Quainton. *Harvest of Light: An Artist's Journey*. Victoria: Orca Books, 1991.

Steinbeck, John. *The Log from the Sea of Cortez*. New York: Viking, 1941.

Stevenson, Fanny. *The Cruise of the "Janet Nichol" Among the South Sea Islands: A Diary by Mrs. Robert Louis Stevenson*. London: Chatto and Windus, 1915.

Stott, Rebecca. "The Dark Continent: Africa as Female Body in Haggard's Adventure Fiction." *Feminist Review* (Summer 1989): 69-89.

Strickland, Ron, ed. *Whistlepunks and Geoducks: Oral Histories from the Pacific Northwest*. New York: Paragon, 1990.

Sullivan, May Kellog. *A Woman Who Went to Alaska*. Boston: James H. Earle and Co., 1902.

Swain, Marian L., collector. *Gilbert Said: An Oldtimer's Tales of the Haida-Tlingit Waterways of Alaska*. Walnut Creek, Calif.: Hardscratch Press, 1992.

Taylor, Diane. *The Perfect Galley Book: Yarns, Recipes & Tips from the Heart of the Ship*. New York: New Trend, 1983.

Thomas, Audrey. *Intertidal Life*. Toronto: General Publishing, 1984.

Thurin, Susan Schoenbauer. "Travel and Tourism." In *Victorian Britain: An Encyclopedia*. Ed. Sally Mitchell. New York: Garland, 1988. 817-18.

Tinling, Marion, ed. *With Women's Eyes: Visitors to the New World, 1775-1918*. Hamden, Conn.: Archon Books, 1993.

Tippett, Maria, and Douglas Cole. *From Desolation to Splendour: Changing Perceptions of the British Columbia Landscape*. Toronto: Clark, Irwin, 1977.

Toth, Emily. *Regionalism and the Female Imagination: A Collection of Essays*. New York: Human Sciences Press, 1985.

Trachtenberg, Alan. "Home as Place and Center for Private and Family Life." In *Home: A Place in the World*." Ed. Arien Mack. New York: New York Univ. Press, 1993. 211-12.

Trueblood, Kathryn, and Linda Stovall. Introduction to *Homeground*. Ed. Kathryn Trueblood and Linda Stovall. Hillsboro, Ore.: Blue Heron Publishing, 1996. 9-12.

Tuan, Yi-Fu. *Topophilia: A Study of Environmental Perception, Attitudes, and Values*. Englewood Cliffs, N.J.: Prentice Hall, 1974.

Upton, Joe. *Journeys Through the Inside Passage: Seafaring Adventures Along the Coast of British Columbia and Alaska*. Anchorage; Seattle: Alaska Northwest Books, 1992.

Usukawa, Saeko, ed. *Sound Heritage: Voices from British Columbia*. Vancouver: Douglas and McIntyre, 1984.

van Boheemen, Christine. *The Novel as Family Romance: Language, Gender, and Authority from Fielding to Joyce*. Ithaca; London: Cornell Univ. Press, 1987.

Vancouver, George. *The Voyage of George Vancouver, 1791-1795*. Ed. W. Kaye Lamb. London: The Hakluyt Society, 1984.

Van Kirk, Sylvia. *"Many Tender Ties": Women in Fur Trade Society in Western Canada, 1670-1870*. Winnipeg: Watson and Dwyer, 1980.

Vicinus, Martha. "Introduction: The Perfect Victorian Lady." In *Suffer and Be Still: Women in the Victorian Age*. Ed. Martha Vicinus. Bloomington: Indiana Univ. Press, 1972. vii-xv.

Vlasopolos, Anca. "Staking Claims for No Territory: The Sea as Woman's Space." In *Feminist Explorations of Literary Space*. Ed. Margaret R. Higonner and Joan Templeton. Amherst: Univ. of Massachusetts Press, 1994. 72-88.

Wardman, George. *A Trip to Alaska: A Narrative of What Was Seen and Heard During a Summer Cruise in Alaskan Waters*. San Francisco: Samuel Carson and Co., 1884.

Warren, Karen J., ed. *Ecological Feminism*. London; New York: Routledge, 1994.

Webb, Jess. *Going North*. LaConner, Wash.: Lone Star Press, 1985.

Weed, Alberta L. *Grandma Goes to the Arctic: As Told by Lola Kirkland*. Philadelphia: Dorrance and Co., 1957.

West Vancouver Yacht Club, Ladies Sailing Group. *Galley Slave's Guide: Recipes and Helpful Hints for Cooks with Limited Facilities*. Vancouver: Brock Webber Printing Co., 1969.

White, Linda. *The Independent Woman's Guide to Europe*. Golden, Colo.: Fulcrum, 1991.

White, Richard. *Land Use, Environment, and Social Change: The Shaping of Island County, Washington*. Seattle: Univ. of Washington Press, 1980.

Wickham, Hilary. *Galleywise: Not Just a Cookbook*. London: Pelham Books, 1971.

Willoughby, Barrett. *Spawn of the North*. New York: Triangle Books, 1942 (1932).

Winthrop, Theodore. *The Canoe and the Saddle*. New York: Dodd, Mead and Co., 1862.

Wolf, Enid. *A-Boating We Will Go: A Cruising Manual for Women*. New York: McGraw-Hill, 1958.

Women and Geography Study Group of the Institute of British Geographers. *Geography and Gender: An Introduction to Feminist Geography*. London; Dover, N.H.: Hutchinson, in assoc. with the Explorations in Feminism Collective, 1984.

Wood, Viola. "Roses in December: Memories of the Charlottes." In *Raincoast Chronicles Six/Ten*. Ed. Howard White. Madeira Park, B.C.: Harbour Publishing, 1983. 8-14.

Woodman, Abby Johnson. *Picturesque Alaska: A Journal of a Tour Among the Mountains, Seas, and Islands of the Northwest, from San Francisco to Sitka*. Boston: Houghton, Mifflin and Co., 1889.

Wright, E. W., ed. *Lewis & Dryden's Marine History of the Pacific Northwest*. New York: Antiquarian Press, 1961 (1895).

Zepatos, Thalia. *Adventures in Good Company: The Complete Guide to Women's Tours and Outdoors Trips*. Portland, Ore.: The Eighth Mountain Press, 1994.
———. *A Journey of One's Own: Uncommon Advice for the Independent Woman Traveler*. Portland, Ore.: The Eighth Mountain Press, 1992.

INTRODUCTION*

*Bold numbers indicate illustrations.